To Wit

and

To Pie —

Who introduced me to love, laughter, and Jacques Tati!

All my love always,

Marianne

21/3/90

BY THE SAME AUTHOR

Novels

One by One
A State of Change
The Cutting Edge
Mortal Matters
A Woman of Singular Occupation

Short Stories

Nobody's Business
What's It Like Out?
Splendid Lives
Quotations from Other Lives
They Sleep Without Dreaming
Lingo

To Wit

In Celebration of Comedy

PENELOPE GILLIATT

Weidenfeld & Nicolson
London

Published in Great Britain in 1990 by
George Weidenfeld & Nicolson Limited
91 Clapham High St, London SW4 7TA

Some passages, much amended, and copyrighted, of this book have appeared in the *Observer* and *The New Yorker*. The author thanks the editors for their grace.

British Library Cataloguing in Publication Data

Gilliatt, Penelope
To wit
1. Humour
I. Title
808.7

ISBN 0–297–81028–6

Photoset by Deltatype Ltd, Ellesmere Port
Printed and bound in Great Britain by
Butler & Tanner Ltd,
Frome and London

Contents

For Vincent Canby

Preface

E. B. White once said to Thurber that someone trying to explain humour 'had comedy by the elbow and now it's nearly on the floor'. Something like that.

Goethe, no slouch, said, 'to explain is to destroy.' Something like that.

His brother in thought, Professor Freud, though not established in Earth-time as having met him, illustrates this with unknowing exactness. He says in *Jokes and their Relation to the Unconscious*, a solemn tome, that 'we should bear in mind the peculiar and even fascinating charm exercised by jokes in our society.' Careful study of the joke literature enables him to make the point that 'it is quite impracticable to deal with jokes otherwise than in connection with the comic.' In his analysis he therefore always distinguishes meticulously between *funny* jokes, of which this is an admired example:

> Two Jews met in the neighbourhood of the bath-house. 'Have you taken a bath?' asked one of them. 'What?' asked the other in return. 'Is there one missing?' This example calls for graphic presentation: The first Jew asks: 'Have you taken a *bath*?' The emphasis is on the element of 'bath'. The

> second replies as though the question had been: 'Have you *taken* a bath?' The shifting of the emphasis is only made possible by the wording 'taken a bath'. If it had run 'Have you bathed?' no displacement would have been possible. The non-joking answer would then have been: ' "Bathed?" What d'you mean? I don't know what that is.' But the technique of the joke lies in the displacement of the accent from 'bath' to 'taken'.

– and jokes that, as he puts it, though they may be undeniably in the *nature* of a joke, do not give the *impression* of a joke. He offers examples of these, too.

Jokes, according to Freud, are a matter of intersecting lines. The lines connect words. If the lines intersect, you have a joke of success. If the lines don't, you have a joke of failure. To some of us, the jokes of the non-intersecting lines may well be funnier than the jokes of the intersecting lines. Freud goes on a lot about 'the jokework'. As in woodwork. Given manual labour, something funny will come crawling out of the jokework.

Jokes of Freud's analysed sort behave as acts of seduction and rape. They are like Don Giovanni about his women, the Don's jocularity about his romantic conquests, laying waste the world with pride in victory and never entering the world of love. There is a Rotarian feeling about these sorts of jokes. People around a table accost each other with them. It can be a hideous ordeal of the chauvinism of the clan.

There remains the genius of funniness. In many forms, in many countries, at many times. The stoic poetry of Beckett and Buster Keaton, 'rotten' jokes, high-bred farce, the physics of silent comedy, the satiric inspection of the pre-Revolutionary Russians, the panacea of fast wit in the American Depression of the 1930s, the wakening powers of Swift and Brecht and Lenny Bruce and Mort Sahl.

Funniness is the wild card in the pack. It plays the part of the Bastard in society, as drama used to see society. It inhabits the marginal. The Bastard hasn't received an assigned place in society, nor has funniness. Edmund in *Lear* is not a legitimate member of his society. Humour is subversive. The Fool in

Lear is in a position to subvert and immensely befriend Lear with his peculiar questions. Comedy can lift us into days which are parenthetical: hence New Year's Eve as it can be, hence Lear's heath, which is a nowhere. Boon nights and false noses, interpolated time allowing the infinitely possible. Does all funniness throw settled things into doubt? Pantomime. Think of a New Year's pantomime. It is totally apt on that night that a girl should play the principal boy.

The elephant is a basic measurement of comedy. This law has only recently occurred to me. We get over-obliging about what we accept as fun in grown-up life. Think of the unspoken melancholy of leg-shows, for instance, or practically everything on American TV network comedy and of Las Vegas-bred comedy from Europe, or, preserve us, Japan. And then remember circus elephants. How does adult situation comedy, or television's monologues beamed at the devotees of the 'rich-and-famous', compare with elephants' standards of humour, ensemble playing, honesty, astonishment and daring? Second City, going on to Mike Nichols and Elaine May, is up to their achievement; Keaton, Beckett; Robin Williams, Carol Burnett, Ken Dodd, The Berliner Ensemble in *Arturo Ui*, Morecambe and Wise, *Così Fan Tutte*, *Some Like it Hot*.

Nothing but a very strong memory of pleasure in elephants could keep us going so optimistically to some of the comic enterprises now. The inextinguishable hope can't come from anything but a childhood of going to the circus and of listening to the elating transactions of harmonic changes in music. Humour, wit, satire turn the tables.

At the circus, children find the colossal things colossally interesting. The pin-sized trapeze artists up in the roof leave nearly all children unmoved. In grown-up life our eyes alter and it is often the microscopic that we are enchanted by, so that passionate opera-goers will lean over the gallery at Covent Garden and fall helplessly under the spell of fifteen-stone contraltos the size of ants. Perhaps Hollywood should consider making films not bigger but very much smaller, on the reversed elephant principle: *Cleopatra* might have acquired the fragile and precise charm of comedy if Elizabeth Taylor's entry into Rome had been the size of a pea.

Sometimes in circuses there is a complicated car that chugs into the ring and goes sensationally defunct, throwing up spare parts like a girl in a farce tossing her underclothes over a screen, and slowly subsiding into a defeated pile on the sawdust. The victory in destruction is absolute: it is a fundament of fun. When a toddler takes an alarm clock apart, it is only the sentimental who can pretend to themselves that he is wanting to find out how it works: anyone with a longer memory knows that he is murdering it. The interesting thing is that it is only the murder that is enjoyable, not the death. That is why jokes are ideally pleasurable. They are an act of assassination without a corpse, a moment of total annihilation that paradoxically makes anything possible.

The physical namings of the humours in the titles of the next chapters are, of course, in memory of the ancients. No longer spleen, bile, phlegm, sanguity. Significant of the difference between the ancients' condition and ours that humour in our sense is not a humour.

In the travels of my life so far, I have been lucky enough to have watched and sometimes even worked with quite of few of the people whose predictions I try to evoke in this book. There was summation from the prodigiously practical George Devine. He said, driving his Alvis round Sloane Square long after midnight in the midst of his untired mounting of month-by-month productions at the Royal Court Theatre, that all problems are technical. Given talent. Many distinct and particular comic talents I have merely witnessed in retrospect. Anyone must bow to the rattling intelligence of the Thirties' romantic comedies. And to the speed of Manhattan wit:

I saw, many times, a stocky rich man coming in alone to the Algonquin to lunch. Coat, briefcase, hat, muffler handed to the hatcheck girl. Three-course meal alone. One day he gave his stingy nickel to the girl and she said, 'Thank.'

Great comedy, great wit makes the ceiling fly off, and suddenly liberates us again as we were when we were much younger and saw no reason not to believe that we could fly, or become someone else, or bound on a trampoline and not come down again. Fellini captured the mood forever in the scene at the end of *8½* when the dream-nagged grown-ups suddenly join hands on the film set and walk round and round as if they were on the rim of a circus ring: it is an image of pure fable, outside the rules of limits and death, like the character of Falstaff; or like elephants.

Spine: Poets of Stamina

Buster Keaton used his august and stoic profile as a sort of mainsail, braced against great winds in search of the compass directions of a moral order. Chaplin was once said to have given comedy its soul. If so, it was Keaton who gave it its spine and spirit. He made it heroic, because he never looks for sympathy for his characters.

'You don't go out of your way *not* to talk in a film,' Buster Keaton said to me, 'but you only talk if it's necessary.' Two-minute pause. He was then sixty-eight, two years from his death in 1966; sitting in his rather poor ranch house in the San Fernando Valley, quite a drive from the stars' hangout in Beverly Hills. (Keaton always talked about making films in the present tense, and you don't easily use any other about him.) He is trying to explain to me, on the basis of what he started learning in vaudeville from his parents' act when he was rising three, the machinery of silent jokes. The pause goes on, and the beautiful profile looks out of the back window onto the plot of land where he has built his hens a henhouse that has the space of an aviary and the architecture of a New England schoolhouse. He doesn't think that a chicken coop is much of a place to live in, even for hens, so he has built a miniature replica of his own house for them, with a door that he described to me as being 'six foot high, so that I can go in to see them.' This was his one piece of boasting; the door wouldn't need to be more than five-feet-five to take him.

The great master of film comedy, who is one of the true masters of cinema, suddenly gets up and climbs onto a dresser and does a very neat fall, turning over on his hands and pretending that he has a sore right thumb. He keeps it raised, and then stands stock-still and puts the thumb at pocket-level, acting. 'Suppose I'm a carpenter's apprentice,' he says after a while. Chest out, manly look, like a Victorian boy with his hands in his pockets having his photograph taken. 'Suppose the carpenter hits my thumb with his hammer. Suppose I think, God damn, and leap out the window. Well, I'm not going to *say* my thumb hurts, am I?' He sits down again and thinks. He is wearing a jersey with a piratical insignia on the front, and the sort of jaunty trousers that people wore on smart yachts in the thirties. 'The thing is not to be ridiculous. The one mistake the Marx Brothers ever make is that they're sometimes ridiculous. Sometimes *we're* in the middle of building a gag that turns out to be ridiculous. So, well, we have to think of something else. Sit it out. The cameras are our own, aren't they? We never hire our cameras. And we've got a start, and we've got a finish, because we don't begin a film if we haven't, so all we've got to get now is the middle.'

For all his age, his body and his vigilant movements still look very like the photographs of him when he played his first professional date, aged three, as the Human Mop in vaudeville. He and his parents used to tour as an act called 'The Three Keatons'. Even before he found his niche as the Human Mop he was taken on to the stage; they used to prop him against a wall, presumably because he was too young to stand.

His father was an Irishman, though he would call himself a Jew in a bar if a Jew was in trouble. When they went to a hotel on tour he would fill up a whole page with the family's names, written out in fancy billing. Mrs Keaton, who stood four-feet-eleven, seems to have been a woman of steel. She once gambled all night to get bail-money for her husband.

As far as I can gather, the act between the two male Keatons consisted mostly of Pop trying to kill Buster, by throwing him through walls, hurling him on to the big drum and wiping up the floor with him. This went on as long as Buster was small enough. When he had grown up a bit, the act developed into Pop and Buster trying to kill each other. While all this was going on, with a lot of custard pies, molasses and shaving-mirrors on rubber catapults, Mom would stand downstage ignoring the chaos and blowing a saxophone.

'Sometimes Pop would take off her dress,' says Buster, trying to explain it to me, 'and she would go on playing, wearing a swimsuit and this dressy hat.'

We lit a fire then because of his bronchitis. His house looks like one of the early American houses in *The General*. He has managed to find an old telephone that hangs on the wall; the rooms are low, with lots of pictures and photographs. He especially likes the place where he keeps the drinks, a Western saloon that is about the size of an ironing-board cupboard, with Victorian nude paintings each side of the bar.

He spends most of his time in a room that looks on to the land at the back of the house. It has a pool-table in it, a small television, and an old black stove like an ancient railway engine. He plays patience for hours, with a table beside him that is cluttered with cough mixtures and bags of sweets. He sits dead erect, cigarette-holder clenched in his teeth.

It is wrong to say that he doesn't understand verbal humour. When he was gag advisor to MGM (after he had had the sack as a film-maker from Louis B. Mayer) he suggested mildly that a comedy with Esther Williams called *Swimming Beauty* should be renamed *The Fatal Breast Stroke*.

He loves good gagmen and he puts Bob Hope in his long list of favourite comedians, whom he takes care to divide according to the rigorous old vaudeville classifications. Bob Hope counts as a high comedian, because he uses words. Buster is a low comedian: 'You're a low comedian as soon as you get into character clothes.' He wouldn't want to stop anyone else using words in the cinema. It is just that he personally doesn't think you need to talk much, in life or in art or anywhere else. He said, between long silences and coughing fits and stompings around the room: 'Say I'm working in a blacksmith's and I'm the blacksmith's assistant. It's perfectly natural for me to work with him for hours without saying anything.'

Two-minute pause.

He lays out a game of solitaire. The room has a lot of old photographs in it. On the table between us there is a card that a studio magnate left stuck in his dressing-table mirror one day soon after the talkies had come in, giving him the sack in three lines. 'In the thirties, if there's a silence,' says Buster, 'they say there's a dead spot.' Stills from his films come to mind: images of that noble gaze, austere and distinct even when the head is up to the ears in water after a shipwreck, or when Buster is in mid-flight of some sort. Partly because of his vaudeville experience and partly because of his temperament, he obviously reserves great respect for those who retain a stoic attitude toward calamity and imminent death in the middle of being flung from one side of life to the other. He admires the character of a performing animal – a gorilla, as I remember, called Peter the Great – who expressed a Senecan serenity as he was being thrown around the stage when Buster was a child.

Presumably because of his violent babyhood, Buster seems to look on himself as a sort of Zeppelin. 'When you go through the air,' he says gravely, as though I were about to, 'you use your head as the rudder.' He demonstrates swiftly. Then we went out to walk round the garden, he coughing and showing me his fruit trees. For all his bronchitis, he still smokes all the time, using a long cigarette-holder that juts out of his mouth like a bowsprit. We look at his grapes and his apricots and the barn in the middle of the land. It has pulleys on it like the beautiful rigging in *The Navigator*. He starts talking in his gravelly voice about a stunt fall he once did for Lew Cody at MGM, when he was already a highly-paid star. The accounts department sent him a stuntman's cheque for $7.50, which pleases him whenever he thinks about it.

'I'm making *The Cameraman*. One day we have a hold-up, so I'm roaming the other sets. Lew Cody's in tails for a dinner party. He's supposed to come down to the cellar and hit a cake of soap. Well, I got down there and I saw a double do it. It was kind of a brutal fall and it wasn't funny. So I said, "Hell, give me the clothes." No dressing-rooms then. So I do the fall' (demonstration), 'my coat-tails cover my head, perfect. You cut to Cody and no one knows. When they showed the rushes they didn't have the chalk marks between the shots and Thalberg thought it was Cody.' Pause. 'Poor Cody. He couldn't fall off a table without breaking his neck.'

★ ★ ★

In 1906, when he was eleven, Buster played little Lord Fauntleroy. There exists a photograph of him in which he exhibits no enormous trust in the part. He wears a black velvet suit with a big lace collar, and suffers the ignominy of ringlets. The huge dark eyes look as if they had never blinked, let alone slept, even at that age. They express a dignified alertness to the possibility of storms or custard pies which might wreck the abhorrent costume in this short-lived – with any luck – reign of fortune's saccharine smile.

Victory over Fauntleroy came soon, with Keaton's film entrance in *The Butcher Boy*. His character is clear at once. We are in a world of slapstick chaos, but he emits a sense of wary order. The scene is a village store. Everyone else moves around a lot, to put it mildly. When Keaton enters, the unmistakable calm asserts itself. He is wearing shabby overalls, and big shoes with a hole in one sole (which later turns out to be usefully open to some spilled molasses), and already the famous flat hat. He then goes quietly through a scene of almost aeronautic catastrophe and subsidence, the whole parabola photographed in one take. Only a child brought up in music-hall mayhem from toddling age could have done it. The shop is hung with posters promising 'Fresh Sausages Made Every Month'. It is run by a Roscoe Arbuckle who puts on a fur coat to go into the freezer locker (Keaton never calls him Fatty: it is always Roscoe). It is inhabited by a club of aloof card-players with Abe Lincoln faces clustered around a stove. It turns into a whirlwind. Molasses sticks, and bodies fly, and flour powders the air. We are in a world of agile apprentices and flung custard pies and badly made brooms that Buster scathingly plucks by the individual bristle, like suspect poultry. And through it all there is the Keaton presence; the beautiful eyes, the nose running straight down from the forehead, the raised, speculative eyebrows, the profile that seems simplified into a line as classical as the line of a Picasso figure drawing. After a bit, Roscoe Arbuckle throws a sack of flour at him. Throughout his life, to many people, Buster has repeated his admiration for the force and address of that throw.

A description of a film thought lost, in celebration. When Buster was twenty-five, in 1920, he made his first feature film, called *The Saphead*, the film version of a Broadway play called *The New Henrietta*, in which Douglas Fairbanks was enormously successful. In the year it was made, Keaton was under exclusive contract to Joseph M. Schenck, who agreed to lend him to Metro. Fairbanks himself suggested that Keaton should play the saphead, whose name is Bertie Van Alstyne. He is a millionaire's son who exudes a surprised and passionate intensity about the windfall of his life. He wears the most elegantly cut suits, and a topper so shining that it looks polished for a turnout class in a horse-show ring. Served breakfast by a butler who even puts the necessary four lumps of sugar in his cup and stirs them for the Master, he nevertheless feels so uncertain of the boon times' durability that he occasionally makes a movement of his hand toward his white carnation as if to protect it from a blow.

Bertie Van Alstyne is a rich nitwit, the first of the loaded figures whom Keaton, alone among the line of comedians born of vaudeville, was able to make funny. Other silent comics (Chaplin particularly) have never made heroes of the well-off. There is something about the antithesis between Keaton's apprehensively anaesthetized face and his classically graceful and courageous body which makes the feat possible. He is one of the few comedians who have managed to be shy, stoic, and dashing at the same time. There is nothing of the tramp about him. He is always impeccably dressed, shaven and chauffeured.

As in *The Navigator*, he is desperately in love in *The Saphead*. His darling this time is Agnes, an orphan adopted by Bertie's father. At the sheerest possibility of sight of her, he leans forward as if his feet were glued to the floor and a gale were blowing his body ahead. The father – played by William H. Crane – is so angry about his son's marrying Agnes that he buys him off with a colossal cheque ('Cutting him off with a million,' says a subtitle) and tells him to get a job. Knowing little about jobs, Bertie looks around him and sees that two people he knows are brokers, so he buys himself a seat on the Stock Exchange. It costs him a hundred thousand dollars. When he hears the price, the Indian-chief face grows more withdrawn than ever, concealing shock courageously. 'Well, furniture is way up these days,' says a subtitle. Thrown out of the house by his father to keep him away from Agnes, he moves into the Ritz, and conducts his life without losing self-esteem or looking at all like a black sheep. As always, his gestures are nobly expressive. Though kicked out of his home, he opens some double doors in his hotel suite for himself with a flourish, as if he were his own two footmen.

Taking his costly seat on the Stock Exchange for the first time, rubbing the arms of a chair with wonder at the cost of a rather ordinary piece of furniture, he finds himself with a piece of paper on his back to identify him to the well-heeled others as a new boy who should be made welcome. It is a welcome in the Evelyn Waugh tradition of the upper classes at their joshing worst. His cane is pulled off his arm; his hat is knocked off again and again. Screams and hoots are emitted by the cognoscenti of this posh boarding school, which parades itself as a place for grown-up men to run the economy of the country. We are in the presence of sunken-continent wit emerging from a few expensively educated idiotic young millionaires who keep their heads above water to bay with laughter at the expense of the rest of the population. Bertie, though a saphead, has more delicacy of spirit. He simply observes the phenomenon, and later remarks unresentfully to Flint, his father's broker, 'All they do here is knock off hats.' Pause. 'But I like it.' Trying to fit in with the custom of the incomprehensible place, he agreeably knocks off the hats of two startled door attendants as he goes out. His clothes for the initiation ceremony are very fine: top hat, morning coat, spats, black and white spotted ascot, gloves with stitching on their backs.

Bertie is not one to make trouble. Knowing his sapheadedness, and having found himself adoringly giving an empty engagement-ring case to Agnes – he had handed the ring itself to the servant for safekeeping, and forgotten what he'd done with it – he equips himself with five wedding rings for her, so that he can have one in every pocket. She seems thrilled. Girls are always very nice in Buster Keaton's films, taking his faults tenderly and trying to buck him up. Nearly fifty years have passed since there was a public screening of *The Saphead,* believed lost. It is a wonderfully funny love story that gives stature to slapstick, and poetry to practical jokes. Where other comedians often yap at your ankles for a response, Keaton treats audiences as if they were not there, and devotes his whole attention to the dilemmas in which he finds himself.

In spite of the peculiarly heroic austerity of his comic temperament, Keaton maintains firmly that he is a low comedian. There are also, among others, tramp comedians and black-face comedians – a category that was stylized for purely technical reasons but that drew some of Keaton's shorts into looking Uncle Tom-ish. The system of vaudeville comedy that he works by is methodical, physically taxing and professionally interpreted. 'Once you've got your realistic character, you've classed yourself. Any time you put a man into a woman's outfit, you're out of the realism class and you're in *Charley's Aunt.*' There are one or two films of Keaton's, early in his career, in which someone wears drag; leaving aside the modern unease about androgyny, the device goes against what Keaton can do.

Keaton's logical and vitally realist nature gradually got rid of the far-fetched, or what he amiably calls just 'the ridiculous'. His comic character is too sobering for that, though infinitely and consolingly funny. Nothing much changes, it says. Things don't get easier. He will be courting a girl, for instance, and have to make way for a puppy, which the etiquette of the girl's demonstrativeness demands that she hug; the proposal that he meant to make to her goes dry in his mouth. He leaves with an air. Seasons pass, the puppy grows to frightful size, and he is still outwitted by her intervening love of pets. Finally, against every sort of odds, and only by great deftness, he manages to marry her, but the chance of kissing her is still obligatorily yielded to others – to the minister, to the in-laws, to the rival suitor and to the now monstrous slobberer, which ends the picture by sitting between the wedding couple on a garden seat and licking the bride's face.

Whatever the mortification, Keaton is never a pathetic figure. His heroes stare out any plight. Perhaps because he has an instinctive dislike of crawling to an audience by exploiting any affliction in a character, including any capacity for being victimized, his figures never seem beaten men, and after a few experiments in his early work he never plays a simpleton. He has perfected, uniquely, a sort of comedy that is about heroes of native highbrow intelligence, just as we have seen him to be the one comedian who has managed to establish qualities of delicate dignity in characters with money. Buster Keaton as the fortunate, debonair, tongue-tied central character of *The Navigator* is one of the rarer creations of comedy; rich, decorous, possessed of a chauffeur who rides him with a grand U-turn all the way across the street to his fiancée's house, infinitely capable of dealing with the exchange and mart of high-flown social marriage, jerking no heartstrings. Keaton's world is a world of swells and toffs as well as butcher boys, and mixed up in it are memories of his hardy past in vaudeville that give some of his films a mood of the surreal. In *The Playhouse*, which he made after breaking his ankle on another picture, he plays not only nine musicians and seven orchestra members but also a music-hall aquatic star, an entire minstrel show, a dowager and her bedevilled husband, a pair of soft-shoe dancers, a stagehand, an Irish char, her awful child. We see the Keaton brat dropping a lollipop on to Keaton as a *grande dame* in the box below; the dowager then abstractedly uses the lollipop as a lorgnette. He also plays a monkey who shins up the proscenium arch: something that must have been rough on the broken ankle. The film has a peculiar aura, not quite like anything else he made. It is dreamlike and touching, with roots in a singular infancy that he takes for granted. Vaudeville is what he comes from, as powerfully as Shakespeare's Hal comes from boon nights spent with

Falstaff. In *Go West*, there is a music-hall set piece about a slightly ramshackle top hat that is kept brilliantly in the air with repeated gun shots. 'It has to be an old hat,' says Buster. 'You couldn't use a new hat. Otherwise, you don't get your laugh. Audiences don't like to see things getting spoiled.'

Keaton has a passion for props. Especially for stylish things like top hats, for sailing-boats and paddle-steamers, and for all brainy machinery. He finds ships irresistible. A short called *The Boat* forecasts *The Navigator*; there is also *Steamboat Bill, Jr*. Facing many calamities, Buster as a sailor works with a sad, composed gaze and a resourcefulness that never wilts. In *Steamboat Bill, Jr*, he leans on a life-preserver that first jars his elbow by falling off the boat and then immediately sinks; Keaton's alert face, looking at it, is beautiful and without reproach. In *The Boat*, where he is shipbuilding, though deflected a good many times by one or another of a set of unsmiling small sons, his wife dents the stern of his creation with an unbreakable bottle of Coke while she is launching it; Keaton helps by leaning over the side to smash the thing with a hammer, and then stands erect while the boat sinks under him in water that comes quickly up to his neck, leaving us to watch the august head turning round in contained and unresentful bafflement. In *Steamboat Bill, Jr*, his last independently produced film, he turns up, looking chipper, to join a long-lost father who runs a steamboat. The son will be recognizable by a white carnation, Buster has bravely said in a telegram, delivered four days late. He keeps authoritatively turning the carnation in his lapel toward people as if it were a police badge. No one is interested. His father eventually proves to be a big, benign bruiser, and not the man his son would have expected; nor is Buster the sort of man his father immediately warms to. He is much put off by the beautiful uniform of an admiral that Buster wears to help on the steamboat. It is not, maybe, fit for running a paddle-steamer, but it is profoundly hopeful. It represents an apparently mistaken dapperness and an admission of instinctive class that turns out to be as correct in the end as the same out-of-place aristocratism in *The Navigator*, that poetic masterpiece of world cinema. There is nothing anywhere quite like the comic, desperate beauty of the long shots of *The Navigator*, when Buster, the rich sap, is looking for his girl on the otherwise deserted liner that has gone adrift. The rows of cabin doors swing open and closed in turn, port and starboard in rhythm, on deck after deck; the debonair, tiny figure with the strict face and the passionate character runs round and round to find his dizzy girl, who is looking for him in her own quite sweet but less heartfelt way. The flower-faced fiancée played by Katherine McGuire in *The Navigator* is a typical Keaton heroine. She is rather nice to him when he has got into his diving suit to free the rudder and has forgotten, with the helmet closed, that there is a lighted cigarette in his mouth. (This apparently happened while Keaton was shooting. 'They closed the suit on me,' he says, coughing, the memory bringing on his present bronchitis, 'and everyone thinks I'm just working up a gag.')

Keaton's characters are outsiders in the sense of spectators, not of nihilists or anarchists. He isn't at his best when he hates people (unlike W. C. Fields, for instance, about whom he talks with regard, doing a brotherly imitation of the voice of men who are martyrs to drinkers' catarrh). A short called *My Wife's Relations* has some of the Fields ingredients, but Keaton muffs the loathing. The picture submits its moments of recoil. The wife is a virago with Irish relations who are devout but greedy; the only way to get a steak, Buster discovers, is to turn the calendar to a Friday. The blows that he manages to give her in bed when she thinks he is only thrashing in his sleep are pretty funny. So are the hordes of rapacious brides in *Seven Chances*, rushing after him on roller skates and wearing improvised bridal veils to make a grab for him because he will inherit a mint if he marries by seven o'clock.

Keaton is at his best when he is being courtly. He has great charm in a feature called *The Three Ages*: about love in the Stone Age, the Roman Age, and the Modern Age, when he stands around among primordial rocks in a fur singlet and huge fur bedroom slippers chivalrously helping enormous girls up boulders. In the Stone Age, prospective in-laws assess the suitors by strenuous blows with clubs, and people ride around on mastodons that are clearly elephants decked out with rococo tusks by Keaton's happy prop men. In the Roman

Age episodes, Wallace Beery as the Adventurer has a fine chariot, and Keaton has a sort of orange crate drawn by a hopeless collection of four indescribable animals. The Romans throw him into a lions' den, but he remembers only the most pleasant thing to remember about lions, which is that they behave well if you do something or other nice to their paws. He takes a paw, washes it, manicures it and dries it. The interested beast responds affably. We switch back to the Stone Age. Keaton, looking more than usually small in the surroundings, is dealing courageously with the colossal opposite sex and hoping privately for more lyric times. He gets them for a moment in the Roman sequences: there is a wonderful shot of a girl's worshipping face as she thinks of Buster when she is in the middle of being pulled by the hair in some impossible Roman torment. But nothing vile in antiquity, Keaton implies by the sudden pinching end of this revue-film, can equal the rich follies of Los Angeles; the Stone Age and Roman Age episodes both finish with shots of Buster and his bride surrounded by hordes of kids in baby fur tunics and baby togas, but the Modern Age episode finishes with a happy couple walking out of a Beverly Hills house followed by a very small spoiled dog.

Such minutes of tart melancholy are often there in Keaton. They go by fleetingly and without bitterness, like the flash in *The Scarecrow* when a girl takes it that his kneeling to do up a shoelace means that he is proposing. His beloveds sometimes have overwhelming mothers; one battle-axe, in *The Three Ages*, causes a pang when she makes him produce his bank balance, which is in a passbook labelled 'Last National Bank' and obviously not up to scratch. One thinks, inevitably, of the hard time that Keaton was to have with his ambitious actress wife, Natalie Talmadge, which left him flat broke when the talkies came in. The Keaton hero, with the scale he is built on, and with his fastidious sense of humour, is obviously the born physical enemy of all awesome women. The girls he loves are shy and funny, with faces that they raise to him like wineglasses. His idyllic scenes are unsentimental. There is silence from him when his battleship sweetheart in *The Navigator* says, in reply to a proposal of marriage, 'Certainly *not*!'

I asked Keaton why there didn't seem to be any great women clowns apart from Beatrice Lillie. He said that he thought the lack was because actresses try too hard and want to be liked. 'What you have to do is create a character. Then the character just does his best and there's your comedy. No begging.'

While he was talking he kept having to walk away and bend over with his hands on his knees in a terrible fit of coughing. He ignored it stonily, as he ignores danger in his films.

The actress he really adored was Marie Dressler. 'She didn't give a thing what you thought of her, you see.' For his own films he needed romantic heroines; shy girls with remote expressions and plummy thighs. He said with his usual terseness that he never insisted on their having a sense of humour, though it was nice if they weren't too stupid.

'I'm shooting this scene, and there's this actress who's the niece of the head of the studio or something. She has to say "I'm glad", and she has to say it through her teeth. She says it looking happy. I say, you're not to look happy. She can't do it. She just can't see how you can say something and mean the opposite. Yuh, it was a silent shot, but I wasn't going to alter the line. I say to her, you go and cancel your date, you're going to do it if it takes me all night. Just a common ordinary close-up and it took me eighteen takes. In the end she was so damn mad about the dinner she did it.'

When Keaton was a director he owned his own cameras. The actors were with him from one year's end to the other, and the only outlay when he wanted to do a day's work was on the film stock. 'Think of it,' he says, 'having to get an okay to do a retake. It's like a painter having to get a permit to do a painting over. If I thought I was going to need a retake I'd just tell the actors not to shave their beards off until I'd looked at the rushes . . .'

'They have too many people working on pictures now, you know,' says the aging, unsoured man. The talkies threw him on the dustheap, though he probably could have gone on making great films in any new circumstances, on a minute budget and editing in a cupboard. 'We had a head electrician, a head carpenter and a head blacksmith.' The blacksmith seems to have been crucial. There was a lot of welding to do. Keaton himself did his stunt work, magically and beautifully. Who else? He could loop through the air like a lasso. When he is playing the coxswain in *College*, and the rudder falls off the boat, it is entirely in character that he should dip himself into the water and use his own body to steer with. The end of *Seven Chances* is an amazing piece of stunt invention, inspired by cascades of falling boulders that would have killed Keaton if he hadn't been an acrobat. Most of his stunt stuff isn't the sort of thing that can be retaken, and Keaton doesn't care much for inserts. 'I like long takes, in long shots,' he says. 'Close-ups hurt comedy. Cinemascope hurts comedy. I like to work full-figure. All comedians want their feet in.'

He has just been asked to the première of *It's a Mad, Mad, Mad, Mad World*, which he has a part in after spending decades doing nothing much but commercials. *Mad World* is in the mode of wide screens with a vengeance. Buster has seen the picture. It can't be much to his taste, but he doesn't say so. He likes working; even making commercials doesn't strike him as such a cruel outcome to a life. He wants to go to the première. He looks vigilant and spry.

The wife of his last years thinks he shouldn't go to the première, because he might get a coughing fit and have to leave.

'We have aisle seats,' he says.

'You're not well,' she says.

'I can take my cough mixture,' he says. 'I can take a small container. I can get ready to move in a hurry.' He was the poet who thought as an acrobat.

★ ★ ★

Alert silence. The deepest comic gift. Keaton and Beckett share it.

If one is to seek, as one must, solid terrain, it will be the axis of courageously satiric and wondering matter. The land of Keaton and of Beckett. Both cling on to the cliff-face of our given lives with no mention of the little purchase accorded, no grievance, all conviviality conferred. Who can say more than the heroine of *Happy Days* as she lays out her toothbrush, up to her neck in sand as she is: 'Another happy day'? She means it.

Good old Earth, silly old Earth, says Beckett.

A professor at Columbia University was lately telephoned by the Nobel Prize Committee to ask whether he could swear on the Bible that Beckett was not a nihilist. Or a pessimist. Or anything conveying the end of a life, or lives. 'Oh, sure,' said the professor.

Good old people, silly old people.

Beckett's *Waiting for Godot*, revived by the English Stage Company in 1968 at the Royal Court in a production as fine and keen as its own prose, first arrived in London in 1955 like a sword burying itself in an over-upholstered sofa. The serious theatre in London in 1955 was a theatre of posturing and flab; the English Stage Company didn't even yet exist, and the frugality of Beckett's play seemed an affront. He had done far too much on far too little. It was hard then for people to sit comfortably in such an ascetic presence, watching a comedy about existence that had no plot, no climax, no star parts, no rousing rhetoric, not even a dilemma apart from the dilemma of how to live, which had long since dropped out of the repertory of questions that could properly be asked in a modern play in England.

There is nothing formidable technically about this greatest of contemporary comedies. The people who called it obscure or pretentious must have been finding labels for their own disquiet, for the method of the play is as clean as a plucked bone, and if the content were insubstantial the situation of the two tramps waiting on the road for a key to their lives could never have become the powerful myth that it has. The only puzzling thing about *Godot* now is not the play, but the way we took it: why on earth did it ever accumulate such a reputation for determinism?

Part of the trouble is perhaps the way Beckett has been bracketed with Ionesco. Ionesco's characters often, by author's intent, talk like ticker-tapes, and they are pushed around helplessly by the circumstances of the world, by goods and chattels and uninspected banalities; Beckett's characters are freely eloquent, with a speech that flies up out of the mundane and tugs in the air like a kite, and they live in a void which they alone have any power over or any obligation to change.

Ionesco's plays are crammed with disagreeably dynamic objects: cupboards that assume the initiative and chairs as fertile as rabbits. Beckett's plays habitually happen in an unfurnished void where the only significant object is the human figure, more or less ugly or infirm but all the same often wonderfully oblivious to handicap. Beckett's characters are anything but pure-dyed pessimists. Like most people in real life, they are capable of feeling at one and the same time that existence is both insupportable and indispensable, and that they are both dying and amazingly well.

'How like a man, to blame on his boots the faults of his feet.' Beckett insists that the tramps' predicaments are their own. The tramp called Vladimir – in one revival he was marvellously played by Nicol Williamson, with whirling arms and the vast skimming lope of a town-born tramp moving over pavements as though they were heather – is prohibited from laughing, but it is a right he has waived, not one that has been removed. A Beckett theme. The urns and mounds that encumber the people in the later plays are not imposed. They are annexes of the characters' temperaments, traps created by their own pasts. Their physical equipment may be grotesquely inadequate for their tasks, but it is all they have, and they are constantly and comically pulling themselves together to mount another feeble attack on the objective, which is 'to represent worthily for once the foul brood to which a cruel fate confined us'.

Beckett's characters are perpetually trying to carve out of the boundless grey flux a piece of time that will have some form of gaiety. They are devoted to trying to make art out of the unpromising material of life, and to bringing off at least one achieved stylistic feat as a way of beating the dark. If this is determinism, I don't recognize it.

In *Godot* the two tramps behave as though they had a sacred obligation to turn the day into a piece of music hall. It is impossible for them to sustain the effort for long, but they keep nerving themselves to have another go, standing back after a burst of backchat to have a look at the result as though they had to be their own audience in the void. 'That wasn't a bad little canter,' says Estragon encouragingly to them both after one spurt. *Godot* is a very affectionate play. Vladimir and Estragon are locked together in a relationship that is a haunting celibate replica of a marriage. They are pitiless in waking each other up for company because they are lonely, thereby restoring one another to the horror of their situation. Part of the great power of the second act is that by then each has discovered that the other is better and happier without him, and is trying not to admit that the same might be true of himself, for fear that this might force solitude finally upon them.

Anthony Page's production for the English Stage Company in 1964 – much less broad than Peter Hall's of 1955 – was characteristically self-effacing, with an ear for the rhythms of the text. Pozzo – played by Paul Curran in clothes like a Jorrocks groom – had a boss's accent that crumbled quickly into brotherhood with the tramps. For he and Lucky are as beleaguered by panic as the tramps. Pozzo is linked inseparably to an idiot who was once his good angel and is now tormenting him to death. In the first act the idiot – played in the Anthony Page production by Jack MacGowran – has a twitching tirade that employs a breakdown of language with more grief and horror than any other speech I can think of in our half-century of experiments with incoherence. Placed where it is, it might well have subdued the whole of the rest of the play if it weren't for Pozzo's great outburst in the second act. The tramps ask Pozzo when his idiot went dumb:

> When! When! One day, is that not enough for you, one day like any day, one day he went dumb, one day I went blind, one day we'll go deaf, one day we were born, one day we'll die, the same day, the same second, is that not enough for you? They give birth astride a grave, the light gleams an instant, then it's night once more.

When a man writes with this noble comic stoicism he can break any rules that he likes.

* * *

A note, about the shared quality of common sense that above all links Beckett to Keaton and that gives birth to brave comedy.

True or not, the story goes that the quizzical artist Jasper Johns, visiting Beckett, showed him the drawings for *Fizzles*, their collaborative book. They were Johns's cross-hatch drawings. Each line crossing another's path. *Ad inf.* Beckett, his sight failing, took up a drawing and, holding one edge very close to one eye, peered across the surface like someone checking wood for warpage. Johns waited quietly as Beckett slowly rotated the drawing, keeping his eye close to the edge. Finally Johns broke the silence with offer of explanation. Beckett refused. 'No, no,' he said, 'I see what you're doing. Every time it wriggles, you hit it with a brick.'

Mind, Face and Wishbone

There is an obstinate comic truth in T. S. Eliot's 'Mankind cannot bear too much reality,' and it is borne out with due pained comedy by Genet, Pirandello, Ionesco. The last of Genet's remarkable books, *Un Captif Amoureux*, has to do with the feeling he had for the Black Panthers and unswervingly for the Palestinians. He found happiness in being with the Palestinians in the Jordan civil war. Few such fiercely comic playwrights have written so gently of nomads. He was himself one, and in Palestine's difficulties he found his mortal kin. Through Palestine's predicament, representative of what he had always understood, he was freed to write about a society insensible to bisexuality and open to the apparent paradox of the delight that Mozart transmits in his *Requiem*. Mozart, of all people who beggared death. Thus Genet's high response to his mind, most specifically in *Un Captif Amoureux*.

So. Great spokesmen on the wander that we call comic, for lack of other adjective sufficient: quitting the world of censors and politicians to traipse space in search of both wilder and more ordinary things.

* * *

The film of Jean Genet's *The Balcony* is very funny about forbidden, grave matters. Maybe this is one of the reasons why the then film censor in England refused to give it a certificate in 1963 but left it to individual local councils to license it. For *The Balcony* uses as its device an enormously enlarged and inventive idea of sex. It employs sex as a code for religion and power and rebellion. And anything that extends the limits of physical experience like this, and worse still presents it as comic, has a hard time with the watchdogs.

The Secretary of the Board of Film Censors told me that he admired it very much. He thought it 'marvellous for intellectuals', but was doubtful about the others, which sounds like the legal *Lady Chatterley* argument about would-you-give-it-to-your-wife-or-your-maid. He said he was anxious for the film not to get into the wrong hands; but what are the wrong hands for a good film? Supposing it were taken up by every blue cinema and advertised with the most misleading X posters out, what on earth would it matter? Supposing tens of thousands of lonely men in raincoats bought tickets hoping they were going to see the usual awful film about prostitutes, would that be a bad thing?

The Balcony was directed by Joseph Strick and scripted by Ben Maddow from Bernard Frechtman's translation. It keeps about half of Genet's original, and what it keeps is the better half, the first act. After that the play flies apart into fragments of symbolism, but the film script holds firmly.

Genet's brothel, his House of Illusions, is set now in a film studio. Outside a savage revolution is going on; inside the tarts are waiting for custom and being told by the Madame not to sit on their costumes. A bride in full fig is soaking her feet in a mustard bath. In one of the private rooms, visible in Madame's office on closed-circuit TV, a worker in a boiler suit dressed up as a bishop has just heard confession from a tart dressed up as a widow. In another room a mock general is treating a whore as his horse, and in another a mock judge is irritably trying to stop his defendant confessing her crime too soon.

The clients in the film have very little expert knowledge of their fantasy jobs, which is one of the things that make them moving characters. The bishop in the stage play has read enough theology to say that the Devil is an actor, which is why the Church has anathematized actors; but the bishop in the film has the vaguest ideas about religion and knows only that he wants to see real tears of repentance, 'wet as a meadow'. The general addresses his imaginary army in a surge of excitement about militarism, but in the end all he can manage is a feeble salute to 'this vast hup-2-3-4'. The chief of police, a real character deeply hurt because nobody wants to borrow his uniform, has a vast vision of patriotism when he addresses the populace from the studio gantry, but he comes out with a piece of gibberish oratory that is mischievously like an American president talking in his sleep. The character who underpins them all – much more than in the play – is the Madame. She treats her clients gently, as though she were in danger of startling sleepwalkers. She also seems to regard them as though they were all small boys, which I suppose is what makes her seem a specifically American character. Shelley Winters plays the part beautifully, with a caustic, grown-up sensuality that is rare. Simone Signoret was one of the few other actresses who had it.

What makes *The Balcony* questioning is the intelligence of the way it is organized, and the springy humour of the script. The dialogue in the opening scenes is written in an electrifying comic idiom, a sparring severity that is half mocking but at the same time meant to be obeyed. This isn't a style that is special to the vicious, as censors seem to think; it is used by most people who understand play, including children.

Like Genet's judge and Genet's bishop, children playing know that things have to be done in a certain order, that details have to be insisted on in fantasy, and that out of this peculiar mixture of pretence and self-exposure a more vivid kind of reality emerges. *The Balcony* is about people's need to understand things with their skins as well as with their minds. It is a work in the great surreal tradition of comedy.

★ ★ ★

Ionesco's *Le Piéton de l'air* begins rockily but ends magnificently. Like his great full-length play *Exit the King*, it is about a man called Bérenger who is suddenly aware that he is going to die. Along with the rest of us, he has managed for most of his life to obscure from himself the prospect of extinction, and when he arrives in England with his wife and daughter at the beginning of the play he is absorbed by naively-seen appearances. The landscape he drops into looks like a primitive, with glowing toy-farm trees and a grapejuice sky like the one in Chagall's *Poet Reclining*; and the grazing is occupied by a set of characters who are deliberately simplified English archetypes.

For the first part of the play – which Jean-Louis Barrault in celery-green once played in a dehumanized mood – the hero behaves very like Ionesco himself in his own puckishness. He gives morosely funny interviews about being tired of actors and of playwrights fighting yesterday's injustices. When Bérenger speaks of 'the years going by like a lot of sacks we send back empty', and a middle-aged lady suddenly voices the universal thought that it is only other people who ever make us know that we are older, the comedy grows as powerfully as *Les Chaises*. It moves from the waking to the sleeping world: back to the skills we have in dreams, which make Bérenger joyfully able to fly; and to childhood nightmares of lost parents.

At his best, which he is in this play, Ionesco is a transcriber of dreams, a witness to fears that we spend a third of our lives inexorably remembering and can forget only in the daytime. In a scene that works with a child's sense of play, Bérenger levitates and cycles off into the cosmos to explore the afterlife: his report of heaven, which no one believes, is of a monster's world full of columns of guillotined men, men with the heads of geese licking monkeys' behinds, a paradise where the blessed are burned alive, and beyond that nothing but abysmal space. *Le Piéton de l'air* follows a daring split scheme: it is seized in the second part by vertigo and anguish, but it is consistently funny with a straight-faced acceptance of life's absurdity that is Ionesco's mark.

★ ★ ★

The sight of actors at a rehearsal when they are not acting happens to be one of life's natural theatrical draws. Next to men making tea around a hole in the middle of Piccadilly, the prospect that opens Pirandello's *Six Characters in Search of an Author* must be one of the most crowd-gathering spectacles of non-work that there is.

Giorgio di Lullo's production in Italy: the stage was bare. The cream brick walls of the stage, towering and dirty, dwarfed the human figures like the perspectives of one of the early nineteenth-century Romantic engravings of asylums. The company of actors hectically doing nothing included an aging leading man, an ancient trouper who says that the lines are the thing, an ingenue in a purple sweater that upsets a superstitious actress, an old-guard leading lady dressed in a lumpy beaver coat with an artificial flower pinned on the shoulder. Onstage there was an upright piano, two full-length mirrors, and the characteristic Italian prompt-box downstage rising out of the floor like a conning tower.

With a typical lick of rancorous humour, Pirandello makes the play that they begin to creak through his own *Rules of the Game*, nothing to do with Renoir's. And Giorgio di Lullo added a conceit of his own: before the actors loafed on to start *Rules of the Game*, he showed them loafing off to make their entrances in *Six Characters in Search of an Author*. The play within the play. Within another play.

The companionship of these people is obviously tenth-rate, but all the same ebulliently confident. It is a bit like the playing of a Sicilian brass band. Into this amiable chaos of exhibitionism, where an ambitious prompter fails to contain himself during the leading man's best pause, wander six creatures from another system. There is a grey-lipped widow clutching two children, an older son, a remorseful father with a moustache like mule-panniers, and a vengeful red-headed step-daughter. They are lost souls from an abandoned play, and for Pirandello the salient difference between them and the other characters is that their identities are fixed because they are fictional, whereas the 'real' people are suggestible existentialists for whom everything is in flux.

The 'real' people feel themselves to exist only through other people's apprehension of them. The characters looking for an author, on the other hand, are in a determinist trap where they feel dependent upon someone else to write the very narrative of their lives. The fierce figments who have wandered on to the stage are apparently consigned to an existence of doodling, re-enacting their characteristics over and over again and finally watching the purple abandoned draft of their lives being performed by members of the hack company.

The father, a harrowing middle-aged lecher in a grey mac who walks with a flat-footed lope and looks like a rapist on the last tube train, sees himself embodied by a dandy elocutionist and finds that the act of representation has changed everything for him. His own past no longer seems to belong to him. Lines to his step-daughter that have become unbearably painful keep striking the producer as merely marvellously theatrical.

Pirandello's form is partly a stand against the dead conventions of theatre that subordinated people to plot and pumped out three acts of motives like motor fuel. But it is a lot more than that. It often seems to be suggesting that there are a great many people in the world apart from the six characters whose lives are spent waiting for parts to be written for them. Pirandello's twentieth-century desolation goes with a fondness of feeling that is less obvious. There are enormously touching flashes of contact between this group of people who feel themselves to be irredeemably someone else's raw material and the ones whose occupation as role players has robbed them of the sense that anything is to be counted on. Why Pirandello is ever put with Shaw, apart from chronology, I can't imagine. Shaw asks 'What?' and 'Why?' and 'How?' Pirandello asks only 'Who?', absorbed in fatalist questions about the self that lie in the mainstream of Christian thought and often seem close to T. S. Eliot's.

The plot is of a love triangle in which every conventional characteristic is reversed. The lover is cautious and punctilious. The husband is plump and acquiescent in a city suit and happily gives his wife a freedom that infuriates her. And the wife, a slinky post-cubist beauty with hand movements off an Egyptian jug, finds her lover too subjective and incapable of abstract thinking.

Di Lullo's late sixties' staging had a quick child's way of twitching back the curtains on his trio. The domestic interiors made a stylish vessel, hardened into a pastiche of 1920s' smartness drawn with the bright perspectives of a de Chirico painting. Romolo Valli's performance as the husband, eyes sharp as needles but vacant at the same time, made a very funny study of an Olympian obsequiousness. The character cooked augustly in his library and mouthed the responses of both sides in turn when he was involved in a fight with the two other people in the triangle. Most of the time he preferred to engage himself in an effort to exist as little as possible, successfully smothering the others with the weight of his self-effacement.

Six Characters is a play written with suave wit: peekaboo is all right, as long as we too are behind the curtain.

* * *

I don't believe that the general public is anything like as devoted to the old narrative conventions as it is still assumed to be. The avant-garde hostility to the well-made comedy isn't a closeted snobbism; it expresses a doubt about whether the form still has the power to be genuinely popular. A real popular comedy is simply one that can excite and exhort and amuse a very large majority of people into reacting with the greatest density, interest and recognition of which they are capable, and it seems perfectly possible that today audiences aren't stimulated by the same things as audiences of twenty years ago.

Perhaps the chaotic and the censorable are more recognizable now than the ordered and the generally admitted. Maybe the deliberate provocation of shock and scepticism that has been experimented with in comedy by Genet and Beckett and Brecht isn't the prancing of a coterie in a corner, but an attempt to discover the devices that might give back to a large audience the pitch of theatrical experience that we still find in Shakespeare but no longer find in *Mrs Tanqueray*.

There is a lot to be learnt from the success of *The Goon Show* and *Son of Oblomov*, where the whole device is one of holding the well-made anything up to ridicule and cheerfully facing an audience with its long-suppressed knowledge that actors aren't really the people they are playing. We readily accept the shortcuts of the surreal, especially in comedy. The funny is always a shortcut. It has no need to explain itself or to represent a literal world. Harold Pinter, Swiftian observer, for instance: he can magnify his characters' jumping nerves and trigger fingers in giving them urgent lines about the seemingly inconsequential. Assumptions that the arts using language must be literal are chains that comedy shakes off. All social satire does it. The shortcut is to sense.

* * *

Satire shows self-deception. It is the more pitying when the self-deception is enforced by ruling fashion. *Tartuffe* at its greatest is played not as a study of an outrageous hypocrite, but as a study of a middle-aged man hopelessly bamboozled by youth. And satire shows us man as animal, ruled by sense of terrain, and the suspicion that speech may be a mortally misleading means of communication sprung on the species rather late in the day. When people say to each other 'What did he mean by that?' they don't want to know what the words meant but what you think the speaker said them for. They want to know if you caught sight of a knife being whipped out from nowhere. The tramp in Pinter's *The Caretaker* is haunted by suspicions of malevolence, but he has no one to ask about them; so when he is talked to, he often says 'What?', not because he hasn't heard, but as a hopeless way of gaining time and puzzling out how much ground he has just lost.

The fact that people often talk like this, replying not to the meaning of speech but to what they can guess about motives, is such a simple and compassionate observation that it is hard to think how so many writers of dialogue have managed without it for so long. Unless your characters are Jesuits, to follow a question by the answer that makes logical sense is a very stylized way to write lines.

For thousands of years, artists with a watchful mind have been drawing people in profile showing them to have two eyes. Trudging pop entertainment, sunk full fathom five in literalness, says 'Hey, there's only one.' In the ellipses of the funny, the clinchingly satiric, to follow the line 'Where were you born?' with the form-filler's answer throws not much of comedy's light. The scared tramp of *The Caretaker* makes the characterized reply: 'What do you mean?' The stinking, wary old man answers like this because he thinks the brother who has given him a bed in his lumber room is trying obscurely to get at him. If he could get down to his papers in Sidcup, everything would be all right. He has talismanic feelings about Sidcup, just as he has about his shoes.

The Caretaker is very funny. It is by nature also painful: the tramp is a study in terrible servility. He has a persistent gesture as though he were touching his cap, and sometimes fills in a pause with 'Good luck' like a beggar. The second brother seems sent to plague him and to take away the puny hospitality he has won; but however much the tramp hates him, he is ready to abase himself to please him. His brain goes over both the brothers' words without getting anything more out of them, like a defunct carpet sweeper that has stopped picking up the dust. Every reflex he has is secretive: he eats with his mouth open, in an elaborate mime of honesty that seems designed to show onlookers exactly what he has in there, but he instinctively waits to swallow until no one is looking. He pretends to be asleep when he is awake, and he wears his clothes as though he were hoarding them. When he sits down in his filthy overcoat he lifts the skirt like a pianist in tails.

Pinter's *The Homecoming* is an exultant achievement. Quite apart from the extraordinary experience of seeing a modern play that demands to be produced in a style as achieved as the best we do for Shakespeare, it is the stirring spectacle of a man in total command of his talent.

'It's a question of how much you can operate *on* things, not *in* things,' says a character voicing the theme; 'I mean, it's a question of keeping a balance between the two.' This is one of the notions that Pinter's conflicts spring from. There are people who can only operate *in* things, like the name-character in *The Caretaker*, and people who can only operate *on* things, like the name-character in *The Servant*; in situations where they are incapable of keeping a balance they are thrown into fear and fury. The inch-by-inch fighting that makes up the matter of Pinter's plays is never to gain the points that are openly declared. It comes out of a mutually murderous mood between a man who feels himself to be floundering in a swamp and a man who loathingly sees himself to be keeping his feet dry.

In *The Homecoming* there are five men in the family. Mum is dead. Their home is a vast open-plan North London living-room: working-class tat in epic concrete. In its first production the magnificent structure by John Bury was furnished with a Welsh dresser painted Berlin-black and a smoky-cut armchair. The whole set was in monotone blacks and greys, the colours of mashed newspapers and cigarette ash and old socks. Uncle Sam, who holds the reins of the kitchen, is a diluted man who works as a chauffeur and has some dim sense of importance about taking his bosses to London Airport. Dad is a retired butcher with a perfect grasp of the fact that half of the grating comic power of the dialogue comes from speaking a line against its surface meaning; roaring hatred when demanding a hug, or vilifying his puny life when his words are apparently boasting about it.

The two sons at home are a beefwit demolition expert who boxes in his spare time and a neat lad who turns out to be a pimp of dapper and glinting ferocity. The visiting son is a doctor of philosophy, a cut above them and equipped with a rilingly sexy wife. Like the pimp, their habit of character is to operate on things, and their effect on the three who operate in things is enraging and hideous.

The comedy in *The Homecoming* is not the plot. In Pinter it never is. It consists in the swaying of violent people as they gain minute advantages. A man who does the washing-up has the advantage over a man sitting in an armchair who thinks he can hear resentment in every swilling tea-leaf. The member of the married couple who stays up late has the advantage over the one who goes to bed first. A father has the advantage over his children as long as he can make them think of their birth and not let them remind him of his own death: the sons are condemned to ruminate interminably about what happened 'the night they were made in the image of those two people, at it'.

Pinter must stylize more than any writer in England apart from Ivy Compton-Burnett. His people are entirely creatures of manoeuvre, hence the peculiar freezing mood of their moments of randiness. The sexual instinct in Pinter isn't at all emotional or even physical; it is territorial. There is one woman in *The Homecoming*, his recurring character of a tarty bourgeois wife who contemplates promiscuity as evenly as if she were counting the doilies, who looks on her body rather as a landlord would look on a corner site. The moment she has apparently been exploited sexually, she has the advantage because she owns the property.

* * *

Congreve's comedies aren't about people who see sex as a pleasure. They are about sex used as a form of currency to purchase something else. In the theatre of sophisticated periods this often seems to happen. In a lot of modern American plays, the hero uses conventional sex to buy proof that he isn't a social deviationist. In Noël Coward's comedies, sex sometimes seems to be a coin to pay for the company of a wit at breakfast. In Congreve's *Love for Love* it is used to buy money, with every courtship in the plot wooing an estate; love for loot.

Congreve wasn't actually a Restoration playwright, as he is taken to be. His period of work was William and Mary's, when people had stopped celebrating the end of Cromwell's austerity and started to be enthralled by trade. It was the time of the rise of the merchant class, of coffee houses 'full of Smoak and Strategems', of emptying churches and growing piety about shop-keeping. *Love for Love* is filled with images of money. Conscience is 'a domestic Thief', a poet 'sells Praise for Praise', the woman who gives most pleasure is the tart who can be bought. A key passage has a horrible image of sexual vigour as an old man's bank balance, with Sir Sampson Legend pawing a desirable heiress to give her 'a Rent Roll of his Possessions'.

Often now, Congreve productions look more like an estate agent's dream of a past updated to glossy than Congreve's own reeking new world. The clothes seem dry-cleaned, and you could eat off the whoring Mrs Frail. But some details withstand anything: the background of ragged business figures, the hero's booby brother, seen as a stinking tar-barrel whose dreadful but original jokes make the secondhand wits in the play recoil as sharply as his garlic breath. The most promising and long-lived character is always Tattle, played by, among the thousands of others, Olivier, in 1965: memorable as a marvellously funny study in the frantic perceptions of the supposedly stupid.

Congreve, Genet, Pirandello, Pinter, they write about an eternal subject of comedy: face. Tattle maintains it with all his might. As von Stroheim did till nearly the end of his career, when the detectives in worldliness found him wanting in high birth.

Wallace Stevens has genealogy in its proper context, describing it as the science of correcting other genealogists' mistakes.

* * *

Apart from Orson Welles, there can never have been a great comic director whom the industry treated as badly as Erich von Stroheim. Eisenstein may have declared that he was one of the three men he most admired in Hollywood – the other two were Chaplin and Disney – but the studios loathed his guts.

They hacked his pictures to shreds, and they did their best to make his creativity look like arrogance. Though he wrote and partly edited *Greed* himself, believing that 'no twelve people can write a book or paint a work of art', they paid him only for directing it, so that he had to mortgage his house and his life insurance. And in spite of being the first director to provoke the phrase 'sex appeal', which must be the most money-making notion there has ever been, they insisted that he cost them too much.

Stroheim in fact made a great deal of money for Hollywood. *The Merry Widow* alone cleared five million dollars for MGM. One of the many ironies of this cruel industry is that it seeks to extinguish the very men who eventually produce the biggest profits. The line is always to pretend that they are financial risks, but it is really their talent that hurts; when art is run by accountants, talent seems too obstreperous.

Stroheim was about a quarter of the way through *Queen Kelly*, with Gloria Swanson, when Al Jolson opened his mouth in the first sound picture, and Hollywood seized on the excuse to be rid of him. They panicked, ignored his suggestion that they might add a synchronized soundtrack and drove him out. The scenes he had shot were put together end to end by Gloria Swanson, and that was the last Stroheim ever released.

Mauled and re-edited as they are, his extant films are some of the most mindful works of satiric comedy in the cinema. Beside them, nearly everything else seems what he once called 'a metal hamburger'. Like D. W. Griffith, whom he worked with as an extra and then as an assistant director, Stroheim can somehow fill a frame with such extraordinary flickering life that it now seems twice the size of one of the loping wide-screens. He made films about what he called 'the real axis of things', with a harsh emotional shrewdness; and this is just as true of the extravagant, sarcastic stories set in Viennese palaces as it is of *Greed*, about working-class America.

Lotte Weisner quotes him as saying that the difference between him and Lubitsch is that, while Lubitsch shows us a king on his throne before showing him in his bedroom, Stroheim shows the bedroom first so that we have no illusions left by the time we get to the throne. *The Wedding March* begins with some wicked scenes of royal awakenings. Prince Ottoker and his languid wife are stretching in an atmosphere of long-established loathing, and their son, played by Stroheim, is making a pass at the housemaid in the middle of a foul hangover. During the son's loveless marriage to a rich cripple there is a metaphor as shocking as any in Swift because it is so savagely placed: in the middle of the cathedral scenes encrusted with the peculiar Stroheim glitter, there is suddenly a shot of a skeleton's hands on the organ.

Like everyone else, Hollywood always believed that Stroheim was lashing a Viennese world that he knew backwards. Peter Noble's *Hollywood Scapegoat*, which is based on Stroheim's own documentation, gives him a father in the dragoons and a mother in waiting to the Empress Elizabeth. It was a piece of research by Denis Marion published in *Sight and Sound* that revealed that the whole famous Stroheim character was a fiction, and that he was really the son of a Prussian-born Jew who made hats.

The deception doesn't at all diminish him. Stroheim lived his whole life by bluff. When he first came to America he managed to eat by working as a guide, inventing information about buildings he had never seen before. He was right to twist the tail of any community like Hollywood's that despised his genius and vastly respected his grandness. He once referred to the mediocrities who had power over him as 'the lousy buttonhole makers'; he identified the enemies of his work with his own bourgeois past, which was perhaps why he had to be rid of it. A satirist's position. A farce-maker's position.

* * *

Tricky situations in English farce happen in drawing-rooms, not in bedrooms. They are physical, but only about the physically ungainly; they are not what English censors called 'gratuitously sexual', a phrase now archaic, but still used in America. It lasts with the manager of the Whitehall, house of farce. He once reprovingly wrote to me: 'We don't have sex. That's not our style.' When trousers come down in English farce, it is because they *fall* down.

An evening at the Whitehall draws its public partly because it offers an absolutely reliable world, a code of values that is never questioned, and a set of characters who are never troubled by an adult ambition or desire. Class distinctions are accepted as inalienably right, constables wipe their boots before coming in for a cup of tea, and no one in the play would dream of being found with anything but the most unchallenging cliché on his lips.

There is a verb that should exist in English and French, and that is the verb 'to trouse', meaning to set a farce in action; that which so acts is a trouser. '*Le drame trousera*', they are about to be let down by their trousers. '*Il se trousa*', he went and troused himself.

One of Feydeau's nippiest works about the bottom half of men's clothing is *The Birdwatcher.* The hero is a doctor who writes swelling verse in his spare time and shouldn't be caught in his combinations in a hundred years. In a fine production in London, he sometimes leaned against an invisible gale, like a dog straining against a leash, quoting a dreadful line while he was on his way out of the door to get some champagne for an irredeemably prosaic married woman. 'Oh, poetry,' she says, 'that is nice'; like 'Oh, Ovaltine.'

Physically the performance was spruce and rubbery. When his wretchedly wronged and debagged frame had been used to propel a new bout of plot, it bounced up into position again like the figure of a footballer in a pinball machine. In emergencies, which is to say in underclothes, he danced as though the world were scalding the soles of his feet. He expressed an exquisite confusion between the proprieties of a brisk GP and the proprieties of a rotten poet, having hygienic principles for other people about not making a fuss but also upholding his right to a good wallow.

An overriding sense of propriety is the key of farce. Where tragic characters feel pain, farcical characters in very much the same extremities will merely feel offence. Often they have to endure professional ruin as final as the Macbeths'; they may well also be cursed with the family of a Lear and the ill-luck of an Oedipus, whose lifelong capacity to be in the wrong place with the wrong information at the wrong moment would have equipped him to do very well in the Civil Service. But in spite of all this, they suffer nothing. Like the heroes of antique tragedy, they submit to a hostile fate at the level of etiquette.

The characters in *The Birdwatcher* feel only social humiliation, not a sense of damage to life, and when the long arm of coincidence smites them it is only the leg of an incriminating pair of trousers.

* * *

Shaw once wrote that his chief objection to monogamy was the existence of its offspring, farcical comedy. No. Mormon polygamy, if it has a historic dramatic reservoir, would lead to nothing but an alternative ordinariness. Attempted adultery is aborted in great farce with a carefully carpentered technique that can lead to one of the great modes of humour.

People who dislike farce often say that their reason for hating it is that the characters are inhuman, making the form unfunny and frivolous. I think 'inhuman' is the wrong word. The people in classic farce are not so much inhuman as partially human, men with half their characteristics cut away. Characters in farce undergo the most severe stylization in all drama, because everything superficial is uncompromisingly isolated. Far from being responsible for making the form unfunny or frivolous, it seems to me that it is exactly this process that can make farce hilarious and serious.

The character in the middle of the appallingly funny action of Feydeau's *A Flea in Her Ear* is a brisk Parisian bourgeois who has suddenly grown impotent in bed with his wife. If he were a fully described man – if he weren't stylized, but existed instead in something like a drawing-room comedy – this wouldn't be much of a joke. It becomes more tempting to laugh when Feydeau establishes that the thing that has put the poor man off is a Customs officer, of all sure-fire erotic wet blankets: a figure that he thinks of constantly, in which a seduction scene is wrecked by an official who bursts in saying 'Anything to declare?'

But the fact that most makes it possible to laugh is that the character's violent feelings are not about sex, but about etiquette and face. Albert Finney, in a National Theatre production by Jacques Charon in 1966, gave a very funny account of the sexually slowed hero with everything but brisk expediency disciplined out of it. He also doubled as a slow-witted hotel houseboy who gets intricately mistaken for the anxious bourgeois; facing a theatre full of born class experts, it was a difficult thing to bring off.

The houseboy is incessantly victimized and bawled at, but nothing shakes him. Like all figures in farce, his self-esteem is impregnable. In the stylizing process his capacity for pain has been cut away. Another character achieves the unlikely task of making a cleft palate hysterically funny for exactly the same reason; unlike any real afflicted man who has ever been, he has no idea of the way other people see him. In his own loving eyes he is a perfect enunciator, and it is the other people's ears that need cleaning out. 'I' a bi' thi',' he complains sourly. In the meantime the world tells him, with vintage heartlessness, not to talk with his mouth full.

The mumbler has great charm and no neurosis at all. When he suddenly loses his false teeth he dives after them in a mood of mere pooh-poohing irritability, like a man chasing a lost bowler in a high wind. He is never mortified by his affliction: he is only huffy.

Seventy-five percent of the action of farce springs from huffiness: the rest from panic and architecture. The architecture in this particular production, designed by André Levasseur with a pristine sense of the taste of the square but doggish in the 1900s, has an alibi hotel bed that can be swung round in a crisis to present an identical bed on the other side of the wall with a bitterly non-adulterous old man in it. Someone in the play says that men and women are the only two of God's creatures who lie. As far as farce is concerned, an even more crucial characteristic about us is that we are the only two of God's creatures who possess the evil gift of suspecting lying in others. The agent of the action in this play, which is mechanically perfect, is the sniffy nose for fibs possessed by the hero's wife, in Charon's production a redhead in a tabby boa, overplayed with electric attack and funniness by Geraldine McEwan. She may have based some of her performance on Groucho Marx: the same 'aha!' head movement, describing an arc like a lobbed tennis ball; her eyes swivelled lewdly from side to side, sometimes narrowing as though over an obstreperous cigar. The effect in a pretty woman is very funny. It was the best female performance in a farce that I had seen in England.

It isn't really lechery that gets the characters in farce into trouble, because they never feel an emotion so conscious of anyone else. Their undoing is their disastrous mixture of rock-hard vanity and jelly fluster. The two vainest lovers in the play are non-French, perhaps because Feydeau anticipated the difficulty of getting a French audience to see anything funny in Frenchmen being sexually proud of themselves. One of the butts is German, naturally; the other is a jealous husband called Carlos Homenides de Histuanga, best to be played with an exquisite Spanish lisp, sucking in lurid cheeks below lime-rimmed eyes and dragging his toes as though to the applause of a crowd in a bullring when threatening *crimes passionnels*. He is suspicious on principle, even about a doctor who has only carried out a test on him: 'Why did he make me pith?' he yells, ready to kill.

The passions in the play are all like this. They are the passions of throwing down duelling-cards, steaming open letters, snubbing invitations; the play is like a deckle-edged Greek tragedy with an RSVP at the end of it, and this is exactly the note that John Mortimer's social ear caught so funnily in one translation. 'I am ready to commit a folly,' writes a lady graciously on scented paper. 'Will you join me?'

Feydeau's *Hotel Paradiso*, revived, translated, and directed by Peter Glenville in 1956, is a now ninety-three-year-old farce of clockwork cunning and, once you accept its postulates, impregnable plausibility. A hen-pecked husband takes his best friend's wife to a shady hotel on the very night when events are conspiring to bring almost everyone he knows to the same squalid rendezvous, which is run by an Italian voyeur who drills peepholes in the walls. Verbally, little is memorable: what matters is the dazzling economy of the construction. Feydeau wastes nothing. If an elderly barrister has a habit of stammering whenever it rains, be sure that this infirmity will play a vital part in the dénouement. The naked offstage woman who demands a pack of cards is not merely funny in herself; she also establishes at a stroke the atmosphere of the hotel.

Irene Worth is a deeply intelligent actress whom we associate with the roles of women interestingly doomed. But in 1956 she appeared with a top hat jammed over her chin. Martita Hunt was formidable, a wounded pterodactyl, indulging in regal dismissive gestures which suggested that she was conducting an invisible symphony orchestra; yet when she was made to fence with a hatpin, one got the same happy, tripped-feet feeling as when Irene Worth wore her topper or when Alec Guinness was compelled to put his head up a chimney and emerge covered in suave soot. The joke is not so much about the characters in the play as about the dignity of the august people cast to play them, an outrageous humiliation which suits the ignominies so nobly brushed aside in farce.

Qualms vanish, for Guinness is giving a display of such exquisite stealth that it transcends all objections. We have seen him in this vein before: the chubby, crafty little fellow obsessed by an urge to break out and show the world his mettle. Twinges of remorse occasionally contort his face, but, once resolved, he will live dangerously. What though his plans miscarry? He will have made his tiny protest, like that respectable resident of the Ritz in Paris who one day smuggled into his room five white mice in a paper bag and set them free in the corridor with cries of 'Mice in the Ritz! Mice in the Ritz!': cries, alas, which nobody heard.

Not the least wonderful thing in Guinness's performance is its sheer physical dexterity. In the 'morning after' scene he is almost unmasked as the black-faced sweep of the night before. 'He was about your size,' says someone suspiciously. 'Oh, no. Much taller!' cries Guinness, crumpling into a chair and shrinking before our eyes to the dimensions of a pickled walnut. Most creative *farceur*.

★ ★ ★

I have worshipped Ben Travers's farces ever since I was a

schoolgirl. This is a stumbling love-note, slipped across the desks under cover of a revival of his *Thark*.

Ben Travers, the hero of the pre-war Aldwych Theatre, was a comic master. *Thark* itself is a title of genius: better than *Hamlet*. The world of archetypes that Mr Travers created, the brow-beaten husbands and dithering fiancés and suspicious, critical matriarchs called Bone or Twine, is ripe and timeless. He has an instinctively radical spirit, and his beautiful style has most often made me agog with laughter even in bad weekly rep productions.

The great thing about his characters is that they have exceptionally fast brains. The lower orders in the Aldwych farces put up with murder alertly. When Mrs Leverett is identified by vague young men as 'Mrs Flannelfoot' and 'Mrs Thunderguts' it seems a petrifying impertinence. A butler in *Thark*, a morbid visionary quite properly called Death, has to change his name to Jones to oblige a nervous mistress, but it is obviously as absurd as rechristening Jehovah.

Faced though they are by wage-paying battle-axes and living in an atmosphere of bedroom fluster that they find very offensive, the employees preserve a stoic isolation and tend to become the umpires. They make their positions darkly plain and speak with the tongue of convention. Their verbal mannerisms are elliptical, to put it mildly, but they never have the patronized oddity of, say, charwomen in middle-class pop entertainment. The quirks of Ben Travers's characters are more surreal than that. Mrs Leverett, who is given to shooing away an imaginary cat, has some inversions that catch like German measles. 'Earlier than that I cannot be,' for instance. 'No.' 'Yes.' 'Nein.' 'Ten.' 'Finish.' This is a typical Ben Travers exchange, with monosyllables bouncing off the sides of meaning like a ball in a squash court.

His typical beset young hero is always very sweet to girls. He calls their dresses frocks, and worries when the bottoms of their satin pyjama trousers get wet with dew or when they sit by mistake on a loofah. Sometimes, he will get absorbed by the loved one's inner works. Gerald in *Rookery Nook* is suddenly enchanted by the way his girlfriend's fingers flop back when he plays with them, 'like a piano'.

'You dare to come here, crawling upstairs like a balloon . . .' When they have their backs to the wall, pinned there generally by a middle-aged woman, the male characters talk very strangely. They speak before they think, which is a characteristic of people in farce, and the reason why farce can be played faster than any other form of theatre. Speech propels speech, almost without mind intervening. Told reprovingly by a landlady that he doesn't write very clearly, Peter in *Cuckoo in the Nest* instantly provides the excuse that he has just had some very thick soup.

Ben Travers's men are always floundering suspiciously. The only reason why the women ever neglect to follow up the suspicions is that they regard floundering as man's estate. Whether they are booming dowagers or girls with laughs like cuckoos, the women have minds evilly bent on sexual rumour. Their view is that man was born sinful, even though he may have spent a wretchedly innocent night wrapped around the plumbing of a hotel handbasin. Ralph Lynn has some racked business in a film of *Cuckoo* when he tries like a little dog to scratch a place for himself to sleep. 'You call yourself a couch,' he says furiously at last. 'You're nothing but a *sofa*.' When women round on men, men have no one to blame but things.

Ralph Lynn was the great improviser of the original Tom Walls–Robertson Hare company at the Aldwych Theatre before the Second World War. In later revivals he would often direct the cast in the midst of acting, turning away from the audience to clutch the forearm of an actor who had got a laugh to show him how to get another. 'Wait for it,' he would say; 'wait for it; wait for it; *now*.' Like all good farce actors, he was exceptionally spry and used to spar round a joke like a boxer. At seventy, he told a young actor in a revival of *Rookery Nook* to go out and buy a skipping rope. He thought it was a good idea to be able to tap-dance; he believed that if an actor gets his footwork right in farce, the rest follows. Ben Travers made the matching technical discovery about writing. In 1925 he suddenly found that if the words are right, a dramatist can get laughs where a paraphrase with a different rhythm will produce silence.

Cuckoo in the Nest was written first in 1922 as a not very successful novel; the situations are much the same as in the play, but the style is literary and the comic engine sputters. The fascinating thing about the work at this stage is that it is a vehement tract about middle-class hypocrisy, acid about young women who are afraid of public opinion, and murderous about the overbearing Mrs Bone. ('Waterloo . . . was won at the childbed of a large number of big, haughty, rather contemptuous and absolutely indomitable women.') Three years later, stripped of fury and written like a metronome, the novel became a play and tamed a whole audience of Mrs Bones at a blow.

Stripped of fury: that was part of it. The disciplines of farce are classical, and the romantic emotions are ruinous to it. A psychologically thought-out production of *Thark* makes the mistake of smudging the outlines with neurosis. An Actors' Studio version of Ben Travers doesn't work. If the characters and their situations are not too painful to be laughed at, theatre's style can make them stable and indestructible.

★ ★ ★

There is a ravishingly funny thirty-five-minute farce by Feydeau called *Ne te promeňe donc pas toute nue*. Like most good farce – even a farce as apparently anti-traditional as Henry Livings's *Eh?* (see onward) – the play is about a set of people who are impeccably servile to custom and who are called upon suddenly to face a single, unmissable gaffe which they can deal with only by behaving as though it isn't there. The gaffe in *Eh?* is the central character: the gaffe in *Toute nue* is a nightdress, which is worn with Sunday hat and button boots by an otherwise devotedly conventional woman, and which every man in the play does indeed consumingly regard as though it weren't there. Madeleine Renaud in a Paris production was naked to every imagination on the stage while the dialogue trots desperately around the point, chatting about civic affairs and the weather.

The appalled fusspot husband, a Deputy with ambitions of becoming a Minister, talks to his election rival with a ghastly lack of conviction about dressing lightly for such a clammy day, while his wife uses the skirt of the nightdress to whisk a wasp out of the marmalade. Madeleine Renaud played the character with the crushing energy of a woman spring-cleaning, using a bossy trudge that is very funny when it is conducted in lingerie, and putting down male dreams as though she were swatting them. The Deputy was played by Jean Desailly, who so perfectly incarnated the bourgeois Frenchman's spirit that even the shape of his tiny moustache began to look like an irritable shrug of the shoulders in the *mairie*. Like the rest of the company, he understood the crossness that is the cardinal mood of farce: not neurotic, but crabbed in a happy mood of total self-absorption.

Farce traditionally depends upon order and the existence of a set of widely shared assumptions. French bedroom farce came out of an attitude to wives and mistresses that was as systematized as a theology. English farce before the Second World War was rooted in a middle class which agreed that the Church of England was serious, making a de-bagged parson funny, and that any decent Englishman locked in a hotel bedroom with a girl would keep his monocle in and sleep under the washstand.

Since then the atom has been split, but conventional farce still assumes cohesion. The Whitehall farces, for instance, take it for granted that their audiences are firm in agreeing that modern art and homosexuals are funny. The unfortunate substratum born of our money-merry and benighted century is of a sort that distils a carefully judged mixture of saloon-bar bragging about sex and the most intimidated conventionalism about it. It is addressed to the standard that infidelity doesn't count as long as it's on a trip for the firm.

A stronger step. Henry Livings's *Eh?* may be the first really anarchistic farce. It is a bold, wild attempt to reflect our disorder and stop pretending that anything is stable in the flux; the result is obstreperously funny and perturbing. The only conventional element of farce that the author has allowed himself is a door. Farce is impossible without doors. In an earlier play called *Nil Carborundum* he wrested more out of lavatory doors than Feydeau could have dreamt of. The device in *Eh?* has been pared down, which is to say that the door has no walls around it. It has a comic function rather like a recurring gag about a man who can never get beyond the first sentence of a story: it emits a cut-off burst of industrial bottled music every time it opens.

The room it gives on to is not a bedroom but a boiler room, which John Bury originally filled with a grunting brontosaural structure of ovens and funnels and sprockets. The monster needs a keeper, to sit in front of it on a green swivel chair and turn a knob every four hours: the man who applies for the job, first played by David Warner, is a hunched, combative, apprehensive eccentric who wears a brown swallow-tail coat and chestnut-coloured boots with black Cuban heels. Mr Warner in this play looked vaguely eight feet tall, with a length of arm that seemed curiously arbitrary; and he had apparently left the coat-hanger inside his jacket. He was constantly surprised by the turns he took, and blew sometimes into his cheeks so that they pulsed like the throat of a frog.

Conventional farce depends on non-stop activity. What happens in a society that is trying to *eliminate* activity? Valentine Brose, fighting off the horrors of lethargy in a world fit for boilers, attempts to people the void by growing mushrooms in the throbbing cellar and then by moving his new wife covertly into the bottom bunk, which very nearly ends in boiled bride.

The works manager, made to be played with a hissing head of steam, is a hysteric driven mad by the way life cannot be contained. He is a man fixed at the moment of infant fury when we discover that the external world exists and can defeat us. It is no good trying to interpret the character as anything so generalized and definable as an archetype of trade unionism, any more than the sunnily stupid heroine can be made to symbolize psychiatry just because she tells Valentine Brose he is a schizophrenic: people's jobs and uniforms in this farce belie their natures.

A clergyman has the most inconstant relationship with his dog collar, dissolving often into a rugger blue or a visionary atheist. In the second act he has a colossal pagan speech about dragons that is the centre of gravity around which the flying chips of the play revolve. Men invented dragons where reality provided nothing worse than lizards; by the same process, the machines made for mankind's ease by our clever and constructive talents are turned by our insensible and chaotic genius into objects of mythic fear.

Eh? is about a world of Protean men who are possessed by maverick impulses and sometimes almost obliterated by their own surprising vocabulary. The play makes the entirely modern observation that words can often precede meanings and touch off feelings instead of following them; the arguments in it follow a pattern as formal as a fugue, with people getting engrossed by someone else's keynote and taking it over so that the lines of the quarrel merge and change sides. The action reflects the combats pent up in our skulls, where we are simultaneously lords and convicts in solitary.

★ ★ ★

One of the great natural differences between farce and comedy is that farce is about people who are impervious and unshakeable. Its characters are exorbitantly alert to the outside world, to the dangers behind bedroom doors or the dragons in boilers; it is about people with such massively engrossing and indestructible characteristics that the outside world bounces off them like grapeshot off elephant hide.

Oedipus Rex would be a farce if, with the plague of Thebes running through their drawing-room, the royal family remained blind to their people's agony and thought only about being attractive to each other. Noël Coward's *Hay Fever* is one of the great modern farces. The Bliss family have invited four wretches for the weekend whom they proceed to wrack with inattention, starting with no introductions, going on to no explanations of a party game at which the theatrical Blisses shine, and ending up leaving them coldly alone with some unpleasant haddock at Sunday breakfast from which the outsiders tiptoe back to London, worn out with histrionics.

The Blisses don't notice: they have the hermetic family infatuation of the Greeks.

And the manners: Ivy Compton-Burnett's wit about ancient families' disloyalties in cataclysmic public surroundings seems made for the theatre. *A Heritage and its History*, adapted by Julian Mitchell, was the first of her novels to be staged and it animated murderously well. The depth of the stage was used for ruthless interjections, so that a comment to kill could be lobbed from the back of a drawing-room.

A Heritage is really about what is expected of us, by ourselves, by others and by the process of life, an inexorably opposed triangle in which all the positions are precisely visible to everyone concerned but an infinite number of possibly fatal choices may be made about stating them. This is etiquette on a monolithic scale, the manners necessary at Mycenae. To apply a version of modern upper-class politeness to a plot involving classical incest is a personal feat. Miss Compton-Burnett has matchless command of the appalling skill of the high-bred Englishman in courteously destroying outsiders, and she has an ancient and most royal Greek's feeling about heirs and births; where a child is born, there is the spearhead of the house, and to her the word 'house' means the House of Atreus.

★ ★ ★

Two phenomenal summoners of character through spoken language: Kingsley Amis and Ruth Draper. Both are scathing of fashion and mannerism, gentle to people. Language is paramount.

Kingsley Amis's *That Uncertain Feeling*, which he wrote in 1961, has a title whose references hit any lover of *Lucky Jim* bang in the face and with knobs on. But the film industry, or some equivalent goon, turned that into a wincing *Only Two Can Play*. Mr Amis's work survives.

It is clear from his 1988 novel, *The Old Devils*, that he has become the unrivalled heir of P. G. Wodehouse in finding a narrative idiom that comes in twit's clothing but knowledgeably and agreeably slaughters snobs. *That Uncertain Feeling* was written for the screen by Bryan Forbes. In the opening shot the hero, a Welsh assistant librarian played by Peter Sellers, is lying awake in bed. The room is in the grip of the last hush before the alarm; the geyser is quiet, and the stags on the living-room wallpaper are out of sight, smothered under three coats of *House and Garden* pink, but still rampant. Modestly, the librarian begins to assault his sleeping wife. She rebuffs him affectionately out of her torpor and he turns back to the ceiling.

Like all true comic heroes, John Lewis is full of gloomy self-knowledge. He understands, for instance, that sex for him is something to be contended with rather than enjoyed: sometimes his world seems to be awash with breasts in the bus and girls playing tennis, but the energy they arouse in him always gives out at the post. He habitually evolves situations that demand a man capable of guiltless promiscuity and vast sexual optimism, but his temperament remains monogamous and given to unhappy self-inspection: it is obvious that his character is as farcically unsuited to the work he loads on to it as a hammer made out of Plasticine.

After he has collared the local equivalent of Mrs Thrale at a literary party, where the sanctification of posturing Welsh-speaking nits has buoyed him up on a wave of rage, he quickly loses his nerve and asks her carefully what she would do if he kissed her. The anxiety of his question is obviously well-founded. In his melancholy obsession with women ('You know. Women in general. Women *apart from men*') he is aware of an inborn tendency to muff it. From the Old Welsh verb, to muff from a great height.

John Lewis is hot on Old Welsh, or 'things Welsh', as the enemy would probably put it. The Welsh character is all right: he has a good deal of it himself, carrying on a war with his landlady that is marked by the same engrossed contempt as the gaze of the conductor who daily gives hard attention to his efforts to leap on a moving bus. It is Welsh culture that does him in. Even more than his own moodiness, caution and hypochondria, he loathes the charlatanism and pomposity that the game of Welshness supports. When his Mrs Thrale comes into the library looking for a book on national costume, he blackly offers her a choice of *Memoirs of a Welsh Hatter* (signed by the hatter), *A Concise History of Cod-Pieces*, and *Expediency and Morality in Welsh Dress*. The scene of his fatal refusal to endorse literature like this, in the presence of a Library Selection Committee manned by a claque of touchy bigots, is one of the cornerstones of his character. Like most of England's comic-heroic figures since 1950, John Lewis is not as arrogant as he looks. He is rather a timid man: his spurts of impossible behaviour come out of a deep and often self-sacrificial resolve to earn the scorn of people he knows to be phoney. The comic triumph of *Only Two Can Play* is the dialogue. For the first time I can think of in the history of British film comedy, a screen marriage is as grown-up and as rich in private jokes as the set-up between Katharine Hepburn and Cary Grant in *Bringing up Baby*. And the film has the rich sense of particular talk that was Ruth Draper's comic, lenient genius.

* * *

In 1922 it happened that Ruth Draper performed before both Duse and Bernhardt. Afterwards Duse told her that she should never play comedy; Bernhardt, presumably having had a surfeit of the pathetic sketches, asked her sharply why she didn't. Looking back on all those reunions with the Draper platoon of characters, one feels sure that Bernhardt was right. At first the monologues were meant as nothing more than drawing-room amusement for her own friends, and it took the encouragement of Paderewski to coax this most unexhibitionist actress on to the professional stage, when she was already nearly thirty. Henry James also egged her on, more opaquely: 'My dear child . . . you . . . have woven, dear child . . . your own . . . very beautiful . . . little Persian carpet. . . . Stand on it.'

A good many of her fifty-four sketches are made of tough fibre, especially the series of rich, spoilt women who were her best subjects: 'The Italian Lesson' is wittily observant of the privileged, and so is 'The Children's Party' and the 'Class in Greek Poise' ('Miss Müllins, will you please give us those slow minor chords? Make them very slow, and *very minor*').

Ruth Draper is – was, and ever shall be – one of a kind in her always mannerly and attentive view of character. A rare thing, to dispose this commodious heed in satire.

* * *

Satire in dialogue is always going to be satire at its most cuttingly comic, because it has no editorializing. We are free to hear. The ear of English-speakers is like a Geiger counter: for the moments when utterance is arrogant, or questing, or go-getting or truly aspirant. There is no other language where unspoken quotation marks can be clearly heard as in English. They can convey irony, or cliquishness, a way of saying, 'Not waving but drowning'.

'No, no, no, no, no.'

English society: I am in it but I am soon going to be out of it. Oscar Wilde.

I have seen a production in London of Oscar Wilde's *An Ideal Husband* when Sir Robert Chiltern and Lady Chiltern, blackmailed politician and relentlessly moral wife, were like a pair of seals trying to fence. But Wilde's language prevailed. The most Wildean things in the play are the butler, best played as though carved out of one of Moses's tablets, and the epigrammatic Lord Goring's father. There is an enchanting line when the bemused old buffer asks his son, after a torrent of paradoxes, if he really always understands what he is talking about. One of the troubles for any cast in Wilde is the danger of appearing to mean what they say. Wilde's people don't really use speech for anything so craven as expressing themselves; butlers and all, they use it for suppressing others, as though they were putting down risings in the Colonies.

The Importance of Being Earnest is our modern comic masterpiece. It uses every ancient convention about doubling, and concerns everything that is more than ever to be put right now about the marriage-mart; the caste sytem; the breeding power of money; the money power of breeding. No one is likely to forget the scorn of Lady Bracknell about the wrong side of possibly the most beautiful square there has ever been,

Belgrave Square. Or her feelings about a baby having been left in a Gladstone bag at Victoria Station; bound for the Brighton Line ('the line is immaterial'). Her manner of catechizing is exactly the way of those ambitious matrons still potent, matrons with the bosoms of roll-top desks who stomp on more timid and less married spirits with parasols as weaponry. Dear parched Miss Prism, the faulted governess forever hoping to be courted by Canon Chasuble.

Great comedy calls large matters into question. Wilde and Jane Austen, like Shaw and Congreve, do it for English-speakers. Shaw's *Major Barbara* is the most startling twin to *The Importance* in its matter and in its characters. Lady Britomart is a dreadful sister to Lady Bracknell, and the thunder of her questions has all the manner of Wilde.

Lady Britomart: 'Really, Barbara, you go on as if religion were a pleasant subject. Do have some sense of propriety.'

⋆ ⋆ ⋆

In league in my own overnight mind:

A voice: But God is everywhere.
A voice: Why?
A voice: Because he's sentimental.

⋆ ⋆ ⋆

Oscar Wilde said of a prisoner handcuffed in drizzle en route for prison: 'If this is how Her Majesty treats her prisoners, she doesn't deserve to have any.' Brendan Behan shared this view. His play *The Quare Fellow*, staged by the terrific Joan Littlewood, who came to her fiercely Republican sovereignty at Stratford-atte-Bow after years of traipsing through the surrounds of Manchester with a company in a lorry, showed us a Dublin prison where the prisoners spend a long night in the unreachable company of a condemned man who is going to be ritually hanged next morning. No attempt to defend the IRA activities of the prisoner. The Swiftian offence of Brendan, now dead, was to question the gravity of capital punishment.

Brendan's convicts behave with exalting humour. No complaint is voiced. The quare fellow – the name given by prison inmates to a fellow about to be strangled – remains offstage. The hangman, in bowler hat, is addicted to his trade, but we are allowed to see him only as a man doing his job. Your average butcher, your average hard hat/skid lid. The prisoners move around him through unslept hours. The waiting is horrible, made more horrible by the way the prisoners have come to accept it as ordinary. We come upon it for the first time. The recoil is ours. It is an unforgettable piece of theatrical tact. The terrible night, with its morse slogans of a hanging-to-come sounded out on pipes between cells, comes to a dawn when the warders appointed to share the condemned man's last hours have some time ago laid aside their wristwatches. Tomorrow occurs, though barely to the hanged one, and the other prisoners accompany his going with a ceremonial clatter of tin plates on iron bars. The exercise yard holds its hush and all one suddenly hears is the voice of some scraping funster commenting on the walk to the scaffold as though it were a race-course commentary. 'The chaplain's leading by a short head.'

The Quare Fellow is stinging and compassionate political theatre, armed by an Irish dramatist's language out on a sprint and ready for battle.

People are wrong who suppose that Brendan was a writer soaked by Manhattan celebrity. Not so. He spent the early part of his life in jail as a Borstal boy. As an adult, with nothing but unproven talent behind him – no references, no money – he wrote *The Quare Fellow* in school exercise books. Spare us the nonsense that the sixties in England were swinging. That is weekly news magazine jargon for consumers, and consumer-editors catch on late to anything but fashion. The sixties were already worrying. Such efforts as the Campaign for Nuclear Disarmament had been made for a long time. Possible change seemed only to be in the hands of economists moving to the right. It was in the fifties that such things as *The Quare Fellow* could erupt, and however young we were – or unborn, and absorbing the past through reading and talk – we can hear the jerk of that rope, the sound of a body's drag. Brendan had those exercise books with him; no money; nor I; but a change in the hanging laws was possible, because England's state was long before its chill anointing of Mrs Thatcher and even the acceptance of the false bill of goods of the Common Market. Brendan wrote a story for me in a school exercise book, just as I had read his play. A brainy man. The story had his signal brave funniness about the rough elbows of South of England prissiness. The title, which conveyed something – not everything – of the content, was *Sunbathers Cover Their Faces in Sweden.*

⋆ ⋆ ⋆

One of the missing ancient humours, even in their original medical senses, is this wit of pure braininess. It took Shaw to have the brains to know that it could dwell in women. His *Mrs Warren's Profession* is ninety-five years old, but let no one tell you that it works in spite of the passionate topicality it had in 1894; it works because of it. The play is still flintily apt in what it has to say about our capacity for humbug, our double view of ambition as admirable in men and disagreeable in women, our high regard for greed when it is called the profit motive and the particularly English conviction that immorality always means sexual immorality. The wit in this play pulls wishbones of change.

Mrs Warren's profession – bordello madame – was her one social blunder. Her energy and thrift, the ingenuity that rescued her from life in a fried-fish shop in the East End, were virtues that Victorian England deeply admired. If she had no training to live by, no one in 1894 regarded that as a crime, nor indeed does anyone now. The most respectable people still believe that a woman's best bank balance is her body: finishing schools and the law of alimony are instances of perfectly legal ways of trading in sexuality. Mrs Warren's mistake was that, instead of marrying for money or milking a living out of a divorce, she agreed to run a classy chain of European brothels to fill the pockets of a nice-looking squire called Sir George Crofts, who tells her blandly not to mention his hotels because the word makes people think you keep a public house.

Every man in the play finds her indispensable, including a porty vicar to whom she has borne a wastrel son: but her job gives everyone the right to patronize her, including the clever daughter whom she has trustingly educated. The last-act combat between the two women is agonizing, and full of a charity that isn't often recognized in Shaw. The play is a superb theatrical organism, able to call on the old energies of Victorian melodrama but gifted with the most even and fine-drawn sense of particular temperaments in conflict. What a play Shaw might have written after the Profumo/Christine Keeler/Cliveden case. Stephen Ward, then someone unprotected by the Homosexual Law Reform Act, eventually committed suicide in a sequence of publicity-hounding that could only cause those of us who sent a wreath to his virtually unattended funeral to label it 'To a victim of British hypocrisy'. Except that Shaw, if he had written the play, would even now be accused of 'mere' sociology, of 'attacking well-worn targets' of hypocrisy with 'Mr Shaw's wearily familiar wit'. The tide has swung away again very fast from social concerns in plays. Shaw would have hated the alternative that seems to be replacing it, a fad for the sort of writer whom he once caustically defined as a hopelessly Private Person.

Shaw was – luckily for us – ready to be a Public Person, at least in his mode of address to us. In *The Devil's Disciple*, a particularly intelligent production had Marius Goring as General Burgoyne. The part was played with a lizard wit close to the author's. It is a very Shavian trick, to write what he blandly described as 'a threadbare popular melodrama' and equip it with a sophisticate who stands outside the structure and explains away the florid architecture as being entirely what the public wants. General Burgoyne is a sort of Preface on legs. By writing himself into a play, Shaw could mock a public taste at the same time as feeding it buns.

He never failed to provide his own forewords, his own codas for reflection. No harbour of an alibi. He is ready to swear, with no hand on the Bible, that he is speaking for himself, the whole truth, with wisdom and a full mind's mischief. In the middle of *Fanny's First Play* there is a playlet said to have been written by a character called Fanny. Round this is wrapped a discussion between four footling drama critics who swear between footles that the piece is a characteristically pig-headed and derivative work by Shaw. The whole unmistakable parcel was presented in 1911 as being by Xxxxxxx Xxxx, fooling no one, and giving the author huge pleasure as a device combining modesty, trumpet-blowing and critic-proofness in one fell swoop. He does it again and again. In *Fanny's First Play* he has a sly good time when a *bourgeoise* clucks over a whole lesson dealt out to St Peter. A high-flown person has been elaborating on the theme that people who depend on religious dogma are liable to be shocked when they can't walk on the water. An owlish butler called Juggins is (as Shaw says, eagerly getting it in first) shamelessly derivative from Barrie's Crichton. The critics are reported with acerbic exactness, especially the one called Mr Gunn, who is a representative of the school that 'goes for the newest things and swears they're old-fashioned'.

Shaw's *The Philanderer* is the companion Unpleasant Play to the Pleasant *You Never Can Tell*. In it he deliberately uses the devices of farce – a form that he disliked because it produces a galvanic sort of laughter rather than a real one – to scourge the human contents of the play. Shaw's eye here is cold and glittering, not least because he described so much of himself in it. Nothing inspired less sympathy in him than his own emotions: to his ideas he was an unswerving friend, but his feelings were inspected in chilly and moving enmity.

When Shaw is recommending recklessness about sex to the young he often sounds hollow, over-assertive, and harrowingly alarmed beneath; but whenever he writes about parents and children he becomes very moving. In *You Never Can Tell* the young lovers and the lectures about getting married are eerily unconvincing, but the long-separated middle-aged parents and the waiter discomfited by a QC son are seen with the wit of grief. Shaw's intellect made him a radical who has no fear about the future, but his sensibility made him a timid man capable of infinite regret, and I'm not sure that his cowardice wasn't an even greater gift to him as a dramatist than his courage.

'You are greatly changed,' says the outmoded New Woman heroine, facing her impossible roistering husband after an absence of many years. While the heroine was away in Madeira bringing up her children, the times left her behind. The seaside resort she has returned to is swept up in knickerbockers and bicycling. Her elder daughter has grown up into a terrifyingly theoretical girl, and her twins are an alliance of chatterboxes who justly see it as barbarous of her not to say who their father is. The reunion lunch with her husband, with an appalled waiter taking cover in fussing over them like Chekhov's Firs, is one of the most comically piercing scenes that Shaw wrote.

She calls the waiter William, though his real name is Walter, because he reminds her of the Shakespeare bust at Stratford. (Ralph Richardson once played him unforgettably, knees buckling in creaseless trousers and arms stretched out for people to hang things upon as though he saw himself as a living coat-hook.) He is proud of his QC son but he is also sufficiently intimidated by him to be sent scuttling into the worst intricacies of English servant snobbery about him. The waiter's life, like the heroine's, has not gone as it should. *You Never Can Tell* is rightly said to be a comedy, which allows it the bite of pity.

Defending himself in advance about his wickedly funny *Man and Superman*, Shaw said in his dedicatory preface to the critic A. B. Walkley that 'your favourite jibe at me is that what I call drama is nothing but explanation'. It is true that Shaw is always hugely exegetical. His characters never do anything that another character does not forecast, comment upon, and then tell us to see as totally characteristic of that sex, that class, that upbringing, that period; but when they do it with Shaw's shrewdness they can be explanatory until the cows come home.

The England here is the one that Shaw most detested, a 'moral gymnasium' where we would rather flex our own principles than attend to other people's necessities. His symbol of the New Man, the chauffeur 'Enry, seems to drop his aitches to oblige a caste system that likes things cut and dried. The hero, John Tanner, is hard to play, being written as a dashing prig. Touching about Shaw that his Don Juan character should be a man petrified by women, and one who doesn't do a single piece of adventuring on stage.

Heartbreak House seems to me Shaw's disarming great achievement in the comic. It is as though his stage direction to himself to write 'in the Russian manner' was a way of seeking the courage to expose what he usually strove to hide about himself: the trait in the Russian's character and art that Mary McCarthy once fixed on as 'an artless preoccupation with the self' comes hard to him. Some of his plays suffer for it, but in *Heartbreak House* his ravenous secret emotionalism is declared as nowhere else. Beneath the usual level Shavian surface, in which the characters habitually talk to one another as though they were pinned to the floor through the heels at ten-foot distances from each other, there are admissions of passionate hope made in the vein of farce that Chekhov so often asked of himself and his actors. Shaw here writes about heartbreak with a curious remote intensity, as though it had happened a long time ago; and, like D. H. Lawrence, he cannot help revealing his unconscious fear that sex makes men look ridiculous to women. He also cannot help recognizing his own compulsive pleasure in administering the stings that cause him suffering himself: 'If only one could find the sort of cruelty that didn't really hurt.' The symbolism in the play of the class structure of English society is bulky, even the irony that old Captain Shotover is really much more enterprising and spirited than Captain Mangan. I love and admire the play most because it is the one in which Shaw wrote most expressively, and with most cost to himself, about longing.

★ ★ ★

Elaine May in *Enter Laughing* – from the Carl Reiner book about show biz in the thirties that was adapted by Joseph Stein into a play and then turned into a film, directed by Reiner – reminded me of Beatrice Lillie in *Exit Smiling*, subject and title apart. Elaine May, cast as the lanky daughter of José Ferrer, who plays an actor-manager of the old school of bossy boomers, has an off-centre practicality that is every bit as engrossing as Miss Lillie's. (She is also much more skilful than most strongly individualized performers at playing scenes with other actors.) *Enter Laughing* is a tame container for her, but it is impossible not to be riveted by her funniness and her brains.

The dubiety expressed in the long, beautiful, yawning-dromedary face is part of her comic temperament. So is the intelligence, which is characteristically obdurate and out of step at a time when comedians often trade on being victimized and gormless. A lot of the acting now regarded as funny in films has been wretchedly debased by the response- begging of television performances. Elaine May asks nothing. Her personality is there to be taken or left; she does nothing to sell it. She is like a buffoon in Dostoyevsky – aware of her existence as profoundly ludicrous but never of her manner as funny. She seems lovingly self-created, with idiosyncrasies rooted in her own sensible incredulity about commonly accepted states of affairs. At the simplest physical level, her point of view is expressed in the position she seems to take toward her clothes. In *Luv* and in *Enter Laughing*, she obediently dresses as a woman is supposed to when she wants to be womanly, and keeps having a go at high heels and spangled cocktail things that have the glum glitter of those neon signs saying GAS-EAT, but she sometimes lets slip a hint of enormous longing to wash her hands of the whole dumb endeavour. One's own strong impulse is to reprieve convention's uncomplaining hostage and put her in jeans and gumboots. Like Bea Lillie tangling with a stole, Miss May has a scene in which she contends pleasantly with a red feather boa, and you can see her quelling a small pang of worry about wearing only a slip as she welcomes a man into her dressing-room. She says, though, in her typical tone of nervous reassurances, that he must come *in*, this is the *theatre*.

* * *

In the *Born Yesterday* story, directed on screen by George

Cukor, Judy Holliday plays the girl of a big-shot junk dealer and swindler called Harry Brock, whose hotel booking in Washington is for a whole wing. Broderick Crawford plays the swindler. Miss Holliday's character is called Billie Dawn. Her given name was Emma; she could never face the test of living up to that one, though. Her man behaves to her like a pig, but she gets through things by pretending not to notice, just as she uses her shortsightedness as a glamour puss's excuse not to have read anything. When Harry is being most boorish to her, she bawls cheerfully to him from a window of their posh hotel wing, opting for comradeliness in this millionaire's hangout that they are trying to browbeat into a slum. The hotel manager, clinging to fake politesse in the chaos like a drowning man clutching at a stone, refers to her cattily as Mrs Brock. Harry stops that. 'Not Mrs Brock,' he says. 'There's only one Mrs Brock, and she's my *mother*, and she's *dead*.' He nods toward Billie and briefly classifies her. 'She's a *fiancée*.' There are Mrs Brocks and there are fiancées, and fiancées are trash. But this trash is blessed with good lungs and a roaring spirit. She was once in the chorus. And not just the chorus, she protests later, in that ripe, high, expostulatory voice; she spoke lines, actually. Five, she says. Ask anybody. But Harry didn't want to share her with the general public.

Billie Dawn is a fine character for Judy Holliday. It is the character of the girl who carefully copies what the dolts do but who obviously knows more than any of them. When William Holden starts feeding books into her and persuades her to wear spectacles so that she can read, it is clear that her brain is better than anyone else's in the picture, including that of Mr Holden in the part of this more upright than engaging pedagogue, who has been hired to teach her about Paine and Jefferson and the opus number of Beethoven's Second Symphony. Miss Holliday, you feel, could have *been* Paine, and nothing on earth would incline her to think her life well spent if she put it to numbering symphonies. Her whole comic character is a natural forerunner of Women's Lib, in a way, but managed without weight. When she caricatures the dopey, pampered woman her men think they want, she is throwing a bone to admen's creatures, and she does it partly because she finds the disguise a useful decoy that gives her space to think. Whenever there's a row in her films, the blade of her mind whips out. Harry Brock, the capitalist who supposes he has bought Billie wholesale, finds that her loyalty to him is not such a plangent harpstring to play on as he thought. When she questions a reekingly dishonest contract that he wants her to sign, and he accuses her of double-crossing him, she says back, 'If there's a fire and I call the engine, so whom am I double-crossing? The fire?' Harry had thought, in his invertedly romantic way, that his juicy girl was a buyable voter; she ends by summing him up objectively as a social calamity.

Some of the script seems politically cautious and dated now, with its veiling of McCarthyism as 'Fascism', in the guise of Harry's cartel-making versus Billie's conscience, and with its unavailing care not to make the heroine more than a being of instinct when it is obvious that she has a rare mind. Billie, one of the best parts that Judy Holliday ever played, is typical of her style. Her comic task as a smashing-looking girl was always to cover up great boredom at having to shimmer around in lamé pyjamas and pretend to be a dumb broad. There are ravishingly funny scenes in her films when she will furtively interest herself in other and cleverer things in the middle of man-made, typecast seductive circumstances – dancing expertly by herself to a radio turned on in a corner, or beating a chap on his own ground with a startling hand of gin rummy, or managing the chewing of gum as well as the technicalities of a long cigarette holder, or dealing a death blow to pedantry with a magnificently simple mutter of sense after some smart-aleck thinks he has made a crushing point. Judy Holliday was of her time in the way she had to hide her brains from men. A girl character probably couldn't do that now without seeming coy. But maybe concealment of one kind or another characterizes a lot of American humour – W. C. Fields concealing his booze and his bank accounts, and Groucho Marx his terror of Margaret Dumont, and Laurel and Hardy their fear of being only two, and Lenny Bruce his panic at the way things in the world were going.

Many rights long won, many to go. Women as actresses still

have demands made of them to be primarily dishy. Judy Holliday's gentle looks held the screen, but it was the intelligence behind them that will always rise up to salute her. Like most of the funniest performers, she has an attitude in her films of alert scepticism. There is something fishy about this planet, she implies. She is ready to be grateful for its small mercies and she is infinitely educable to our ways, but we may all, she hints, be nuts. She makes her entrance in Garson Kanin's *Born Yesterday* with a corsage hanging behind her right ear like a displaced bunch of grapes. Apart from Beatrice Lillie, no one can ever have expressed a more quizzical view of fashion. Judy Holliday is perfectly polite to her clothes, but they seem visited on her, like mannered guests whom she can't wait to be rid of, although native absorption keeps her interested in their arcane reasons for being around. She is not one of us. She behaves toward the corsage, though courteously, as if she were an uncomfortably intelligent horse decked out with bells and flowers for some festival held by another species.

Miss Holliday was one of the most touching American comic actresses. To any luck dealt out to her in the parts she played – diamonds, nice men, high living – she extends a powerful disbelief. Orchids and sequins obviously arouse in her a very strong suspicion that the orchidless and sequinless times must be just around the corner. Her assumption that her grand clothes are a disguise to fool nobody is wonderfully funny. She has the knowledge that she is obviously a down-and-out to anyone with eyesight. She shared it with Marilyn Monroe. Both of them were breakable-looking waifs struggling to stay hidden inside their misleadingly confident rubbery bodies. They plainly felt themselves to be pretenders, and they had a very American inkling that they weren't going to get away with it for long. It made them beautiful clowns.

★ ★ ★

Even with Brecht now dead, his Berliner Ensemble Theatre expresses the way he wanted theatre to be: skimming, speculative, beautiful, fun. To watch his Hitler play, *Arturo Ui*, is like watching a bunch of tumblers or men on a trampoline. Physically the actors are phenomenal. Even their moments of relaxation have a fierce life. The substance of the play is an acrobatic feat in itself: it is a farce about the rise of Nazism, mockingly mirrored in the career of an unimpressive American gangster, who blackmails a mayor called Dogsborough (Hindenburg) into allowing him to organize a protection racket and move in on a town that symbolizes Austria.

The scenes are set inside a circus big-top, and the ringleaders are presented by a huckster. Goering is a cleft-chinned jokester in a white suit who collects the hats of his victims; after a murder he is inclined to open his jaws on a mirthless, cavernous howl. Like all the cast, he is brilliantly made up, with a cheesy green skin that makes his mouth look shrimp-pink. The betrayed Roehm, assassinated in a St Valentine's Day massacre with car headlamps glaring straight at the audience, wears plus-fours, black lipstick and a magenta scar. Goebbels (Hilmar Thate) looks like an Oriental monkey, with damson-stained lips and an Adam's apple that lurches at religious music. The physical images of Thate's performance are distinct and unforgettable. In one scene, plotting with Hitler-Ui in a hotel room mined with treacheries, he sits on a very low stool at a very high table drumming excitedly at a blotter under his chin, and then races Goering for Hitler's handshake, bouncing along on his stool like a satanic toddler. In another he sings a song astride the barrier of the dress circle, leaning perilously over the stalls with one leg jabbed into the rails like a grappling hook.

Ekkehard Schall's performance as Ui starts from a paradox that is pure Brecht. To define a man incapable of shame, it first records that he is bashful. Ui clearly longs to be an actor, but he is locked in a rictus of stage fright. Whenever he is near a window he goes to it instinctively, like a model-girl to a mirror, and prepares to harangue the street: but his gestures fall foul of one another, the left arm ambushes the right, and his feet hang down from his abject mackintosh like the feet of a dummy in a shooting gallery. When he is yelling he will suddenly gag, or change dynamic level uncontrollably, as he does in a deafening diatribe where the recurring word 'faith' is each time spoken on a soft indrawn gulp. His neck is scored with two black lines of make-up, the tendons of tantrum, like a frantic pullet, and after a stint with an actor hired to teach him Shakespearean delivery, he acquires a Hitlerian clasp of the hands that one suddenly sees to be the primordial gesture of male modesty, as used by a naked Popeye.

* * *

Great satirists catch the breath by pursuing a flip solution to its limits. Swift was only escorting the rabblement to its logical conclusion when he proposed solving the Irish Question by the eating of Irish babies. Nigel Dennis, an Englishman now living in Malta, must count as one of the rare living satirists writing fiction in the English language. His wit questions the absolutes in a way that exists now in English only in the best of cartoons and of maverick political journalism. He wrote *Cards of Identity*, first as a novel and then as a play; *The Making of Moo*, a play about the arising of religion that Buñuel and Swift would have signed; and *August for the People*, a play about a sceptic who cannot help being regretfully aware of the gap between the idea of democracy and the achievement of the people called upon to demonstrate it. It is also scathingly funny. In the definition of H. L. Mencken, whom Nigel Dennis brings to mind all the time, the sceptic is a man who has observed that 'no man is worthy of unlimited reliance – his treason, at best, only waits for sufficient temptation . . . One may believe in an idea absolutely, but not in a man.' *August for the People* is written in a mood of harshly humorous inquiry about the flaw in mankind's gift for philanthropy. It is a concept in which Mr Dennis would dearly like to believe, but which was mercilessly undercut (by the evidence of the sentences on Bertrand Russell's Committee of 100: a hundred people standing out for unilateral disarmament, some years after the roots of the movement in the colossal Aldermaston Marches, and the malicious fatuity of the popular press). 'We're opening an academy to find out what happens after democracy and before extinction,' remarks the hero at one point. It is as good a definition as any of the concern of the play.

The hero, played originally with wild cold comedy by Rex Harrison, is a high-born eccentric called Sir Augustus Thwaites. Like all sceptics, he has a good deal of the stoic about him. He views death with quizzical unsurprise, and mistrusts the human instinct for dramatics, including his own: as a sceptic, he is sometimes worried by the passion of his scepticism, which against his will has an inflaming effect that his mistress wryly notes. 'I have been challenged into passionate instability', she says, 'by your repellent passivity.'

Mr Dennis does not endorse his hero's position wholesale. He gives the mistress some passionate and sympathetic arguments. 'The times are feminine,' she says, affronted by her lover's male scoffs. 'Mercy and pity are the only alternatives to whips and jackboots.' In the view of the play, it is our appetite for dramatics that has given us wars, snobbery ('there are no classes, only our own excitement') and the popular press. When the journalists in the play round on the hero, hypocritically scandalized because he has suddenly voiced the same contemptuous view of the public as provides their daily feast, he can only look at them with self-loathing, recognizing our own faces in them: 'You are our spite, our greed, our love of lies, our pleasure in the pain of others, our perfect emptiness.'

Next to cant, misused emotionalism is what the hero distrusts most. Warnings against the dramatic instinct run all through the play. Theatricality springs, as the hero sees it, from boredom, the same boredom that nourishes the yellow press and that he regards as the legacy of pre-democratic societies: 'You are tasting the tyrant's boredom and you are dying of it.' The clichés of the half-crown visitors who traipse around his home as they peek into gossip column paragraphs constrict him like a harness: clichés are the product of boredom, and boredom reduces the heroic to a travesty. As Sir Augustus puts it, in a characteristically bilious apophthegm that no one listens to: 'He gave his blood that we might be bored again.' Or as he says angrily to a visitor who would let him put his foot on his neck: 'Have you no haughty dreams?' To pretend regret that man does not see himself as noble is key to this immaculately witty play.

★ ★ ★

A showbiz agent in Elaine May's *Ishtar* queasily rules the theatrical business. He pours whisky into a glass.

'Telling the truth can be very flat,' he says out of nowhere.

He represents Warren Beatty and Dustin Hoffman, who have hit most flat circumstances. Dustin Hoffman leads into an uplift song obligated for senior citizens' anniversaries. He has just invented it. Hope. Satisfying the audience. Something called 'empathizing'. Hoffman sings to gently aglow married couples that they are going into the big sleep. 'When life is nearly over.' The audience of the blue-haired and the toupéed is, in a baffled way, furious, but has to seem grateful; for it is, of course, nicely meant.

We move gently into the desert, and the world of a blind camel. Warren Beatty and Dustin Hoffman are on their hands and knees. The camel has its head more than usually raised, being blind. In sand, Hoffman confesses that he is not the kind of guy Warren Beatty thought he was: he lived with his parents until he was thirty-two. Warren Beatty, all-American, looks as worried as a man on hands and knees with sand in his eyes can be. He would be saluting the flag if it weren't for the sand he is in, and for solicitousness for the nearly off-frame camel. Hoffman: 'I'm a fake. I'm on the ledge. Don't tell anyone in show business.' Dry mouth. There is a kind cover-up by Warren Beatty. And by the camel. Other camel-owners, not responsible for the blind, scent trouble. Hoffman bravely says out of the dust that he doesn't believe the line-up of camel-owners talking nice gobbledygook in Arabic in response to his believable but invented dialect-yells can understand that this mission is no longer covert.

The blind camel looks like Kissinger in dark glasses in China.

Many are the possibilities of aspiring musicians pursuing desperately rhyme-weary lives, but many more the possibilities of covert camels.

Few are the writers capable of questioning Hollywood's inextinguishable sense of worth or profit. The dream-factory is not the extinct dinosaur it is said to be. It badly needs camels.

Mute

Max Linder was a famous comedian of the golden age, though a good many people by now have never heard of him. His comic style is most akin to Keaton's, of the great silent comedians. He did most of his work in France, from 1905. By 1914 he was world famous. He was wounded at the Front in 1916, went to Hollywood, got pleurisy, came back to Europe in 1919. In 1923 he made *Au Secours*, co-scripted by Abel Gance. The scenes of a rescued, valuable anthology dredged up from a flea market were made in Hollywood toward the end of his life. Unlike most of the silent comedians, who wore baggy trousers and looked as though they had nowhere to sleep, he was a dapper and debonair man. He wore a moustache of stylish melancholy and looked very like Mastroianni in *Divorce Italian Style*.

Linder was obviously mad about children and animals; he has a comic horse that seems to be walking on tiptoe, and there is a surreal ending to one story when the screen suddenly sprouts with dozens of two-year-old Max Linders, staggering about like puppies wearing long trousers and silk hats. He seems to have been deeply attached to one actress, a woman with a monkish profile who turns up as an aunt and again as a bossy queen in a spoof of *The Three Musketeers*. It is typical of Max Linder that, though this film is played in heavy period costume, the queen suddenly uses a typewriter.

Laugh with Max Linder is a dapper anthology of the work of a man who was making silent comedies at about the same time as Keaton and Chaplin. He had an elegant nose, purplish full lips like a Gibson Girl's, a taste in clothes that tended to waisted coats and spats, and a private, dandyish sort of humour engrossed by japes and sly surprises.

The film was put together by his daughter Maud Linder after his death: in 1925 this natty, prankish man, who seemed from his art to find such persistent pleasure in the small details of being human, took his own life.

⋆ ⋆ ⋆

If Max Linder has the doughty three-piece suit look of a man who would cross the Atlantic in a properly functional and neat balloon, if Harold Lloyd looks like a schoolboy who is hitting the awkward age and who is also a bit of a swot, Harry Langdon looks like a small girl with high hopes of one day being eight. The exquisite Bessie Love face is hung with panniers of puppy fat. The makeup, which weirdly manages not to seem androgynous, gives him the likeness of a child who has been mooning for hours in front of a looking glass with its mother's lipstick and mascara. The mouth looks babyish and jammy, and the eye-black has been put on in a state of trance; the whole face has then been dreamily smothered in talcum powder. When Langdon gazes into the distance in a film – when he is playing a soldier looking for his regiment in country too hard for him – his lineless, unpanicked face is the mask not of a mind hard at work, like Keaton's, but of a mind gently lolling at rest, like a punt. He seems to be contemplating not a problem but his own reflection, with an interest too infant to be called vanity. Any intrusions of thought would be perilous, like noises that could make a sleepwalker break an ankle. The face exudes great sweetness and placidity. When cunning takes over, it is the response of someone pre-moral. Langdon is very much an only child, and it has made him a duffer at games. As a 1914–18 private in *The Strong Man* – the only private in the whole army who might easily fail someday to absorb the fact that the war is over – he takes abstracted aim at a tin can and then at a German officer's helmet, using army biscuits from a catapult. Only a girl would find such a rotten form of bullet, and only a girl would be so thrilled and surprised to get a hit: a girl with aspirations not to be a butterfingers, but doomed in the hope, and solitary. Langdon automatically goes his own way, without troubling himself to get in touch with the rest of the world. The position seems to be shared by all the great cinema comedians; the movies' double acts, the fables about alliance, derive from the stage, and never seem to be as glorious on screen as they can be in music hall.

When Langdon is in mufti – when he isn't being a soldier, or isn't dressed up in a morning coat to marry some scheming, avaricious bride – he generally wears a hat with the brim turned up all the way round, an outgrown jacket of which only the top buttons will fasten, baggy trousers, and large, amoebic boots. He stands with his feet in the first position of ballet, toes out: again like a girl without much of a clue. There can never have been such a spry comedian who gave such an impression of unathleticism. He looks as if he couldn't run for toffee. The best of his films – including some that he directed himself – reflect his schoolgirl torpor and move along with a beautiful dumb-bell liquidity. He has a child's blitheness in egoism, a child's greed and hope and otherworld criminality, and if the characterization ever slips into a moment of adult, this-world proneness to wounds, the film falters. Keaton is entirely grown-up, stoic, decisive, ancient; Langdon seems most himself when he is unformed, born before time's knowing conjurings. He is a virtuoso of infant twitches that signal some tiny, fleeting worry, and a master of the beguilingly fatuous motions of beings who are still at the stage of experimenting to find their muscles. He can be especially splendid when he is working at a slant, trudging around the precipitous floor of a shack in a cyclone as if he had only just learned to walk.

The girls in his films are filthy grown-ups, treacherous and not very pretty. There is a terrible harridan in *The Strong Man* who cons him into thinking that she was the flower-faced girl who was his pen pal at the front; back home in America, she slips a stolen wad of bills into his pocket to offload detection by a dick behind her, and then faints massively outside her choice of mansion. Langdon is told severely by a servant that one can't leave one's women lying around like that. He lugs her inside as if she were a very large roll of carpet, keeling under her weight and avoiding several nasty blows from her diamanté jewellery. Her neck looks like a boxer's. Langdon staggers, sees the immense curving staircase that she wants to be carried up, and staggers some more. Starting the long haul, he gets his foot stuck in a flowerpot. There is a joyful moment when the overdressed burden, who is still pretending to be in a swoon, has to be propped on the marble banisters for an instant and slides all the way down on her stomach. Langdon anxiously begins over again, sitting down on the stairs and carting the woman up step by step on his lap. He has indoctrinated himself so sternly into making the taxed movement that he plugs on with it, still backward, up a stepladder at the head of the stairs, right to the top of the ladder, and then beyond and over. It is a marvellous passage of mime. Maybe inflexibility, automatism, abstractedness and unsociability are great staples of funniness; Langdon's films sometimes have them all.

Unlike Chaplin and Harold Lloyd, he doesn't wheedle. We might as well not be there. He is subject to attacks of entirely private petulance, and doesn't give a damn that they're dopey. He will kick a cannon, or throw things irritably, and with a girl's aim, at a cyclone. In one celebrated set piece, again in *The Strong Man*, he has a cold and attends devotedly to curing himself with stinking remedies in a crowded vehicle. The other passengers object, especially when he rubs his chest with Limburger cheese instead of liniment. A fusspot on his left is incensed. Langdon, hampered by feeling lousy, gives him an effete punch and also manages to spatter cough syrup over the dandyish enemy. His revenges are always serene and his movements oddly meditative. As with the business of lugging the hefty woman thief upstairs, his physical gags often come out of the old vaudeville-comedy discipline of repeating a movement mechanically after the need for it has gone. In *Tramp, Tramp, Tramp* he somehow gets himself into and out of a prisoners' work camp in the middle of a cross-America walking race; he has grown entirely accustomed to walking with a ball and chain when he rejoins the race, and when a train happens (never mind how) to run over the chain and cut it loose he picks up the ball gamely and carries it as if it were a given of life. Sometimes he will stoop to pull up the iron links around his legs because they have dropped like sock garters. You can see that the things have given him pins and needles. He rubs the circulation back. Comedy is to swallow a camel and strain at a gnat.

Comedy is also to be tenacious in pursuit of hermetically peculiar tasks. In *Long Pants*, Langdon tries desperately to train a ventriloquist's dummy to run, doing demonstration sprints again and again, and coming back each time to see if the lesson has taken. He is fine with props and a great punster with objects. Planning radiantly to murder his prospective bride in a wood, he drops his pistol into the undergrowth and retrieves in its stead a pistol-shaped branch, which he carries on with for a while. In England, the Goons used to do this sort of thing in their great early days at the BBC. Spike Milligan would suddenly pick up a passing banana in the recording studio and plant it in his ear as a telephone receiver for an improvised call to Peter Sellers, blandly ignoring the fact that they were doing radio, not television.

Harry Langdon was born in 1884, child of two Salvation Army officers, which was a start. He worked as a cartoonist, a prop boy, a barber, and a performer in a patent-medicine show and then in vaudeville for twenty years before he went to Mack Sennett. It was Frank Capra, a Sennett gag writer at the time, who invented *Tramp, Tramp, Tramp* for him. Capra apparently understood Langdon's comic personality perfectly, and begged to be allowed to work with him. (Later on, it was Capra who directed the two films that are probably Langdon's best – *The Strong Man* and *Long Pants*.) In *Tramp, Tramp, Tramp* Capra correctly shows him coming out on top, as infants do, and winning the cross-continental marathon in spite of infatuation with a girl played by Joan Crawford. The spiritual load for Langdon of loving Joan Crawford is inspired.

In Langdon's most characteristic films, the girls tend to be armour-plated. While he slips them love-notes, they are likely to be immersed in some manly correspondence with other criminals about loot and dope. His attitude toward them is distant and spiked with decorum. He may sleep with a framed poster of his beloved's face in his bed, but this is as far as he will go. The strapping lady thief in *The Strong Man* tries to seduce him; though he is perfectly polite, the occasion is beyond his experience, and all he knows is that it tickles. There are some Langdon pictures in which the misogyny becomes delicately surreal. In *Three's a Crowd*, which he directed, he has a nightmare about having to fight in a brightly-lit boxing ring, with his girl rooting against him, eyes hard as quartz; in the end, loopy with blood lust, she bites her straw hat to pieces. Girls are never much help to Langdon. His best friend is providence: some fall of a stone in the nick of time, some Old Testament collapse of a saloon filled with stronger enemies. There is one cast list in which the characters include 'His Bride', 'His Downfall', 'His Finish'; all three, predictably, are girls. Nonetheless, he is chivalrous. There are standards to be kept up. Sometimes he will explain these standards in a subtitle. They have a charming impatience and oddness: 'Can't you see, Pa, when your sweetheart's in distress, you can't go around marrying other women?' His love-letters have the same straightforward idiosyncrasy: 'I love you, I love you, I love you, I love you, and hope you are the same. Harry.'

The America of his films is grounded in the twenties. It is a world of marathons and patent medicines and bootlegging, of religion that has a thunderous edge to it, of wedding rings in hock, of keeping one's end up. There is an out-of-work strong man who wears a brocade waistcoat for bravado; he boasts, to maintain his spirits, 'I lift the heaviest weights in the world, and when I shoot myself from a cannon to a trapeze it's a sensation.' Sometimes Langdon's films movingly catch the desperate, squalid courage of the epoch. His father in *Tramp, Tramp, Tramp* is a small-time cobbler on his way out because of the coming of mass production. 'I can't battle those big shoe manufacturers,' Pop says tremulously from, of course, a wheelchair. The sentimentality about crafts and private enterprise also belongs to the times; it seems half-mock, but meant, too. The great silent comedians demonstrate a philosophy of me-against-the-world, of small-town decency against metropolitan mayhem, of the loner against the propertied. Greed whirls over the landscape in a dark cone, drawing with it everyone except the tramp comedian and his kin. But though the tramp doesn't have a bean, he has benedictive luck. In one of Langdon's famous stunt sequences, he has leaped over the fence of a yard enticingly labelled 'Private. Keep Out', to be saved from falling down a cliff face on the other side by only a nail. Whoever wrote that notice had a satanic passion for property and no great feeling for the lives of natural daredevils. Langdon's belt catches on the nail, and so does his sweater. He removes the sweater from the nail carefully and starts to unbuckle the belt. Then he sees the drop below him, absorbs it gravely, and does up the buckle, going on to cover up the sight of it with his sweater, in one of my favourite hopeless moments in silent comedy. Langdon did the stunt himself. 'There was no one else to do it,' he told a friend later, after the talkies had come in and his career had hit bankruptcy, 'so I had no alternative.' He was apparently deeply worried at the time because there wasn't a titter from the crew as he hung there. He didn't allow for their being fond of him; he thought it meant the sequence wouldn't be funny.

⋆ ⋆ ⋆

Whereas Keaton looks like some poetic widower, and Langdon an infant dope fiend, Harold Lloyd really only found his comic character when he saw a film about a fighting priest in glasses. According to James Agee's *On Film*, he thought about the spectacles day and night, and once he had adopted them as his own he must have discovered how very like a young cleric he is. He has an anxious, evangelizing stance, and the teeth of the true curate.

There is a fine sequence in one of his films about a nine-foot man with a toothache whose incisor the hero sympathetically lassoes with a rope before scaling his chest like a mountaineer, looking as though he is about to sink an ice-axe in his breastbone. When this fails, he tries sprinting up the street to get a purchase on the rope but the mammoth patient, foggily aware that he has found a friend, undermines the plan by bounding trustfully after him.

Harold Lloyd deals in this sort of let-down. He never does anything that is as beautiful or moving as Keaton does, but he does a lot that is technically brilliant. There is nothing in film comedy to better the sheer theatrical adroitness of the twenty-minute danger sequence in *Feet First*, when he has survived every crisis on the face of a skyscraper and only gives in to panic when his feet are two inches from the ground. This is the real flowering of Mack Sennett. There are other things that are more like germinal Goonery: during a chase, for instance, a very young baby played by a midget suddenly clambers around a pram hood and gives a weird thuggish roar.

★ ★ ★

While I was watching Charlie Drake in *The Cracksman* I kept thinking how much he would have enjoyed making a silent for Mack Sennett. It isn't really his voice that is funny; his accent, a kind of landlady's front-parlour English, is in fact rather ogling. The spirit of his comic personality is better expressed without words, because it is in the spirit of an infant.

With his heavy, troubled head and kewpie-doll limbs, Charlie Drake has the odd look of pre-moral anxiety that you see in newborn babies. Sometimes he gives a furious yell, or moves his hands as though he is thinking of throwing everything out of his pram. In a physical discipline like the one there must have been in the Sennett studios, where almost everyone had been trained in the circus or vaudeville, his childishness could have developed into a comic style as distinct as Harry Langdon's. James Agee once described Langdon as looking as though he wore diapers under his trousers.

In *The Cracksman* he plays a master locksmith who is innocently used as the vital technician in a series of robberies. Thrilled to be asked to show off, he fiddles the locks of Bentleys, safes and rich men's houses with no more insight into what he is doing than a can-opener. When a gangster has parked him in an opulent drawing-room and left the chump happily alone with the cigars while the place is rifled around him, Charlie Drake is still eyeless in a Gaza of brand-name locks. He finds himself looking at a TV play in which an actor is blowing up a safe. The risks that the man takes give him a pain. He is harshly critical of his technique, but at the same time obviously bothered about being hard on an amateur.

Intensely partisan on two sides at once, he is in the sort of split-minded fighting mood that silent comedians used to be able to milk laughs from for five minutes. It is typical of the change in screen comedy that it goes by for a tenth of what it might be worth. I think writers and directors are frightened to make detours from the narrative in case the audience forgets where it is. But most comedy consists of just that: of living inside the skull of a man who is constantly distracted from his objective and who will spend ten minutes picking fluff off his suit when he is standing in the path of an avalanche.

The trouble with *The Cracksman*, like most British comedies, is that the screen clown now has so little to support him. The characters played by Chaplin and Keaton and Harold Lloyd and Harry Langdon lived in a world that was full of comic paraphernalia, including their erotic and exquisitely dismissive heroines: vamps in motorcars, lofty girls whose long drawers kept showing, great strapping Valkyries with ripe thighs and prim little bangs on their foreheads. Their only contemporary equal is the girl whom Joan Littlewood has defined, the chirpy bird who wears a skirt as taut as a balloon and amiably tells men to keep their hands off it. The girls in *The Cracksman* are like the nonentities in every other British comedy: brassy, anti-erotic, impossible either to dote on or to send up.

Nor is there any help from the sets. What is a comedian to do if he is put down against a background that has about as much character and fantasy as a display of three-piece suites? Apart from the charming set for the hero's shop, most of the rooms in *The Cracksman* don't work with any comic style; there is a lot of humourless opulence that I associate with James Bond, a sort of Thug's Luxe that isn't parodied enough to be funny. In the Sennett comedies the screen seemed to fizz with baroque bedsteads and wallpapers and eccentric, beautiful props. The cluttered country parlours in some of Chaplin's films are eloquent about a whole kind of American frontier life. The only person who has done the same sort of thing lately is Jacques Tati. What a gentle prophetic mind.

* * *

Chaplin apparently once told Eisenstein that the reason why he scattered food to the poor children in *Easy Street* as though they were chickens was that he despised them. Eisenstein took him literally and may have been right. Chaplin used hungry kids in his work to the point of gush. This is one of his small aesthetic hypocrisies: in his political life, he derided the idea of anyone accepting slops from society's soup kitchen, in which he would always include swallowing society's conventions.

The tramp of the early films is Chaplin's simplified ideal man. He is totally practical, created by acts, not rules. The incompetent cops and addled factory workers and crazy bank presidents of the silent pictures are retarded by comparison because they react theoretically.

Some linking between Chaplin and Keaton is inevitable, but there are great distinctions. Keaton on screen clearly chooses to be taciturn. Chaplin pines to speak. For Keaton, it seems right that he is silent. The witty subtitles that he himself wrote are, properly, laconic. They reflect his own choice in life not to explain himself: which is the mainspring of his characters' wonderful dignity. Chaplin's films and the exclamatory subtitles carry the sense that the man on the screen is robbed of speech by some pathos of circumstance. 'If only you could hear me, you would know the tragedy of my predicament, the invention I am using to subdue this muteness.' One has much the same feeling about classical ballet dancers when they lean into positions expressing anguish, yearning, loss, with such physically strained long-windedness. If only they could open their mouths. Chaplin is usually in manufactured combat with being silenced. It is a part of the general begging for sympathy that strikes us in Chaplin, this part of it being nothing but a matter of film's technology.

It is not for nothing that *City Lights*, made by Chaplin at the beginning of his first move into sound, should grow in mystery and beauty. You feel that this lighted city might be anywhere. There are exquisite iron grilles on grand houses, poor stairways in ramshackle buildings with bird cages in the windows, romantic statues that engulf Chaplin in startling embraces as soon as they are unveiled. Paris, London, New York, Prague: perhaps it is whichever city one knows best, but recognizable only dimly, as if it were that place some long time before one was born.

Chaplin made the picture in 1930–1, when he could have used sound, but he chose not to, apart from music and the extended wonderful gag when he has swallowed a penny whistle at a party and gets a hooting attack of soprano gulps that attract a taxi and a horde of dogs after he has politely gone outside to be – so the other guests think – sick. The friendship in this film between Chaplin's tramp and Harry Myers's Eccentric Millionaire is a version of Falstaff and Prince Hal, with the Tramp a very slight Falstaff and the Millionaire a very fat Prince Hal, who spends unequalled nights with him when drunk and denies him horribly when sober. The Millionaire's sloshed attempt at suicide in a river after he has carefully taken off his patent-leather shoes is one of the great things in silent comedy, with Chaplin alertly inspecting the knot round the millstone that the man means to drown himself with, presumably to see whether the knot is a reef or a granny.

Chaplin loves visual puns. There is a beautiful one when he starts eating paper streamers instead of spaghetti. It is a moment that seems to give particular joy to children, I suppose because one is always interested as a child in the edible possibilities of the unnourishing, including india-rubbers, and sponges soaked in bathwater. At another point there is a decorated pudding blissfully mistakable for a man's bald head with a paper party hat around it. Chaplin manages the confusion practically and delicately. The Charlie most admired is always the tramp who mixes courtesy with a good deal of stubbornness and quite callous horse sense; the down-and-out in *City Lights* is evicted from the Millionaire's house when his rich chum is sober, but he is given the Millionaire's car when the chum is drunk, and as he drives slowly along the street looking for the fag end of a cigar to smoke he doesn't hesitate to get out and shove another tramp away from a butt he has his eye on.

There is élan when a man in a silent comedy will not fight without first elaborately taking his coat off. All punch-ups, suddenly convulsive, will begin in correct concentration and quickly peter out in some distraction. One of the great fight scenes in the range of silents is the one in *City Lights* where the very small Chaplin, after graciously lifting up the ropes for his second and his trainer, and wearing his coat because he is cold and thin, finds himself able to shelter behind the very large referee, who vainly tries to establish physically that two people are supposed to be boxing and he isn't one of them. As soon as the antagonists do connect, they are both on the ground. The referee counts them out alternately, because they take turns in getting up. *City Lights* is sometimes mawkish but at its best exact, and it has some of Chaplin's best acting moments. A few are quite bitter and angry, with the mouth full of ashes and road dust.

* * *

An interlude. Chaplin's chosen interlude.

Just as the hosts in a visited country will so regularly greet a foreign traveller with the question 'When are you going back?', meaning no harm in the world but succeeding in making the guest feel thoroughly unwelcome to stay a day more, people are quick to turn on anyone who has made them laugh and has then committed the sin of doing something else. They want to know when he is going back, this spoiler of the fun. *A Woman of Paris* – Chaplin's legendary 'serious' comedy, written and directed by him in 1922 and 1923 – provoked just that response. The public expected horselaughs and was furious about being robbed, furious about being given instead a sophisticated comedy (which was greatly to influence Lubitsch, for one). Audiences wanted back Chaplin's baggy trousers and clownish trudge. They paid hardly any attention to a film that forgot the little tramp. In the late twenties, Chaplin withdrew the picture from circulation. The self-imposed ban lasted nearly fifty years. Then, in 1976, he wrote a musical score for it and consented to its theatrical redistribution. The film, which was long thought lost, has been transferred from nitrate to glittering 35mm safety stock. In content, it amounts to a king's ransom dredged up from the ocean bed of sunken movies. It has all of Chaplin's wit and none of his whimsy. Strange, lively, reviving, to see evidence of the innovative mind of the figure too familiar to us in the guise of the little man.

This is a film with a sense of comedy which is debonair and elegant and bitterly close to the bone. The woman of Paris is acted by Edna Purviance, fulfilling a promise of Chaplin's that in their long career together he would one day write a dramatic part for her. As the subtitles announce, the Marie St Clair she plays is the key figure in 'a drama of fate'. We are in a small village 'somewhere in France'. Parted by disapproving parents from her love, who is a glaze-eyed, very silent-film figure called Jean Millet (Carl Miller), she goes to Paris alone on the train on which she was to have eloped with him. She gets involved with a handsome dandy called Pierre Revel, played with a benign wink at craftiness by Adolphe Menjou. The characterization of the figure makes it seem as though Chaplin toyed with – perhaps feared – the idea that he himself was this dandy.

In the cutting of one of the picture's many restaurant scenes, there is a mettlesome juxtaposition of gossip. Revel is called the richest bachelor in Paris by a woman at a far table. Revel, smoking rapidly, remarks out of her hearing that she is one of the richest old maids in Paris. We see him making a study of eating as he makes a study of everything, this scholar and taster of 'the good things of life'. He goes into the expensive restaurant to inspect the cooking. The scene is a Chaplin mêlée of tired and overworked servants observed by an alert and underworked bigwig. His office is his plumply pillowed bedroom, and for doing a rich man's office chores he wears embroidered pyjamas. He gets engaged to an heiress but laughs gaily at the idea that this should in any way perturb his set-up with Marie. *A Woman of Paris* is a film of ironic social acuity, full of women trailing long skirts that they kick aside in pretended irritation with expense, and of *luxe et volupté* that lack any kindness or exhilaration except for what is imparted by the character of the movie itself. Marie's friends have pinchbeck souls, and Chaplin shows the fact. These are people who thrive in margins. They chat indestructibly through everything. They allow the passing of time to make strangers of intimates, and they allow politesse to black out sensibility. Marie is caught up by the charade. Marie is trapped by Revel's fury about her when she says, with all too much credibility, that she's so depressed she doesn't want to go out. Marie is trapped by the Latin Quarter parties at which girls are hoisted like hooked fish to float among balloons. Marie is trapped by the party sight of a striptease done by a girl bandaged like a mummy, who slowly lets go the bandage – which is rewound about the stomach of a fat man in evening clothes – and who goes out of the scene, to poke her head around at us with nothing of her nakedness showing but a gleaming bare arm and a merry head with a finger held to the lips. Marie is trapped by the rich society that, by the duplicity of its kind, encourages her to lead a double moral life so well that she doesn't even notice that her maid has spilled out of her tallboy a man's telltale stiff collar in front of her badly-off Millet. He has followed her to Paris and become a painter, anxiously trying to mend things at least to the extent of painting her portrait. At a fine moment when she is standing for the portrait, she yawns in a pause when he is busy painting her, out of sight behind the canvas; and, by some flight of ESP, infects him with the yawn. More of silent comedy's visual puns.

It is a scene of emotion made strict, of yearning not allowed: Millet has made her promise not to look at the canvas because it presents the girl she once was, and not the counterfeit she has come to be.

There is no lack of wit or fault of sentiment in this film. Marie, in a tantrum with Revel, tears off her pearl necklace and throws it into the street, and then breaks a shoe heel when she has had second thoughts about the necklace and gone after it. Revel laughs at her greed. He consoles himself with a so-called friend of Marie's. Then follows the massage scene, so often described by film-lovers: the heroine is invisibly massaged by an inattentive, angry woman. Only the masseuse's irate hands show in the frame with occasional flashes of Marie's hand. They are intercut with shots of another friend, who is bringing Marie cruel gossip and flicking cigarette ash into a saxophone idly left in a chair. In a last and marvellous celebrated sequence, after Marie has found her self-willed fate, two vehicles meet and pass: Revel's splendid car, and Marie on a farm wagon with a child. Neither principal has seen the other. This is a beautifully put comic moral tale about matters of innocence and ignorance.

Buster Keaton once told me that when he and Chaplin first used the new sound cameras what they most missed in them was the noise. The old silent-picture cameras made a rhythmic racket that both of them had unconsciously taken for a beat when they were acting. Perhaps this is why Chaplin continued, even in old age, to write his own film music; knowing that he was going to be the composer, he could direct a scene with a tempo going on in his head.

To have seen him work on a scene in *A Countess from Hong Kong* was rather like watching a classical ballet master teaching behind glass. The beat that he could hear was out of one's own earshot, but it was holding the work together. Comedy for Chaplin was choreography: placing, movement, the intricate classical disciplining of vulgar energy. His urge to make his teaching concrete and physical was like the nostalgia of a great old dancer taking his thousandth *Swan Lake* class from a chair, unconsciously mimicking a *pas de deux* in a sort of muscular mumble, and exploding on to the set to dance the *corps de ballet* steps himself when some wretched cygnet missed a cue. The dancers in the *pas de deux*, obviously greatly admired, were Sophia Loren and Marlon Brando. One day the cygnet was a ship's steward in the film who had to make an entrance during a scene with Brando and offer a double brandy. With so little to do he fluffed it altogether; Chaplin catapulted on to the set and mimed it himself, and it was like Pavlova with a napkin over her arm.

A Countess from Hong Kong was made at Pinewood Studios, which in their time have produced some of the most deathly conventional films ever made. To Chaplin, then aged seventy-seven, who had made eighty-one films, this wasn't of the faintest consequence. More than with any other of the great classicists of comedy, conventionalism is really just what his work springs from. Rules, propriety, order, loyalty, romanticism, and a sweet decorum were the elements of his style: anarchy suggested nothing to him. A studio that had been the home of other people's technical revolts had little to offer Chaplin. His needs were simple, almost prissily formal, and entirely his own. He didn't, oddly, want location-shooting in his old age, which tells us perhaps that he never did.

I think he was always happy enough in any studio at all, provided it was professionally competent to do what he wanted, and if it wasn't he could undoubtedly teach it to be, because he knew every trade of his craft backwards. The freedom that other directors find in working on location meant nothing to him. The intrusions of commonplace life were not an inspiration to him but a distraction. If he worked outside a studio he found his ideas and concentration 'blowing away on the wind'.

The conditions at Pinewood were what he needed. They were a familiar focus for work, and everything extraneous to that seemed to be invisible to him. The mock-Tudor front offices obviously didn't jar on him, the crew had learned to do what he wanted, and the huge sound stages scattered with sets of a liner made a convention that only aided him to imagine the reality of his film more fiercely, like the genteel flower-curtained caravan on the set that was Brando's dressing-room, and the tea-stall where the technicians stood in line for currant buns and a black brew of tea that laid a coating of tannin inside the mouth like an animal's pelt.

Chaplin at eighty seemed to feel physically forty-five. But the only thing that bothered the outstripped crew was that they couldn't quite recognize him as he was in the silents. I saw one of them holding up a finger against the sight of his distant face to blot out his upper lip and try to imagine him with the old Hitler moustache. With his white hair he looked almost like the negative of his silent-film self. The wide mouth, stretched like a child's eating a slice of watermelon, wasn't quite as one remembered it; perhaps it was always changed by the moustache.

He seemed to feel the cold, but then he had lived out of

England long enough to grow unused to the conditions that the locals dourly called livable. The studio was what fellow citizens thought of as living-room temperature, which is like March out of doors. He wore a thick sweater under a thicker jacket. Usually he had a hat on against the glare of the lights. When he felt debonair he tipped the hat over his eyes; when he was growling at the stupidity of his extras, or at the unwieldiness of conventional modern film lighting, he pushed it impatiently to the back of his head. During hold-ups he often suddenly wheeled away from the stage to find his wife Oona, a shy, beautiful woman who generally effaced herself behind a pillar. He seemed to look to her not so much for advice as for some sort of confirmation.

He kept the technicians at a distance. They called him 'sir', and if he joked with them they watched carefully to make sure that they were right to joke back. 'OK, print that,' he said once at the end of a take, and then he heard an airplane overhead that had probably wrecked it. 'Damn it,' he said; not his furious version of the oath, which was an American-accented 'Goddammit', but an atavistic curse out of his English youth which is practically a pleasantry. The crew noticed the inflection and deduced from it that they could freewheel with him for a minute. 'There's a humming. Why didn't you tell me?' he went on to the sound technician with the headphones, giving the start of his wide grin. 'Because you were talking, sir,' said the soundman daringly because he was suddenly licensed to. The atmosphere on the set was at its warmest, sunny and trustful. But one take later Chaplin said 'Oko' instead of 'OK'. He often pronounced words wrongly when he was in a hurry, sometimes even trying to force them into other meanings. The visual punster could use verbal punning to shelter him when his old mind was racing.

The immediately endearing thing about watching Chaplin work on this picture was the way he went on laughing about it. He didn't laugh at the lines in themselves; he laughed at the way they were executed. One had the feeling that when he wrote them he probably wasn't even yet amused. The pleasure must have come later, when the actors had gone through the lines mechanically, overemoted, lost their confidence, learned their moves backwards, broken through some sort of actors' sound barrier, and eventually found the work as easy as breathing.

It was ease that always made him laugh. He kept saying that this was a romantic film, not a comedy. He wanted to make a film about love that simply happened to be funny, without anyone in the picture knowing it. 'Play for absolute realism, not for comedy,' he said again and again. One could see the details of Brando's performance becoming daily smaller and more meticulous, like the movement of a watch. His attention to Chaplin was total. I found it technically enthralling, and often moving.

Brando was playing a stuffy American ambassador to Saudi Arabia, travelling from Hong Kong with Sophia Loren embarrassingly stowed away in his stateroom as a dispossessed Russian countess. The ambassador's wife, played by Tippi Hedren, is an amused lounger who has been separated from him for two years. She discovers Sophia Loren's bra in his cabin with nothing more than elegant glee that he should so undiplomatically have been an ass. His Excellency is travelling with his valet Hudson, played by a stone-faced English actor called Patrick Cargill: the valet has to be induced to marry Sophia Loren in order to give her his nationality as a way of getting her through American immigration. The valet's resistance to marrying the most marriageable woman imaginable was funny to work on. When the subject is broached, he behaves as though he has been offered the wrong wine with the fish.

Most of the action happens on the ship. The sniffy valet is given his orders in the sundeck lounge. Before shooting, Chaplin sat on the edge of one of the chairs on the set and listened to Brando and Cargill running through their lines. He mouthed most of the dialogue with them unconsciously and made tiny replicas of their movements. When he was rehearsing actors his muscles often seemed to twitch like a dog having a dream.

'You are an American citizen, aren't you?' says the ambassador to his valet.

'I've been an American citizen for the last sixteen years,'

says the valet stiffly, in the most English voice possible. Chaplin laughed at the way he did it. Then the valet is told that he must marry Sophia Loren.

'I'd like you to marry her,' said Brando, so disarmingly that Cargill laughed, but also so lightly that he made it seem like kidding.

'Don't denote anything on your face. Keep your voice up. Insist on the action.' The ambassador did the line again, bland and clear.

The valet paused, then replied, 'If I may say so, sir, this is rather sudden.'

Chaplin: 'More polite. You're disguising your feelings by being very polite.'

Cargill said it again.

'But before you close up, just a shade of shock on that line of Marlon's, "I'd like you to marry her." It lays an egg a little bit.' He laughed. 'So long as you're not suave. A suavity here would kill the whole scene.' This was real comic shrewdness; most people directing these lines would have thought that unruffled suavity was their basis. Chaplin turned out to be quite right, of course. It is like the funniness of P. G. Wodehouse's Jeeves. The comic point about the godly servant isn't that he is totally impassive, but that across the immortal calm there is an intermittent flicker of ordinary humanity. The crack in the Olympian surface has to be microscopic, but it can be gigantically expressive. It is a difficult thing for an actor to do without oversignalling. Lazy American comedians now would tend to make the crack a large crevasse; lazy English comedians would leave it out and settle for unbroken haughtiness. Chaplin was patiently insistent about the point. Finally, the lines made him laugh.

The extras had to walk across in the background. They had been told exactly where to go and how fast, but everything was fumbled and Chaplin watched in agony. Some of the extras were old trouts who habitually went to sleep in the armchairs on the set although one of the masters of the cinema was working under their noses. Some of them were bored young hacks who weren't even alert enough to be nervous. They imported an atmosphere of crassness and laziness that was sniffed by the members of the crew with instant dislike. The fact that they turned up in the wrong clothes is one of the common absurdities of big-budget film-making, but it was enough to upset a perfectionist like Chaplin for the morning. 'They should be in lovely summery clothes – lovely pale shoes . . . ', I heard him saying to himself unhappily between takes. 'They look as if they've just got off the 8:17 at Victoria Station,' said the amiable cameraman with an edge of irritability.

'Remember your tempos,' Chaplin called out to the extras, who did their jobs again. One group had to saunter, the other to scurry. They managed it eventually, looking as awkward and unreal as any extras in any big studio in the world, which was one of the penalties that Chaplin paid for working under conventional conditions. The rehearsals for this scene took a long time. Chaplin himself demonstrated a steward's entrance twice, arriving and pivoting exactly on cue, saying 'So-so-so-*so*; so-so-so-so-so-*so*', as dummy dialogue. It was rather like Toscanini giving an entrance to the triangle-player after a hundred and fifty bars of silence.

Eventually the moves hardened and became mechanical, which was what he wanted. Once the routine was fixed and had started to bore the actors, the comedy began to emerge. He worked from the outside inward: first the mechanics, then familiarity and physical skill, and after that the right emotions would come. It was the diametric opposite of the Stanislavskian style that had become accepted modern dogma.

'Do that line again, Marlon. Quickly. Take off the fat.' The working atmosphere between them was relaxed and easy. Brando is one of the greatest screen actors in the world. He has been trained in exactly the opposite tradition, but he listened and absorbed with an attention that seemed unflawed.

He was doing a close-up shot of the scene, with the cues being given to him by the producer, Jerry Epstein. Brando fluffed twice, saying, 'Husband' instead of 'Hudson', and the producer giggled. Brando found himself infected and started saying words upside down. At the end of the final take he squinted at Chaplin, laughed, and said to the producer, 'Do you want to get some Scotch tape and sew yourself together?'

Epstein was an old associate of Chaplin, and an obvious contributor to the mood of fun that Brando and Loren both sensed on the set. His way of giving Chaplin a prompt when the director was signalling for it looked like the result of years, rather like a surgical nurse shoving the right instrument into a surgeon's hand.

The attention that Chaplin demanded, and got, was fierce and total. Where other directors become most inventive by allowing energy to fly outwards, with Chaplin the pull was always towards the centre. He knew exactly what he was doing. When he was shooting a scene he seemed to be gently chivvying the actors towards something that was already complete in his head. Like a tug edging a liner away from a quay, he coaxed the incomparable Brando into a manner that was just faintly at odds with the one he was known by. The sumptuous, time-taking style, spaciously intelligent behind an opiate gaze, had become smaller, quicker, and sometimes comically testy, just as the histrionics of Sophia Loren's abundant comic temperament had been converted into a very funny flatness. In her work before *A Countess from Hong Kong*, she made people laugh by Latin fluster; in the scenes that I saw, she did it by phlegm. 'He has made me quite different,' she said. 'When I see rushes I don't recognize myself. He doesn't like me to use my hands much, especially near my face. We're trying to do everything as naturally as possible.'

Directors and actors always say now that they are working for realism, of course; it is one of the modern pieties of the profession, but in Chaplin's case it was precisely true. Again and again when he was directing a scene he would cut out some gesture or response that revealed itself the moment it had gone as a hamstrung comic mannerism. His laughs in the picture nearly always came from doing apparently as little as possible very fast. 'Lots of lift, lots of tempo . . .' he often said. The takes that he decided to print were always the ones with the most dash and lightness; sometimes when he was talking under pressure he made a bouncing movement upward with his hand as though he were keeping a ball in the air.

'It wants a beat,' he said to Tippi Hedren, after she had been working on a scene where she enters with the identifiably outsize bra that she has discovered in her husband's cabin. 'This is all a great comedy to you. No malice. You haven't lived with your husband for two years. You come in with great gusto. You're kidding him.' Through the next take he looked worried. 'There was no tempo.' He got up from his chair by the camera, wrinkled his nose and pranced through the moves himself, saying 'So-so-so,' like a groom sedating a horse. 'So-so-so, *Your Excellency*,' he said, pivoting on the words. 'You're mocking him. You're glib. That's it. Can we come in with a bigger spread? I would burst in here. It's sort of breezy. One-two –' He gave her the time, and caught his breath on the upbeat as she entered. 'Can we keep that lovely movement?' In a previous take she had turned on one of her lines and practically flowed on to a sofa; he did it himself to fix the move in his mind, looking comically grand in an imaginary tea gown, and made sure that the camera movement fitted it.

For Chaplin, the pacing of a camera articulated a scene. On the whole he didn't seem to like camera movement very much. ('The actors should be the performers, not the lens.') He didn't care for trick angles and he hated the laziness of cryptically significant shots that show nothing but door-opening. 'Orientation' was an important idea to him. He believed that an audience must always know where they are in a room, and that actors must know exactly where to stop, where to turn, where to stand, whether to talk directly or indirectly. I had expected his physical business to be graphic and hilarious, but I hadn't been quite prepared for the precision of his sense of words. To talk about Chaplin's mime is rather like praising the height of Everest; it is his pin-fall ear for dialogue that was technically so absorbing to anyone fortunate enough to have seen him working. 'There's something woolly in that word, Sophia,' he said; the fuzz was there, an emphasis that was faintly implausible and faltering, but a lot of good directors would have let it go. 'Most films are just in and out,' said the chippie (the film carpenter). 'Not this one. He's definitely got something on his mind.'

When he was coming back from lunch break or inspecting the sets in the morning, he carried his script against his chest as if it were a buckler. Like Keaton, he stood and walked with the arched back of a small boy, perhaps because of the ferocious physical training that both of them had as tiny children in vaudeville. 'He's a perfectionist,' said the director of photography, Arthur Ibbetson. 'When he did his own bit it was rather a day.' (Chaplin appears in the film in a tiny part as a steward who gets seasick.) 'All he really did was sweep the deck with his head down. Other people would have made a production out of it.' Ibbetson did a mime of someone milking laughs. 'There's one passenger asleep on the whole deck and when he's finished he sweeps the muck very neatly behind his feet. That's all he does, see?'

* * *

There is a link between Chaplin and James Thurber. They share a startled gaze at the lesser spirits unable to cope with predicaments of dismay. It still baffles a few hardliners behind the gossamer of what was called the Iron Curtain that we should laugh at Thurber, for they see in his work nothing but despair.

But it is not despairing to know that electricity obviously leaks out of lamps without bulbs. It is not despairing to deal nicely with a first wife who happens to be lying on the top of a wardrobe when you are with people to whom her physical and social positions need explaining. For Chaplin, for Thurber, it is not at all desperate to be in a place peopled with characters briskly intent on unexplained tasks, with agnostic men envying women and cats their atheism, with dogs that sit in attitudes of scholarship, with a pony that has a moose's antlers strapped to his head in a way that is obviously giving him a headache, with a television set in a privileged bathroom where the screen steams up when there is hot water in the bath and the bather uses windscreen wipers. This is simply the world of circumstance that has to be contended with, says Chaplin, says

Thurber. In Chaplin's case he brought that view to bear on Nazism itself, sometimes marvellously.

Long after the first appearance of Chaplin's *The Great Dictator*, though, it still bothers a good many of the people who remember the Second World War that Charlie should have tried to bring off a joke about Hitler and anti-Semitism which rests on political naïveté and schoolboy humour, finally mixed with oratorical mawkishness. Goering becomes Herring; Goebbels becomes Garbitsch; Hitler is Hynkel, played by Chaplin, who doubles uncomfortably as a little Jewish barber. Hynkel is the dictator of Tomania, and his brother-dictator Napaloni (Jack Oakie) runs a country called Bacteria.

The scenes that work best now, when we seem to be at a safe distance from Hitler, if not from dictators, propaganda, and anti-Semitism, are the scenes of kindergarten fooling, such as the one in which Hynkel puts mustard on his strawberries by mistake, and the one in which Napaloni's official train keeps shunting back and forth to find a red carpet. There is aerial pleasure about the dark sequence of fantasizing megalomania where Hynkel plays raptly with a balloon that is inscribed with a map of the globe, practising kicking it up with his heels and finally lying on his back to play with it like a trained circus dog. The moment when Garbitsch arranges for the tiny, panicky dictator to be seated always higher than the looming Napaloni in audience in Hynkel's ballroom of an office is one that Brecht might have much liked – Brecht, who wrote that other perilous farce about the same men, the intellectually dazzling *The Resistible Rise of Arturo Ui*. The trouble with *The Great Dictator* is that Chaplin's political sense is minute, which eventually undercuts the wondrous slapstick. The last long uplift speech about the coming brotherhood of man is a mistake. So is the rhetorical close-up of Paulette Goddard symbolizing Jewish womanhood under dictatorship. She is better earlier, in the ghetto scenes, absurdly banging the SS over the head with a frying pan. It is the political underpinning of the film that strikes one now as being unequal to the huge comic task that

Chaplin took on. All the dreaming vaudeville turns seem true and brave.

Guts

There is a free-booting comic courage of observation through quickened language that only sheer guts brings off. It has to do with cheek, stamina, and a founded suspicion of being at the bottom of the heap. Its voice is the voice of down-and-outs, vagrants, the stateless, the bank-accountless, the fighting born victims who know themselves outnumbered the moment they are in the company of one, the furiously lovelorn who repine only in secret and publicly grumble blue murder about their woman as they brace themselves for another thwack on the head from the handbag of the beloved. It is the sound of the man with nothing more to lose, a yell from the last ditch, the resort of the persecuted, the humour of any American who sees the joke of his being welcomed as an immigrant by the Statue of Liberty with a gracious reference to him as a huddled mass. Most other countries have nothing approaching this particular baleful, disruptive funniness. France hasn't a notion of it, with her serenity in Frenchness, her imperturbable syntax, and her limited understanding of humiliation. The wit institutes of France – farce at the Comédie Française, say – possess nothing so raw and socially unhousable as Woody Allen's anxious confidences about being Jewish and about chasing girls. Poland's famous bad-taste wit is specifically political, a form of gallows humour that comes from being overrun, a policy of going too far personally when your country has been allowed to go nowhere for centuries.

W. C. Fields is the quiet agent of calamity. The tone of his utterance is of a man disclosing his private moods without much expectancy of being heard. He does not so much state a line as dredge it from an obviously very crowded storeroom in the basement, having hauled it up in that much-imitated dying undertone. He will roll vowels around his mouth as though cooling them before they sear a gullet sore with the Scotch he has imbibed with perseverance and patience. 'Imbibe' is a favourite word; so is 'alfalfa', and 'kumquat'. The embarrassment he felt about his nose ('The man had a rather prominent proboscis, after the fashion of eminent men') was perhaps born of a wish to brazen out a childhood of living in ditches when his face was badly hit about, though the people who disliked him, who I fancy boiled down to Mae West, put it down to alcohol. He threw her once, she told me in outrage, by saying to her in the middle of a take, 'And how is my little brood mare?' He valued most of humanity on the low side, including himself, though his forbearance was clearly infinite. In his films, he fended off unfair domestic happenings, including impossible wives, with unwilting benevolence until Christmas Day of 1946, when he was collected by 'the fellow in the bright night-gown', as he always referred to death.

Mae West was a Christian Scientist who did not, of course, believe in death. I met her only once, in the part of Hollywood of which she owned a valuable amount, being canny about real estate and believing, as a good Christian Scientist does, that prosperity is one of God's attributes which his children are duty-bound to reflect if they are not to be in mortal error. Mae West clearly was not in this mortal error. She lived in an expensive apartment, nearly all of it white apart from tinted oil paintings of herself more or less naked. The curtains were white, the carpet was white, the sofa was upholstered in white fur, the grand piano was white, and she herself (in the middle of the afternoon) was in a white satin peignoir bordered with white ostrich feathers. A member of the Mae West fan club, male, wearing a white satin suit and a rose-pink satin shirt, was sitting in the white kitchen eating health-food honey with an Apostle spoon during a break in a discussion about a beach party by the Fan Club at which the members were to wear Mae West's carefully kept costumes. She wouldn't have been good to Fields.

'The time has come,' Fields would moan, with his usual all-seeing meditativeness, 'to take the bull by the tail and face the situation.' He would say it in situations with Mae West, unless he betook himself to the quiet curse of 'Godfrey Daniels', in the quiet caw he used for homemade swearings to flummox the censoring Hays office. Well, I would say he was one of the four or five most courageously funny men we have lately had in the world. There is a myth that women don't really like W. C. Fields, the most prejudiced, unruly and sloshed comedian in cinema history. It arises, I suppose, because he loathed brats and felt genial to mayhem; and the male sex, which chiefly invents myths, along with slang, war, symphonic music and obscenities, obviously has an interest in assuming that women will love children come what may, and that they will always elect to make life work. Once start admitting that women frequently cherish quite urgent desires to thwack infants on the head, and that they may well have the same fellow-feeling as any other human being for W. C. Fields's dogged anarchy, and I suppose that civilization as we know it would come to an end.

Fields is a moving man. The pseudonyms he used when he wrote scripts – Mahatma Kane Jeeves, Otis Criblecoblis – are not only funny but also obviously devised in an authentic moment of instinct for flight. They are part of his system of boltholes, like the elaborate chain of bank accounts that he instituted under a score of names. His early life was appalling; but instead of turning into a victim, he became a fifth-columnist. Where other kids grow strong on oranges and the love of relations, he lived on pickings and solitary sniping operations. By eleven he had left home. He obviously had the deepest sense of grievance about ever being a child, at the mercy of a father who sold fruit and vegetables from a cart and sang maudlin songs. Fields hated 'Annie Laurie' and the human voice in general until the end of his life, and he seems to have become sulphurously bored by the time he could talk.

Required as a minute infant to trail round after his father when he was selling greengroceries, he immediately satirized the parental sales-cry. This led to trouble. He also yelled commercials for non-available commodities like calabashes and rutabagas because he liked the names.

Fields is one of life's losers, and the hell with it. He is not in the race. Fields is truly debonair and his own man, a covert friend to mongrels and a brilliant enemy to privilege, hiding affliction under a murmured outrage all his own. He is Chaplin's diametric opposite. Chaplin's little man can seem to be on his knees and begging for sympathy with his bravely managed suffering, but Fields is on his feet and thinking. ('It is much more easy to have sympathy with suffering than it is to have sympathy with thought,' wrote Oscar Wilde in an essay on Socialism.) Fields is a smouldering independent who asks no pity and who saves himself with eccentrically conceived and harmless vengeances. In *It's a Gift* – which now turns up regularly at the art houses, along with the other Fields works – he tries hard to run a grocery store that is eventually flooded with molasses by Baby LeRoy. Fields lets the little saboteur go unscathed. The incident merely adds a baleful new jot to his analysis of the human condition, and the notice that he hangs on the door of his wrecked shop mildly reads, 'Closed on Account of Molasses'. Surrounded by wives, cross, unheeding soppy girls, and overblessed children, he deals unexceptionably with the immediate situations, walks away with a sceptical expression somewhere around the hips, and implies that the better part of his considerable brain is disreputably engaged with other things. In *It's a Gift*, his battleship wife, Mrs Bissonette ('pronounced Bissonay', he writes loyally on a placard, obeying her haywire snob teaching), makes him halve a sandwich that he then has to eat in the middle of a storm of cushion feathers. She yells, never satisfied, that these were her *mother's* feathers. But Fields has secretly won, all the same, for even if he is getting hell for obligingly eating a stingy half sandwich full of feathers, he is also eating the half sandwich that contains the complete sandwich's ration of meat, which he has neatly swiped from his own greedy child during the forced act of partition. Fields often has a bad time, but he is no masochist. He is fortified because he always holds an opinion, even if the opinion isn't exactly communicated in speech as we know it. Fields doesn't so much speak as amuse himself with self-addressed soliloquies. The to-and-fro of less doughty men is not for him. His is only the fro. In his great films he is always the reactor. He plays the muttering straight man to Life, the counterblow to a punch in the stomach. His surreal retorts are conceived for himself alone, like his endearments and his curses. In *Million Dollar Legs*, as the weight-lifting President of an otherwise rather weedily athletic state called Klopstokia, he tries to do something about the economy and simultaneously deals with his dopey daughter's suitors. One of them is visible out of his window. 'What's his name, Angela?' he says, with native distaste for his own offspring's name, though his hungover Richard Tauber voice suggests that the seraphic fib committed at her christening is only the way of the world and scarcely worth reacting against. 'I call him "sweetheart",' says Angela. 'Hey, sweetheart!' yells Fields vaguely out the window, and thereafter he is so beguiled by the wooziness of the word that he applies it to various sports trainers and members of his Cabinet throughout the film. No one can use endearments more dangerously than Fields. *'Please sit down, honey!'* he bawls at a blind man who is in the process of exploding a pile of electric light bulbs by feeling around him with a white stick. If this sounds a particle cruel, the next sequence shows Fields covering his eyes with terror at the sight of the same man weaving his way through traffic. Secretly alert to everything, Fields pretends to a protective callousness. His kindnesses are clandestine; his open and implacable hostility is beamed at the fortunate, and the armour-plated, and the prissy. This axis includes Deanna Durbin-like stars, mayors, milk, gambling laws, literal-minded listeners, and soupy women, among whom I think he would have put the nurses who tried once, in real life, to look after his own broken neck and were waved away ('It's only a flesh wound') with stories about far worse calamities that had befallen him and that he had survived with the help of Doctor Buckhalter's Kidney Reviver. At the last ditch, which was where he lived from toddling age, Fields took refuge in improvisation, in wild names, in veiled ripostes to child stars whom he sensed to be looking after number one far better than he had ever managed to.

No other Hollywood personality can ever have emanated such steady contempt of the Hollywood idols who were in the same picture. His relationship to the thinly disguised Deanna Durbin warbler in *Never Give a Sucker an Even Break* seems to be one of longing to get her as intoxicated as possible and to use her vocal cords as a catapult. His fatigued voice sounds as if he has been defending himself against creditors and prigs and line-ups of the commonplace all his life. His drawl, which he can throw quietly from any belligerent's sounding-place, as a cat can, is never going to win him a point but never going to surrender one either. A lot of other Hollywood comedians are frantic but inert; W. C. Fields is the opposite, stoic and energetic. His rudeness is afflictingly lonely.

When a friend of mine once met him, he was drinking three Martinis for breakfast and looking at a rose garden. He preferred Martinis to anything else. He told her carefully (she was about eight) that Scotch could begin to taste like medicine and that bourbon led to drunkenness. He genuinely hated drunks for their vehemence and mawkishness, two things that this calmly out-of-step and stoic man despised.

As his biographer Robert Lewis Taylor has recorded, he always used to take a Martini shaker to the studio. He would say that it was filled with pineapple juice. Somebody mischievous once put actual pineapple juice into it. 'Somebody's been putting pineapple juice into my pineapple juice!' he yelled. But he never failed to turn up for shooting, and he generally finished days ahead of schedule. One of the many reasons he drank seems to have been that he was frightened of making the subtly understood technical miscalculation of speaking his lines too fast, which he never did when he wasn't cold sober. He had an outlaw's gift that was matched by no other comedian. Faced by the conventional breakfast, he would suddenly ad-lib an inviting burble suggesting that ordinary food might as well go out of the window. 'How'd you like to hide the egg and gurgitate a few saucers of mocha-java!' he mutters convivially to a waitress who victimizes him. He takes cover in 'Sarsaparilla'. The word engaged him. So did 'my little plum' and a game he called 'squidgalum', and an uncle called 'Effingham Hoofnickel', and foggy snatches of descriptive narrative out of the blue: 'She dips her mitt down into this mélange. . . .' He can make gracious sentences to the dignitaries who are his natural enemy. 'I am Dr Eustace P. McGargle,' he says, elegantly switching from gambling to preaching in the presence of a mayor. 'Perhaps you've read my book on the evils of wagering. . . . I was a victim of this awful scourge. A helpless pawn in the coils of Beelzebub. Beelzebub . . . Beel-zee-bub . . . Lucifer.' Fields allowed himself no sympathy and he joined no one. He was the author of his own life, and he behaved as though he had no kin. He never wanted anyone else's favours. He had the wiser trick of extending a licence to himself, and he died an agnostic, without help, as he promised he would. 'I'll go without knuckling under,' he droned once, about believing in God.

Children are born at the bottom of the heap. W. C. Fields, for all his loathing of spoilt tots, often sensed blood-brothers in the young of the lower depths and would mumble a fraternal fantasy on their behalf. In *International House* he suddenly says, 'A little French baby, and the mother took up French lessons to understand him when he started to talk.'

Truffaut was the ultimate champion of childhood. Better than anyone else in film-making, he understood children's instinct to labour at self-set projects before the grown-up division between work and play has them in its grip. In *L'Argent de poche* (translated either as *Small Change* or *Pocket Money*) a small boy dragged out by his mother to shop diverts himself as he staggers upstairs laden with groceries by using a long French loaf as a debonair cane. A little girl, rapt in seeing herself as abandoned and starving while her parents are merely out for an hour, rigs up an elaborate famine mechanism and yells to the neighbours in the courtyard that she has no food, not a crumb. The neighbours, satisfyingly scandalized, pile provisions into a basket that the tiny arm muscles bravely haul up. In *Such a Gorgeous Kid Like Me*, there is a scene with an infant film buff that is purest Truffaut. Adult characters are on the trail of an amateur photographer who may have a vital piece of evidence. They ask a nice bourgeoise at the door for Mr Farrell. 'Mr Farrell is dead.' 'Oh, excuse us, our condolences; your husband dead. . . .' 'No, not my husband,' inexplicably brightening up, 'my son.' 'But such a fine photographer,' the interlocutors plug on. 'Ah, that would be my nephew,' says the housewife, and she yells for an extremely small boy in an Eton collar, who reaches up to the amateur detectives' waists but nonetheless holds with dignity that he doesn't like showing his rushes before they are edited.

The great *Zéro de conduite*, made in 1933 by Jean Vigo, is a droll poem on behalf of the comic anarchist who stirs in all children under grown-ups' institutional whip. It is set in a boys' boarding school. Like many works of art about childhood, it employs a trick with proportion; but where the usual conservative's way is to show the adult as monumental in young eyes, Vigo knows that adolescents are not so obsequious. To these schoolboys, authority looks not impressive but puny. The headmaster that they are required to respect is played by a dwarf.

All the masters are unctuous, spiteful and full of nervous bombast: they are also, the children observe, comically greedy. One of them, a stool pigeon with sly pointed toes and a hat like Ben Turpin's, steals around the classroom pilfering sweets at break. The adults in the film move as though they were in whalebone corsets, but the skinny children prance blithely about their prison, throwing off the masters as though they were mosquitoes and marching through the dormitory with rakes and balloons on their shoulders in a surreal Peasants' Revolt. The film has no real narrative ending: one sees only that the children continue to triumph through the sense of sustaining proportion that humour's abandon endows. It is a marvellous work.

* * *

Millions of black Americans in a muted clump at the bottom

of the heap? For going on two centuries, yes; but things are changing. A lot of the voices in cinema, theatre, cabaret, and TV are clarion. The acoustic that makes the voices carry is the biting comedy of turning white condescensions upside down.

Richard Pryor holds that a white told him about the wonder for all Americans of the Courts of Justice. Pryor said, 'Yuh? It's *just us*.' His sharpest comedy is based on his certainty that blacks are the only group that any observer could believe to exist. Whites *may*, but they're pretty implausible. At his best Pryor has a demonic take on life. His laugh is to himself, furiously amused by what he sees around him, and distinctly baffled. His deep-sunk eyes are looking at a space that strikes him as being incredible.

Eddie Murphy, cheerfully delirious and foul-mouthed, lopes the stage in *An Evening with Eddie Murphy* in red leather jacket and trousers, throwing us lassoes of lore about sex and faggots and women singers ('that wholesome sentimentality'). He imitates Elvis, Stevie Wonder, a white man's walk, a white man trying to dance ('they got no beat'), a black child putting up with a social worker ('You don't have no ice cream because you are on the welfare because your father's an alcoholic'). His bits of wisdom come at us pell-mell: 'Remember those days when you used to be able to beat women up? In the movies, girls would get slapped and say "Ooh!" Now they're heavily into aerobics.'

Trading Places is a scabrously funny film with Eddie Murphy into shifty big-business and scoring off paler and shiftier financiers. He says confidently that he has a hunch about pork bellies. It works out fine, along with a dabble in angel-dust. He looks after himself with sagacity: 'I'm a karate man. Karate men leave their marks on the inside.' The tax people freeze his account and he has a brush with jail ('a rehabilitated, culturally disadvantaged *prison*' – correcting himself to administrators' English). He takes on the nobs and beats them: 'Haven't you people ever heard of coasters?' When asked, he will present himself in white society as an exchange student from the Cameroons. On *Saturday Night Live* this guide to the white world puts on white-face and a handmade suit to sit on a Madison Avenue bus beside a slouched black drunk.

When the drunk gets off, the all-white busload starts laughing and joking and having drinks. So that's how white folks behave when blacks aren't around. And there are still some blacks who want to get white-educated and be like rich white lawyers and say things like 'This man, *per se*.' Murphy then swivels into an imitation of a black mother who says humbly, 'We never had luxuries like food.'

In these times, one might expect many an enterprise of American going-over-the-top about being black. Melvin van Peebles's *Watermelon Man*, made in 1970, was a forerunner of Eddie Murphy. It is quite a feat of off-key funniness. Godfrey Cambridge, who is black, appears in it first as a bigoted Northern white. The make-up job – it is impossible to look at this film without its giving you a share in its insane bad taste, which is rather companionable of it – is elaborate and interesting. The bigot is called Jeff. He thinks he is popular, but nobody really likes him at all except his wife and children, and the children barely. He is actually a beast. He likes irritating the black driver of his usual morning bus by racing the bus on foot, and he likes needling the black counterman at the drugstore where he daily orders some lunatic health juice of his own recipe. He fancies himself as a humorist. When he finally climbs on to the bus, he says merrily to the long-suffering driver, 'If you were in the South, you'd have to drive in the back of the bus.'

But then Jeff, to his horror, turns black overnight. He puts it down to his sunlamp. He then goes on being exactly the same sort of beast, and the familiar victims of his racism go on taking it on the chin because they are so used to it. His wife (Estelle Parsons), a quiet and liberal woman of great patience, implies somehow in her manner that his blackness is simply a trouble he is going to have to be babied through, constituting only one more of the eccentric tasks she took on by marrying him. After shrieking briefly about the change in him, she becomes solicitous and practical. Jeff bathes in milk, the bathroom floor littered with milk cartons. He buys skin-whiteners by the ton from stores in the black section of town. 'These creams don't work,' he says desperately. 'No wonder Negroes riot.' His wife is soothing. 'I don't think any intelligent Negro expects it to be immediate. Don't be militant,' she says. 'I'm not militant, I'm *white*!' he yells, hopping mad. Worried to death about himself, racing to embarrassed doctors, he keeps up his spirits by roaring at other blacks as usual. They look at him carefully, wondering why on earth they should stand this any longer, and put the change of skin down to a trick of the light. Beginning to be defeated, Jeff retreats to the shower to pray for whiteness. Not that he believes in God, but still, God can be bullied and whined to, presumably. 'Please, Lord, you will see a *nice* person coming out of this shower?' A white person. Pause. 'There are no *atheists* in this shower.' Sob. Godfrey Cambridge is a funny actor who, considering the time when the film was made, left a praiseworthy amount of bile in a satiric tale hard to bring off.

* * *

John Berry, blacklisted during McCarthy time, made his fine *Claudine* in 1974. The film is an inside job about a pretty, thirty-six-year-old deserted black mother with six kids in Harlem. The leftist white creators burgled the place for their picture's jokes, rashness, steady good humour and resourcefulness under fire. Most of the trouble that rains on the unbeaten characters comes from their being poor. Not crime poor, or drunk poor, or junkie poor. Just plain poor. Claudine – Diahann Carroll, slight and spunky – takes the bus every morning to work in Riverdale, washing her way through a pile of dishes for a white couple and leaving behind her kids, who range from a militant eighteen-year-old down to a toddler. Claudine's white mistress doesn't hesitate to grumble about her being fifteen minutes late, although Claudine works herself into a stupor, stopping to admire the cheek of a garbage man called Roop (James Earl Jones, who suggests a mixture of pretended Hamlet misogyny and a Chekhov gift for friendship that won't flag however hard he tries). He makes a stab at flirting with Claudine but has no luck until she sees him decline on official grounds to hoist her employers' overweight garbage bin full of bottles one morning after a party, even though the white boss has taken out the bin himself on a little cart to show, convincing nobody, that he isn't above manual work. Roop turns a bulk of shaking laughter at the sight of a man who doesn't understand that the whole point of being economically superior is *not* to do the filthy jobs. Claudine reluctantly recognizes in Roop a man to call an ally, even though he is another kind of poor. Being a woman, she's working poor *and* welfare poor. Thirty dollars a month per child.

Her eldest girl, Charlene, is about to get pregnant by a boy called Teddy, who has just changed his name to Abdullah. 'Black won't be beautiful anymore,' Claudine says, correctly scenting trouble. Charlene, pouty but dying to be nubile, aged sixteen, is childishly sick after a night out, to the pleasure of little sister Patrice. Patrice is a girl, but named after Lumumba, and she has all the impeccable reporting instincts of a treacherous younger sister. The sometimes apparently numberless kids make loyal and obscene efforts to keep their mother from adding 'another nigger' to the brood. The ranks against Roop are soon closed. They want to know what she's been doing when she's been out with him till 4 am in his apartment building. As he points out to her, it's a place where you meet a better class of cockroach.

Roop is a blusterer with a strong vein of farcical cowardice and a useful ethic about being a man, which lets him get a girl pregnant and then skedaddle back to his usual secluded life with Milhous, the crafty, long-unimpeachable mouse who looks remarkably like Nixon. Roop's life suits him, and he preens himself about managing it pretty cleverly. Having languidly got his date, he gives the exhausted Claudine a bubble bath of liquid detergent and looks forward to rubbing his new chick's back. But this chick, who is no fool, shuts his bathroom door in his face and falls asleep up to her neck in suds.

Accounting for the six kids, she explains that she has had two husbands and 'two almost marriages'. He says he has two sons by a first wife in Ohio, and a daughter in Louisville, who is living with his second wife's mother. To Claudine this isn't the same thing at all. Children don't count in the mathematics of Harlem life unless you are the parent landed with them. She has to cope with babysitting; arguing with her wild eldest son about the language of militancy; coaxing a middle child out of a miserable game that he's invisible and doesn't exist ('I know you *do* exist. I *borned* you,' says Claudine with typical sharp comfort); and protecting her own vestige of privacy ('Momma! You went out with a *garbage* man?' says one of her shocked progeny, followed up by another angel-faced innocent with 'Don't they stink all the time?'). She also has to keep everyone's hands off the toddler; sit the family down early to hot oatmeal, milk, bread, and margarine; and do battle with her lazy, gorgeous hulk of a Roop, whose cleverness is devoted to sidestepping worthwhile jobs because he wants to avoid being hated and envied for them. Sidestepping is a luxury she can't afford, because she's well and truly married: married to welfare. She says to him saltily, 'You know us ignorant black bitches . . . Grindin' out babies for the taxpayers to take care of.'

Claudine and Roop together run up against what amounts to the Catch-22½ of welfare, which has been Claudine's familiar all her solitary maternal life. 'If I marry this lady, I want to make it better for her,' yells Roop in the welfare office. 'But if I spend a dollar you gonna deduct it from *her*. If I buy a little something extra, you gonna deduct it. And I *better* report every penny I spend, because if I don't, I'm a crook. Now, you say if I lose my job I *must* apply for welfare, because I can't be sitting around eating the government's biscuits. That's *fraud*. If I do go on welfare, then there's another lazy-ass nigger living off the taxpayer. OK, fine. Now, let's say I do *not* marry this lady, just sleep with her. Then she's a whore. If I move in and don't tell you, then we're crooks. If I *do* tell you, then we're back to the income and the outcome and the deducting. You'd drive me to drink, then come screaming *fraud* if I spend seven dollars on a bottle of whisky! We can't win.' Claudine isn't even supposed to be working because if welfare knew, her stingy government handout would be cut. In a bar, days later and pretty sloshed, Roop says to the assembly, 'I'm gonna testify. . . . The Lord spoke to me . . . said, "Baby, cheer up. It could be worse." So I cheered up. And the Lord was right. It got worse.'

Claudine is a toughly funny film. In that, and in its sweetness of spirit, it summons up the character of Whoopi Goldberg's monologues. It is typical of the film and its script (by Tina and Lester Pine) that Roop's tirade on welfare should come off with colossal energy in a reigning mood of farce which treats disaster in the gang spirit of some huge family linking arms late at night on Coney Island.

★ ★ ★

Enough of your lip, we are told. But we can hardly afford not to have more. Political satire is the swiftest of comedy's kinds. Since the 1950s American and English tongues have been loosened. They have become as swift as Prague's or Poland's when circumstances of leadership sharpen alertness to stupidity.

The terrific Robin Williams, no backscratcher, says of his colleague, Richard Pryor, 'He performs open-soul surgery every time. Riffing with him is like playing with Bird.' The same Mr Williams, of *Good Morning, Vietnam*, says about the Bush–Quayle administration: 'I'm looking forward to Bush Cassidy and Sundance Kid. How many vice presidents does it take to screw in a light bulb?'

Spalding Gray is a mimic exemplar. In *Swimming to Cambodia*, on video cassette, he does a perfect English first-assistant-director's voice when he is directing the extras to enact further horrors before a flown-in lunch. Through a bull-horn: 'Will the artistes kindly . . . ?' The performance is a Swift reversal about Cambodia. Spalding Gray was cast by the film producer David Puttnam to play in *The Killing Fields*. Cast, or thrown, to Cambodia. His role was to play an officially-appointed aide to one of those acts of genocide that make the world safe for democracy. The film, a dusty answer to the actuality of the USA's war in Cambodia, was costly enough to make Spalding Gray pause about the loss of Cambodian life and effort in the war. In the end he hits, as Swift would have done, on the logical proposition. Make the expensive outraged film, and skip the outrageous happening.

It is as simple as eating Irish babies to solve the problem of the hungry Irish.

Perhaps partly to answer the bequest of suaveness that was left to the entertainment industry by Senator McCarthy, Mort Sahl arose. A hungry sceptic, with a sidelong passion for stationery, I found. Facially he has the twist of mouth called sardonic, but he is passionately earnest. His political monologues break up placid ground. The improvisation goes on a breakneck stammering loop and you think it will never make the circle. It always does. He freewheels a bike on a highwire tightrope with his brain racing and his hands off the handlebars. Incalculable, what his wit has done about the state in which we live. It is what we have created, he insists. A satirist urges our liability to act.

At all moments in a satirist's life he is going to need the muscle of knowing that to withhold a witty conjecture is dangerous to the species, however hard it may be to make it audible.

Lenny Bruce held that view and met that hardship. The cool iconoclast came to England to play the Establishment (a Wardour Street nightclub, started by Peter Cook and a fine *Private Eye* magazine editor). It took a while for London audiences to take in Lenny Bruce. He seemed to be climbing up the wall of the bared-brick club. He probably was. He was arguing with himself. Among his habitual points of purple discursiveness were the bomb, the profit motive, organized religion, racial imbalance. Playing all parts, he would sometimes use a routine in which a Madison Avenue publicist telephones the Pope to get him to wear 'the big ring' on the trip to America and promises him that 'Nobody knows you're a Jew'. This fragile man, whose eyes were both enliveningly witty and premonitorily dead, harangued audiences with the gift of his satiric wit far beyond the conceivable finish of energy. He was Jewish, and his sane short-circuits of wit were Jewish; his methods and sense of rhythm belonged to jazz. I think it was really the pumped-up profit motive that beat him, not drugs. I remember a night when he wickedly persuaded us to believe that he was unveiling a promotional plot to bump up cigarette sales by starting an opinion-makers' campaign asserting that cancer is a top status symbol: 'I was in the Bahamas last night. Practically *everybody* has cancer.'

Satire's convictions on the stand are more than any local Surgeon General's Alice-in-Wonderland cigarette warning now required to be run on the cigarette advertising that props the economy.

★ ★ ★

In England, subversive comedy has traditionally found its form in music hall. Its heirs are in *Not the Royal Wedding*, broadcast by the BBC from France – that off-shore country, if one thinks in terms of Agincourt – with a licence across the Channel to make commonsense mock of yet another Royal Wedding. And in Victoria Wood, who has everything owl-eyed to say about the English class system that its beneficiaries believe to be unalterable.

It is from music hall's roughing up of the English language that revolution is made. England is profoundly a place of words. For all Mrs Thatcher's reign – 'Attila the Hen', according to her Cabinet – England has a deep dedication to unsettling verbal jokes. Other countries may have a town devoted to gambling, like Las Vegas, or to diplomacy, like Canberra, or to the colonic tract, like Baden-Baden, but England has Blackpool, which has given up its maudlin Victorian heart to the form of the feeble pun.

The image of Blackpool to me is of a huge, glum toddler sitting in a collapsible plastic pushchair and blowing on a hot potato chip. In the meantime his parents, frozen out of inhospitable digs as soon as the HP sauce has been cleared away, will talk about the joke level of the season like fishermen assessing the sardine harvest.

The ocean around the island must be alive with gags. Every few miles along the coastline an old pier barnacled with *double-entendres* sticks into the sea, a long silvery arm of jokes encrusted with lights like the sequins of drag-queens in pantomimes, with bright little booths selling unimaginably censorable beach postcards and at the end of it a theatre that is a shrine of the most terrible jokes in the world ('Paris, city of madness, where only the river is Seine . . .').

I think perhaps you have to have been an English child to stomach it, reared on riddles in Christmas crackers and double-meanings at the pantomime. I don't know how else to explain the success of the *Carry On* pictures, which are made like old socks, or the Whitehall farces, which might be directed by traffic wardens, or the Palladium, where English people wait for the funny man as people in other countries wait for the nudes.

Music hall may be dead, but its gags are inextinguishable. They merely transmigrated into other forms: the *Carry On* pictures, for instance, and the radio show *Beyond Our Ken*. The temperament remains what it has been since Hogarth: ribald, brutal, incautious, domestic.

Harsh laughs still go in harness with Victorian sentimentality, 'Ramona' is still sung, and even the buoyant Ken Dodd will belie his nature and silence a house with the penny-in-the-slot melancholy of a number called 'Tears'. The fact that fewer couples have to live with their parents now has enfeebled the mother-in-law joke, but the telly-commercial joke that has replaced it perpetuates very much the same comic impulse, a mood of sat-on derisiveness about bossy home-makers covertly lusted after. 'What is a mum?' 'A mum is someone who has something hot waiting for her husband.' A mum is a nit, thinking that what he wants is a beef-cube, toiling over a hot fishfinger, without an idea of the double meaning in his head.

The butts of English jokes are male and historic: honeymoons, cuckolded mates, paternity suits, homosexuals, women most of all, who are funny because they are gullible, kind, long-suffering, childbearing, without insight into themselves, unable to tell Stork margarine from butter, intent on an irritable life-task of correcting the plumpness that men love them for, and never, never aware that their desirability is comic.

Comedians' acts and funny films are full of a tender hilarity about the way a girl in a job will brush away the fact of her sexiness, like a lecturer vaguely swatting a fly on his pate in mid-flow. They show us a secretary typing a balance-sheet behind a sweater that forbids our meditating anything else, or a nurse severely taking temperatures in the presence of thoughts that need a good slap. A girl in a music-hall act stands about on the edges of the joke much like the lady-helpers who move the tables for acrobats. She looks gracious about it, as though opening a fête, and quite unaware of her astounding unmissable ripeness.

Morecambe and Wise, the great music-hall partners, had a doctor-and-patient act involving a nurse. She has no idea how sexy she looks, but Eric Morecambe can think of nothing else. Experimentally, he calls her 'Sid'. She doesn't notice, of course. They never do. 'Poor thing,' as Frankie Howerd says behind his hand about Blanchie Moore, his ill-used and iron-clad accompanist.

I suppose that women are most of all funny because of the very thing that prevents them from being comedians – because of their vocational pretence that life works, when men can so clearly see that it doesn't, that it is an impossibly ropey engine with most of its crucial parts lying on the ground. It is only a very few geniuses, like Beatrice Lillie, who have had the detachment to seize on this feminine tendency to boil eggs for everyone in the middle of Armageddon and make it funny.

The most profoundly comic jokes I know about Englishwomen are embodied in Mrs Shufflewick, who is played by a man. It is the most delicate drag act in the whole ambiguous range of English humour. The character is dogged and unshockable. She generally makes her entrance wearing red gloves, a damson velvet coat, drop pearl earrings, and a dusty flower hat much like one of the pot-plants that are put carefully *behind* the net curtains for the sake of the neighbours. Her fur, as she says, you won't see the like of again. 'It is known in the trade', she remarks in a voice worn out with booze and the double-meanings seen by lecherous men, 'as untouched pussy.'

To Mrs Shufflewick lewdness isn't a pleasure, it is a condition of life, and she has no objection herself to meeting anyone's demands, except that barmen sometimes victimize her for it. She lives in Wimbledon – 'all cut glass and tennis balls' – and you feel that the people there probably patronize her. She drinks green chartreuse, and she was married once, lonely centuries ago, to a pheasant-plucker. There is something about her doctrine of getting on with it that distils half England.

This is the best of English joking. At its worst it can create a foul mob, boisterous and beef-witted, but the good comedians do something different. They don't make crowds, they divide them, asserting that not much of life can be shared and turning a joke into a sort of undercover contact, as though we were men in prison flashing mirrors at one another or tapping the pipes.

That was the great charm of Morecambe and Wise – it's not on to continue in the past tense, though one partner is dead – the implication that Eric Morecambe is so obviously unfitted to cope with life among the hordes of the adjusted. He is a mild, eager man who might just have emerged from some affable Tibetan monastery. Even his best friend, Ernie Wise, can't help him for more than a second at a time to concentrate on relevant things as a successful citizen must.

Ken Dodd, a brilliant misfit with forgetful Pre-Raphaelite hair and teeth like eaves, has rather the same habit of being ambushed by his own thoughts. Sometimes his speech-pattern can sound like a short-wave radio on three stations at once. He will say something about using a cat in a sack as a hot-water bottle, and then be distracted by the idea of getting granny's legs lagged for the winter.

People confuse him because they keep striking him as objects, just as his hand will suddenly take his eye as though it were a traffic sign. 'Grandad used to stand with his back to the fire,' he confides suddenly. 'We had to have him swept.' Girls alarm him rather. 'I woke up in the morning with misgivings' is a line that sometimes comes up in his act, and both the idea and the pun seem to startle him.

The traditional English way to activate a terrible pun on stage is to set it into a dialogue-rhythm like a tap-dance, with the joke exploding like a stamp of the foot. The metres of music hall have survived the buildings:

'If you succeed with Cynthia, you'll go back to your missus with a tidy sum.'

'With what?'

'A tidy sum.'

'I thought you said a tiny son.'

Vicars are good, and philistinism is a winner. 'The Laughing Cavalier' is endlessly profitable, like the 'Mona Lisa'. The holes-in-modern-art joke never seems to fail. Any modern painting will be a portrait with two noses. Artists stemming from music hall will always walk with the swift, knee-scraping gait that identifies homosexuals in music hall's heirs. 'Go on, Julian, show him your swatch.' English: any word can be forced into a temporary new meaning simply by its context, *viz.* the English joke in honour of an Irish priest who died of shock when two students said they had matriculated together after the girl had seen the boy's thesis. People enjoy supplying the points of jokes in the privacy of their own skulls. The English are indeed a very private race, a nation of do-it-yourself and pigeon-fanciers and collectors of things that nobody else wants.

Perfectly bright people in England adore dim puns, the more laboured the better, as in the question about 'What-is-the-inverted-proverb-about-a-lot-of-provincial-Frenchmen-caught-in-a-revolving-door?' which comes out dazzlingly as 'Having all your Basques in one exit.' Jokes like these are obviously arrived at backwards, with toil. On seaside pier shows a background of hard plotting in the bath is rather admired. No insistence that jokes should seem effortless. That goes back perhaps to training in riddles, which are the pure biceps of humour, all muscle and no laugh, mechanisms children respect for their complication and that they study in comics as seriously as stockbrokers study *The Financial Times*.

What other national sense of humour would put up with the phenomenon of those items on the pages of tabloids which exist entirely as excuses for joke headlines? 'The meal unfortunately ended in an exchange of blows' – Essex solicitor, for instance, is titled SLAP-UP DINNER. Are they *real* items? Next to the work-worn woman sub-editor who proof-reads knitting patterns by knitting them, whoever writes these paragraphs has the strangest job in Fleet Street. I imagine some solitary and impassioned man going over the news-tapes in a trance of punning, looking dreamily for joke-fodder like an elephant moving his trunk over a tray of buns.

★ ★ ★

Language. The reviving comedy of homo sapiens rests in love of language, and knowledge of its freight. Without that, the rest is indeed silence. In the English vocabulary we have an extraordinary possession, and in the present vandalism we forfeit ourselves. When one sees the American romantic comedies of the thirties in a run, it is their utterance and their estimate of the audience's intelligence of it that is constantly a wonder. The dialogue comes out like grapeshot, instead of at the speed of a railway announcement, and the laughs and plot-points go by in a flash; if you miss them, too bad. The heroines, too, are so different from the ones of the present that they are like another race; they have a character and a humour that make most Hollywood women now look like housewives in a television commercial.

What director today, apart from John Cleese, would think of the shot in *Love Me Tonight* when C. Aubrey Smith gets out of bed in his pyjamas and starts to spoof Chevalier by pretending to be singing 'Mimi'? Or of the more slyly directed moment in *Monte Carlo* when Jeanette MacDonald, who has just been buying a train ticket in fur coat and cami-knickers, leans graciously out of the carriage window and sings 'Beyond the Blue Horizon' to fields full of a chorus of toiling merry peasants? Apart from Billy Wilder's *Some Like it Hot*, which was one of the most magnificently witty films ever made, or Blake Edwards's *Victor/Victoria*, when did we last see a comedy from America or Britain that convinced us that the director had a laconic sense of the sophisticated without excluding anyone?

The thirties' films seem to be uniquely capable of sending up their period; but at the same time they are steeped in a sense of it that is instantly accurate and serious. In the dialogue there is a note of last-ditch self-reliance that keeps recurring and seems special to the time. 'I can take care of myself.' 'Nobody can push me around.' In the Depression people were on their own, and there wasn't much more damage the world could do.

The movies that Spencer Tracy and Katharine Hepburn made together: what a reviving part of comedy's past. The pace of action, the speed of backchat between obvious acting intimates, the stamina, the films' imparted feeling for private life, the braininess, the devotion and the rages, the SOS that women with jobs wear pretty hats for gentle reasons, not aggressive, the flashes of women's lib in the sibling feeling of the heroines for equally alert heroes; the gentleness between the sexes, threatened by belligerence, in the way these heroines are shown as intellectually stunning but emotionally sometimes at a loss and often near to weeping, people being fragile, men included: it all seems ripe for restoration. For restoration of everything that romantic comedy now fails to comprehend, and possible if the pulse of spontaneity can still be found under the tread of laugh tracks.

Tracy and Hepburn, Astaire and Rogers, Beery and Dressler, Myrna Loy and William Powell: the wonder of man–woman comic partnerships has been largely lost. Who is there now? The finely intelligent Betty Comden and Adolph Green, by a great piece of luck. Mastroianni and Loren could have been a wonderful double. There was a moment when it looked as though Albert Finney and Audrey Hepburn might become a pair, but they went their own ways.

Spencer Tracy is often talked about as a simple actor, without tricks or sophistication. It is true that he has the apparent solidity and directness of, say, Finney. He weights the screen as a fish weights a net. He has substance without bawling, like some great Russian. But the offhand tough-guy manner is a matter of true style; it brings up Belmondo's and Bogart's. Otherwise, it could never meet the brilliant oddness of Katharine Hepburn. She and Tracy together create a particular comic weather. It is without storms, sometimes self-mockingly despairing on her part, imbued with generosity, blue-skied. It has a special quality of sensuality without sexuality. Miss Hepburn's blend of resilience, frailty, and bravery is not definable as ordinarily feminine, but it is certainly not mannish. Like Tracy's performances, hers imply a moving suggestion that most people tell the truth, and in their own fashion.

Tracy's and Hepburn's best films together – perhaps *Woman of the Year*, *Pat and Mike*, and *Adam's Rib* – are wrapped in moods of excitement and amiability and some magical longevity. They are entirely unhectic. Miss Hepburn's bruised caw acquires beauty and nobility, like her skinny figure, which is in the shape of a dairymaid's yoke across the shoulders and has no obvious right to be as stirring as it is. There is a moment in *Adam's Rib* – in which she plays a lawyer married to Tracy, a lawyer opposing her in a case about Judy Holliday's being accused of a comically improbable and touching *crime passionnel* – when she bends down with the greatest intellectual dignity to look at her husband under the lawyers' table from the opposite end and shows him her petticoat. There is another moment when, with even greater dignity, she bends down for a second time, on the ruse of picking up her pencil, and catches his eye under the table to stick out her tongue at him. But 'You look kinda like Grandma Moses,' Tracy has said passionately earlier, at home, giving her a hat in which she looks ravishing.

The pallor and sunken cheeks and the consuming flame of gaiety are as typical as the inimitable voice. Katharine Hepburn conveys an extraordinary abundance of spirit. In *Adam's Rib* she lets Judy Holliday become a star, allowing her a seven-and-a-half-minute scene done in a single take when Miss Hepburn is supposed to be listening to her testimony in a women's detention room. The take is photographed entirely over her shoulder and on to Miss Holliday, who looks unhappy at being a bit plump. 'After you shot him, how did you feel then?' says Miss Hepburn, the vehement defending counsel. 'Hungry,' says Judy Holliday, miserably. This is the first film in which Judy Holliday's politely soaring acumen really made its comic point. She seems to have the IQ of someone beyond education but to be trying ambitiously to be ordinary. 'Thank you,' she says to Katharine Hepburn's secretary, who is taking down her words. 'Thank you,' says the secretary, fast, surprised. 'Thank you,' says Judy Holliday back, even more rapidly. Not many people could make three 'Thank you's sound witty.

Adam's Rib was written by Ruth Gordon and Garson Kanin (Mr and Mrs Kanin) and directed by George Cukor. The Hepburn character, chirruping away with boldness and buoyant farcical invention, is very reminiscent of Ruth Gordon. The character wonders, with swift sense, not pursued, why there can't be a radio arrangement so that all the good news is on one station and all the bad news on another. She scatters ideas like a bird showering drops in a birdbath. To make a point about the superior competence of women, she calls three women witnesses and gets one of them to recite her endless number of degrees, one of them to say that she has been a foreman for seventeen months without any complaints from the men working under her, and one – a vaudeville star – to do a spectacular flip-flop and then to lift Spencer Tracy bodily over her head in front of the judge. The point of female equality has thus been made, but male pride has also been much wounded. So Spencer Tracy leaves home in a huff, to come back to prove his own superman point by pretending to terrorize his lovelorn wife and the neighbour who is trying to woo her with booze. The Tracy character holds a pistol on them that turns out to be made of licorice. He first makes his wife eat her own words to the judge – a speech about double standards that won the case – and then eats the pistol, which is piling Pelion on Ossa in the familiar plaint about male infantilism, but still.

In *Pat and Mike*, also directed by George Cukor, Mike (Tracy) is a sports promoter who manages Pat (Hepburn), an amazing upper-crust athlete unbeatable at golf, tennis, shooting, archery, boxing, and judo until she ever happens to catch sight of her chatty boyfriend (William Ching), whose fidgety role reverses the convention of the doting wife without nerves or sensitivity. He is her jinx, and she perversely adores him. (A female counterpart of him in character talks bossily to Pat at one moment in a golf championship about tensing her gluteal muscles; Pat looks furious and fully equipped to throw her to the Antarctic.) 'What's your handicap?' somebody asks. 'My fellow,' she says honestly, unable to do a thing about it. She tightens up with muscles like bits of bone when the fellow comes on the telephone in the middle of Mike's massaging her. Pat and Mike eventually join up, as you expect them to because of the Irishness of their pair of names, and long for them to because of the community of their sense of humour. When they decide to get married, they merely shake hands. It is a signal of the complicity of comrades. The promoter–apprentice relationship has been equalized.

It was Ring Lardner, Jr, and Michael Kanin who wrote *Woman of the Year*, with George Stevens directing. Tracy plays a sports columnist and Hepburn a star newspaper opinion-monger. Hepburn speaks every known language with fluent geniality, trailing a rather miserable Tracy after her. He is dazzled by her wits but horrified by her eloquence, her male secretary, and her hysterical news ticker, which gives him the jumps. When they get married, she barely has time to put on a negligée before a famous Serbo-Croatian on the run from the Gestapo arrives at her flat with a train of Yugoslavs. The ticker belches again. Spencer Tracy, with the price tag still on the back of his dressing-gown, leaves the edgy study she has allocated to him as his room and goes into the nuptial suite, which is crowded with languages. He has the quiet acerbity to ring up his amicable neighbourhood bar and invite everyone around. A friendly down-and-out called Flo sizes up the situation and efficiently clears out both the Serbo-Croatians and the bar-room anecdotalists, who are all in full flood but ready to be sentimental about a wedding night. The film earlier has one of the very best Tracy–Hepburn love scenes, full of the sense of private shelter that they uniquely purvey. It recalls the wonderful way Hepburn acted in a stage production of Shaw's *The Millionairess*, that late polemic farce. Hepburn, in her born role of the boss, movingly had a child's look of misunderstanding, hard to comprehend, when she defended marriage for all its risks of damage.

The whisk of accomplishment that defines Hollywood's great comedies of the thirties and into the forties: the supreme Carole Lombard remains one beautifully intelligent sweet figurehead. Remember her in *Twentieth Century* being pricked with a hat pin on the bum to give the correct scream in a melodrama written by, and starring, John Barrymore as the most self-mocking forehead clutcher you could hope for. The Carole Lombard character as his ill-dealt leading lady is clearly capable of any scream she wants, correct or incorrect. She is any barnstormer's match, thinking more deftly. The actual Barrymore, not limited to barnstorming, had a prodigious sense of the absurd, often in lines that he seems to have written himself. He will describe Julius Caesar – in Garson Kanin's *The Great Man Votes* – as having been the first war correspondent, to put down a know-all child who is precociously versed in Shakespeare. In a dressing-gown, pretending to himself that his pauperism and his sense of having a precarious hold on life will go away if he treats them as non-existent, he will grandly ask an intruder 'why his stygian retreat has been invaded'. It is splendid to see an actor using the flag of language in the face of private difficulties. It is also moving to see the Barrymores – John, Lionel, Ethel – working together as they do in *Rasputin and the Empress*, cast by Irving Thalberg. A familial vocabulary reigns in the film. The vocabulary is constant, recognizably aristocratic in this most classless of professions, and funny against all odds. It seems a matter of courage confounding dunces that John Barrymore, whose life was hard and was managed with gallantry, should speak so many lines in so many vehicles for him which are equivalent in meaning to a line in *Rasputin and the Empress*, spoken with the dandyism he cared to affect: 'Punish my impertinence by death if you wish.'

A Pricking in Their Thumbs

The masters of the comic spirit are often our prophets. They can tell us when Shakespeare's 'Something wicked this way comes'.

Renoir's *Rules of the Game* is a work of alert satiric comedy. In the good nature it extends to society's falls and foibles it is to be put with *Così Fan Tutte* and *The Marriage of Figaro*. It satirizes present rules with Mozart's own mixture of biting good sense and blithe, transforming foresight. Like the operas, the film has a prodigality that is moving in itself. Fugitive moments of genius pass unstressed, because there is always infinitely more to draw upon, in the way of the Mozart melodies that disappear after one statement instead of spinning themselves out into the classic a–b–a aria form. The serene amplitude of Renoir's view floods the sophisticated plot and turns it into something else. He thought at the time – in 1939 – that he was simply making a film about a contemporary houseparty. Mozart probably had an equivalent feeling when he was setting da Ponte's librettos. The script of the film – by Renoir himself, with Carl Koch – was written with actual memories of eighteenth-century plays in mind, and it opens with a quotation from Beaumarchais.

Even for a masterpiece – masterpieces often have savage

voyages – the film has had a hard and strange history. It was made in the conditions following Munich. The opening, in Paris during the summer of 1939, was received with fury. Renoir saw one man in the audience start to burn a newspaper in the hope of setting fire to the cinema. Because of the presence in the cast of the Jewish actor Marcel Dalio and the Austrian refugee Nora Gregor, the film was attacked by both the anti-Semitic and the chauvinist press. Butcher cuts were made. In October of 1939 it was banned by the government as demoralizing. Both the Vichy and the German Occupation authorities upheld the ban throughout the war. Until 1956 it seemed that only the mutilated version of the film was extant. Then two young French cinema enthusiasts who had acquired the rights to the film found hundreds of boxes of untouched footage in a warehouse. After two years of editing, under Renoir's supervision, they were able to reconstruct his original film. When it was first shown again publicly, Renoir sat with tears running at the sight of it restored.

Through the intricate gavotte of the film wanders the solicitous figure of Octave, played by Renoir. As he goes through bright welcomes and glances and melancholy accommodations to loveless social rules, through a shooting party and amateur theatricals and good-night scenes in long corridors where nobly born men horse around with hunting horns while a lordlier-looking servant walks impassively past them. Octave is the eternal extra man, the buffoon who really has both more sense and more passion than the others of his class, the one who pines to look after the witless young heroine in memory of her father, who taught him music in Austria long ago. He would have liked to be a conductor. The man whom everyone idly holds dear for being the perfect guest suddenly speaks of himself with hatred for living the life of a sponger. How would he eat if it were not for his friends? The thing is to forget it and get drunk. Though then, after feeling better, he feels worse. But he will grow accustomed, as necessary. He used to dream of having something to offer. Of having contact with an audience. It would have been overwhelming.

There is a true Renoir counterpart in the character of the

poacher, honoured in the film-making. He is catapulted into a world of snobbery-by-proxy and of a chef's adopted airs about making potato salad with white wine. He had always dreamed of being a servant. Limited hopes, delusory debts. He had always liked the clothes.

Rules of the Game has itself the highest talent of comedy. It is delicately good to every character in it, even to the most spoiled or stilted. For the people who are driven to their limits, it has the special eye that Renoir always reserves for men nearly beyond what they can manage. During the last part of the picture, the camera moves about almost like another guest. It must be some quality of Renoir's that makes his camera lens seem always a witness and never a voyeur. The witness here communicates a powerful mixture of amusement and disquiet. *Rules of the Game* was made in 1939, after all. It is not only a wonderful piece of film-making, not only a great work of humanism and social comedy in a perfect rococo form, but also an act of historical testimony.

Renoir held in his hand the compass of disquiet. Since his death, I believe that Stanley Kubrick has been his nearest successor. Through their sage comedy, we are enabled to think of the impossible. Kubrick has been concerned in his mindful career with what mankind with all its knowledge and fragility is liable to do to itself. His *Dr Strangelove: Or How I Learned to Stop Worrying and Love the Bomb* uses an iced tone of comedy peculiarly his to let us know where we stand.

To laugh at annihilation: something that only a pondering satiric mind can properly take on. It can't be done, even in the wonderfully permissive form of the comic, by hurling gusts of bad weather.

Dr Strangelove is perhaps the most devastating piece about the bomb. It is frontal and relaxed in its funniness. Most anti-bomb films and plays are overrun by wet naïveté, a worse disability than usual when someone is letting off about nuclear politics. Anti-bomb plays seem to happen in a folksy vacuum, with dialogue about the good simplicities of life. Anti-bomb films tend to the same tone. They seem to be full of uncharacterized figures who stand for the New Generation, or the Emergent Nations, and the pity of it is that the children and Africans most often charged with this thankless job never, never say anything allowed to be more than symbolic.

This is to sketch in the level of thought that *Dr Strangelove* wonderfully surmounts. In the best sense, the film is sophisticated. It is a remarkable act of worldly satire: that is, satire deeply concerned about Earth. And it is specific. The film happens, not in a vacuum, but accurately in America: in a nuclear bomber, in an echoing model of the War Room at the Pentagon, and at a nuclear base camp where the hoardings say 'Peace is our Profession' and 'Keep off the Grass'. Whereas most left-wing art is concerned to emphasize that nothing is any particular nation's fault, so much so that it seems an act of suspect radicalism to give any characters a recognizable accent, all the people in this film are wickedly localized. The observation of different kinds of American male speech would satisfy Professor Higgins, and the photography seems to be almost deliberately like a reportage in *Life* or *Look*. Kubrick as a lad worked for *Look*. *Strangelove* must be the most anti-American comedy ever made, and only an American would have had the experience and guts to do it.

The premise of the plot is very simple. It is one that the professionals themselves are worried about: the danger that a single psychotic in the right place could start a nuclear war. General Ripper, played by Sterling Hayden, is a broody nutcase who has fluoridation of water on his brain. He sees fluoridation as one of your real hard-core Commie plots to sap the American people's body fluids. After years of fuming about the injustice of it he puts into operation Plan R, originally devised to appease a Senator who complained that the American deterrent lacked credibility.

In the interests of greater credibility – but greater risk of the deterrent going off – Plan R allows an underling to press the button, immediately seals him from contact with anyone who could stop him, protects him with a force of soldiers who proceed to defend him to the death against the intervention of the President, and prevents any of the aeroplanes from being recalled because only the ecstatic madman knows the code. The machine is in motion; no one can stop it, and the moment the first bomb falls annihilation of animal life on the planet will follow because no one, not even the Soviet Premier, can stop the Russian Doomsday machine from going off in response.

The key of the brilliant comic tone of the film is in the title. What makes the picture so funny, terrifying and horribly believable is that everyone in the film really *has* learned to stop worrying, as smokers do about lung cancer after living with the statistics for a bit. Disaster is half an hour away but nobody goes berserk with fear. The President – Peter Sellers, a calm Adlai Stevenson figure – talks to the Soviet Premier on the telephone in the voice of a Mike Nichols character trying to calm down a hysterical mother. George C. Scott, as a midriff-slapping general, first discovered in Bermuda shorts and Hawaiian shirt in a bedroom with his secretary, is so proud of his boys' initiative when he gets to the War Room that he can't quite bear to call them back.

And meanwhile the general who started the holocaust sits at the base camp quietly chatting with Peter Sellers, now an RAF officer, while the place is being besieged by his own countrymen. The general believes in an afterlife, which must be a help. What he is still most bothered about is this fluoridation, a deadly danger that he says he discovered during the act of love. 'I don't *avoid* women,' he says, suddenly worried about his virility image, which is quite something to want to preserve if you're about to go up in smoke, 'but I do deny them my essence.'

The film has a sort of running theme about this kind of priapic hauteur. At the end, with Peter Sellers in a third incarnation as a naturalized German nuclear scientist, everyone in the War Room is entranced by the scientist's suggestion that they will have to preserve the race by going down a mine shaft with ten fertile women to every man. No one quite believes in his own death. The rasping ram played by George C. Scott, swooping proudly about pretending to be an aeroplane while the President asks him questions, really does think he'll be back in bed with his secretary any minute. The Biggin Hill figure played by Peter Sellers runs up against a hard-core hetero colonel who won't let Sellers telephone the President because he thinks he's struck a mutiny of 'preverts';

but what Sellers threatens him with is a Court of Inquiry, not extinction.

Like N. F. Simpson in the theatre, Kubrick is working one of the best veins in comedy: the simple observation that our planet is inhabited by a race of eccentrics who, unlike all other animals, take practically no notice of anything that is going on outside their own heads and have absolutely no sense of priorities. *Strangelove* is a savage comic achievement.

The hot line between the President and the Soviet Premier when the world is blowing up:

> Now then Dmitri, you know how we've always talked about the possibility of something going wrong with the Bomb. The BOMB, Dmitri. The Hydrogen Bomb. Well, he went and did a silly thing. . . . Well, I'll tell you what he did . . . Well, how do you think I feel about it? All right then, who should we call? Where is that, Dmitri? . . . Soviet Air Command in Omsk. Listen, Dmitri, do you happen to have the number on you?

★ ★ ★

Roger Milner's first play, *How's the World Treating You?*, is an appallingly funny nightmare about beefy English sociabilities. In the first act, set in 1946, the location is a transit camp where a Guards colonel is bemused with marchings-past and the ethics of how to behave on dropping a baton. ('If you drop anything, you go with it,' Peter Bayliss snorts keenly, ordering tall men on to their faces on the mess carpet.) In 1956 the scene becomes a doleful deb's dance, and in 1966 a suicides' sanctuary that is run as a sideline by a gas-meter man. Where would we be in the nineties? This play would have known: on a disco planet of savagely baffled young people in all continents, 'wilding', bashing other races, raping, thieving.

Running through Roger Milner's play there is a unity of behaviour personified in three characters played by Peter Bayliss: the colonel, the deb's father and the suicide-worker. *How's the World Treating You?* is pinned together beneath the surface by a fierce dislike of this three-part man's false *bonhomie*, which to the modest hero is a killer. It is what drives him to suicide. This is an England where men assassinate each other not with stabs between the ribs but with slaps on the back.

The plaguily recurring character notices nothing. In the first act the colonel doesn't see that a wretched subaltern he is being breezy with has lost his trousers on a troop train. In the second act, metamorphosed into daddy at a coming-out, he thinks that the seven-month-bulge under his daughter's dejected expensive dress is a case of puppy fat. The ex-subaltern, who dearly hoped to be headmaster of Eton, is forced to marry the bulge and to start flogging not small boys but washing-machines, a substitute that causes him suicidal disappointment; but his breezy social worker in the third act doesn't observe any of it.

The married couples in this play talk to each other with hefty remoteness. The men make protestations of jollity with flowers in their buttonholes, but the thought of their wives openly fills them with melancholy. They dream of killing themselves, gossiping enviously about successful suicides, and they long to murder their wives. The wives know this but gamely try to forget it.

The women are not murderers or suicide cases or any other sort of retaliator; they are insistent, maddening, pitiful triers. To the end of time they will go on making sprightly conversation, putting out the dog and sitting helpfully on the lid of a berserk washing-machine that some man has broken his incomprehensible heart about. The play is hideously funny, but it often makes you feel that you are watching lives hard to bear.

The colonel's wife is a frozen woman masquerading as a nympho to reassure herself. Her name is Violet, and she assaults the officers' mess at sherry time. Obviously she fears that she is ugly, quite apart from the fact that her husband never stops saying so, and she shelters therefore behind Scotch terrier hair, pirouetting shyly in a deflated-looking evening dress that she wears back to front so that the satin pleats on the bosom of the thing show when she is dancing. In the third act she is the suicide-worker's wife, a chirpy but secretly panicky woman who calls herself Rover. On honeymoon at Eastbourne her husband tries to push her off Beachy Head, but she explains with a smile that she wouldn't let him; she says it in exactly the fond voice of a wife who wouldn't let her husband do something kind for her.

Verbally the humour consists mostly in placing side by side meaningless pleasantries and all too meaningful private thoughts. The unspeakable is spoken loud and bald. Holding the play together satirically: not only the comic energy of the performances, nor even the spluttering funniness of the lines, but the author's aghastness at his vision of a mild man trapped in an England that is one gigantic medical-student rag. Like Kubrick in *A Clockwork Orange*, he was saying much about what has happened by now through teenage riots, and not only in the Kubrick–Burgess England. It is on film news footage, in citizens' heads. West Berlin; Japan; China, the big cities of America; the Philippines; Moscow. Much for satire to reflect upon and hand on.

★ ★ ★

The pounce of Bertolt Brecht's wit is the response of keen thought to a German theatre full of bombast and wind, as well as a cool argument against a drama long dedicated to catharsis. I wonder if he wouldn't have risen to events even more cuttingly if he had been working in the context of the Anglo-American theatre today, which is now more than ever a shrine to the cult of the lovable personality, visited by a public yearning above all to identify with a real, wonderful, human person. For all his faith in popular music, I am quite sure he would have detested the Broadway musical in its present form, with its freneticism, its muscle-magazine biceps and its two surging stock themes, which are marriage and the splendidness of momma. The Brecht–Weill musical *Happy End* is Broadway's enemy in every way. Its villain is the system that keeps Broadway obesely alive, its method is a mockery of the conventional theatre-goer's demands, and its themes are cant and money.

Like *St Joan of the Stockyards*, for which it provided a

reservoir of material, it is set in Brecht's simplified imaginary America of thugs and killers and capitalist opportunism. He owned up only to the lyrics: the adaptation of the book was attributed to Elisabeth Hauptmann, though he almost certainly wrote a good deal of it himself, and the original was said to be by an entirely fictitious American writer called Dorothy Lane, rather as Brecht laid many of his anecdotes and apophthegms at the door of a non-existent man called Herr Keuner. It was a characteristic piece of reverse traffic in plagiarism, a right which he believed in as profoundly as he believed in the non-sanctity of property.

Happy End is a supreme political farce about people in two kinds of shaky employment, gangsterism and Salvationism, both trying to wrest themselves a meal a day out of a society ruled by a closed class of bankers. Neither the thieves nor the believers can do it. In the happy end, whose necessity to us in the audience is caustically insisted upon, they unite to form a bank themselves. Brecht believed that the purpose of satire is to teach us how to survive, just as he believed that a man's stature is shown by what he mourns: as tutors in survival both thugs and Salvationists are hopelessly ill-equipped, and as mourners they are muddled. The thugs have only their sten guns, and unsteady regrets for a concocted romantic past; the Salvationists cling to a faith that God, 'the great cracksman', will eventually crack the safes of the rich better than any thief.

The sacrosanct can be questioned. Religion in *Happy End* is seen as a weapon in the economic war. It is merely less efficient than a gangster's gun because it is unloaded. Its intentions are just as belligerent – the two texts in the mission hall read: 'The Lord is a Man of War' and 'I came not to send peace but a sword' – and its motives are just as literally hungry. Brecht's lyric for 'Song of the Brandy Merchant' is a description of an evil boozer at the gates of heaven which the Salvationists infuse with as much rapt imaginative feeling for the details of his sozzled face as the writer of the Song of Solomon for his mistress's marble thighs.

The singer's unintentional admissions are a comment on the narcotic effect of this sort of music. Brecht wrote once with loathing of the brain-washing effects of 'concert-hall music', presumably having had a bellyful of well-fed Berlin audiences swooning through Wagner and Strauss: 'We see entire rows of human beings transported into a peculiar doped state, wholly passive, seemingly in the grip of a severe poisoning attack . . . the worst gangster film treats its audiences more like thinking beings.'

One of the comic devices that Brecht fixes on in *Happy End* is to immerse the singers as soon as they open their mouths in a run-away emotionalism. Salvationist Lillian Holliday, 'the canary of the Lord', gets so carried away by the experience of singing 'The Sailor's Song' that she strips off her uniform and stands exposed in a long-legged swimsuit with SA embossed on the thighs. Woman tattooed by misguided hopes. A theme for satire's help here, as Whoopi Goldberg has gone on to give it.

* * *

The satirist who carries the debonair name of Whoopi Goldberg is, by profession, a superlative inventor. As an improvisational performer she stands alone. She is scabrous and fiercely allied with the out-of-step. Perhaps her deliberate elusiveness and self-effacement are there to leave room for the fictional characters she creates. It is pretty certain that she was born in New York City, in or around 1949, though the surname of her birth stays shrouded. The Christian name she openly made up. That led her to 'Whoopi Cushion', and then to 'Whoopi Cushon', which she says she fancied because it sounded French. In the light of her acting talent it seems apt that she be self-christened. Like Coriolanus, she has it in her nature to claim that she is 'the author of herself and knows no other kin'. She prefers to people a stage with figures who are Whoopi variations. Hence, presumably, Goldberg.

A set of her variations played as a one-woman show on Broadway in 1984. Not many in the profession believed that a single actress could hold a big theatre at Broadway's exorbitant ticket prices, but Whoopi did. Any one performer who can pack a stage can certainly pack a house. Mike Nichols thought so when he first saw her show, off-Broadway at the

Dance Theatre Workshop, in an evening that a lot of others thought suited only to cabaret. He brought it to the Lyceum and then supervised the show again in what has wound up as its sharpest form.

Her improvisational gift is swift and satiric. She insists that she is not a comedian, though she can be ruefully funny and sometimes sulphurous. 'I'm an actor. And I'm not a star, either. For me, stars don't work enough. I want things I can *do.*' Five monologues – written by her 'in my head' – summon up five quite different characters. As Fontaine, a drug addict of heavy social commitment, she comes downstage in a junkie jig and announces in a tone of duty to her fellow men that she is a thief. 'People always got things. People always want things. So I provide a service.' Fontaine is surprising. Mild-mannered rationalist that she is, she scotches the ways of the liberal toadies who busy themselves with line-toeing notions of reform. 'I got a PhD in English Literature at Columbia University. I don't want you people to think I'm just a junkie. I wasn't born a junkie, I got this PhD I can't do a shit with, so I stay high so I don't get mad. My forte happens to be American history.' (It surely is.) She takes a plane to Amsterdam, I should think to check out the Occupation, and goes to the Anne Frank Museum. That the family could not be found by their hunters amazes her. 'Now it just happens that when people are in hiding I always know where they are.' She is also amazed by 'the way they could stand that silence'. A glare. Then she swivels a silence on to the filmed audience, visibly making it discomfited.

The eager Californian valley-girl who follows Fontaine has a crowd of tight plaits that keep falling over her face, and a piercing nervous tic of 'okay' and 'know-what-I-mean'. 'Like, I feel *ecstatically* connected with the *ocean*' – she is a very lonely girl, this starveling of our padded world – 'well, *okay*, this man on the beach said Hi, I said Hi, he said Hi, I totally wasn't into this heavy conversation.' The only escape from the constraint of her vocabulary is to play dumb and play numb. 'So he said okay? so I said okay so everything okay, okay? And I get totally with child like Mary with Jesus except I know who the father is'; and the character turns out to have no one at all who will listen to her, including her mother. So she gives herself a home-made abortion with the help of a wire coat-hanger, and only then tells us that she will soon be all of fourteen.

The next variation is about a girl hitting seven: a black girl who wants to be white, 'with blonde hair cas-cas-cascading down my back, and blue eyes. The optometrists, they got blue eyes in they desk drawers.' A confidence: 'We live near a nuclear reactor. My granny says we gonna grow in the night.' An assertion, louder, after sitting in a bath of bleach, head pushing ever lower in resolve: 'I'm gonna be white, I *yam*.'

The lights dim, and when they come up again we are in the presence of another voice, grown-up, unmistakably Jamaican. 'Now I tell you, this man, he ask me, come to the United States of America. He all wrinkled, I say you look like de old *raisin*. He want me to clean and cook and have a little nooky. Now I don't know what he mean but I can clean, I can cook, I can improvise. So we fly to his place, the house was called Tara. Now these bathrooms was huge and I love a bathroom that is inside. In Jamaica they outside. A while later now de old raisin come upstairs and he was naked and wrinkled wrinkled *wrinkled*, all I want to do is iron him.'

The set ends up with a cripple who dreams of being 'normal'. A blink. 'I meet this man who want me to come dancing and I say no and he say why, is it me? and I say this is not a disco body. Then he ask me swimming. I say, me? when I get in the water I tend to sink. He say, you think I'd let you sink?' A shiver passes through the cripple's body and the knot untangles for a moment to let loose a dancer. Then the cripple takes over again. As 'normal'. The sketch could be mawkish, but the performer's matter-of-factness saves it. Whoopi Goldberg's mastery of spoken language is extraordinary, and best when it is amused, amazed, and sensible.

She has a lot of work under her belt, this woman with the reason of a child, who can create misfits caught always in all too grown-up predicaments. She started acting when she was eight, at the Helena Rubinstein Children's Theatre. She won't say that she studied with anybody, and I believe her. She learns by watching details of behaviour, by riding subways, by eavesdropping.

She says that she was a typical product of sixties Manhattan, 'somewhere on the borderline between the Lower East Side and the spiritual'. She quit the hippies and flower children because 'I had to figure out what to do with my life.' The characters she improvises are always figuring things out. She loves American gangster movies: the ones of the McCarthy era, when the voices of persecuted opinions found outlet in stories about unheeded people at the bottom of the heap. She got herself 'stuck into civil rights marches and radical politics'. In 1974, newly divorced, she flew to Los Angeles with her child on a ticket from a friend. It was a present of such excitement that she didn't notice it was one-way. *One-way only*: a theme. 'You forget you don't have the money to get back.'

Then San Diego, where she meant to be for a week and landed up spending six years, working with the San Diego Repertory Company and the Spontaneous Combustion group, an improvisational company. She played the lead in one of Brecht's greatest plays, *Mother Courage*: ' "The one with the cart", as a matinée lady said once as soon as the curtain went up, okay, okay?' She joined David Schein, a comedian. It was a time of political activity and they were in combat with the anti-abortionists. When reason failed, she presented them with wire coat-hangers as 'the alternative to legalized abortion'. In those days 'my livelihood was welfare', though there were other fugitive jobs: bricklayer, 'cosmetics person, make-up person in a mortuary. The corpses never complained about what they looked like.'

Whoopi Goldberg herself looks like anyone she is playing. Her face is as precise a mimic as her voice. When she senses from an audience a moment for rancour, her lower lip can come out like the beak of a duckbilled platypus. When she picks up another sort of rapport, born of her warmth, she becomes a great beauty. Her talent easily extends to acting a thing: a coat-hanger, for one. Whoopi's political thoughts obviously led to the monologue about the pregnant fourteen-year-old, which has maybe the most ferocious climax in her show. On behalf of all her characters, at the self-abortion coat-hanger moment Whoopi gives an audience a very powerful scowl from the lower depths.

Optics: Intent on the Marginal

Concentrators on the marginal. That is to say, marginal to everyone else. To the person concerned, this margin is the centre of the universe. For reasons clear only to the reasonable, such concentrators are called eccentric.

For instance, in what some zealots call real life, I know an eager person who devoted her not at all well-heeled life to the measuring of flintstones. Her uncle, poor but always sure that fortunes could be salvaged by his passion for inventions, spent nearly all he could make on the equipment to perfect hens' eggs that held nothing but the white. He knew there was a market for them because of the number of children who, like him, felt squeamish about yolks. He lost his savings but never his fortitude in pursuit of the yolkless ovoid, to him a shape more perfect than the free-hand circle that the boy Giotto is said to have dashed off when he was sitting on a mountainside minding some goats. Niece and uncle, these people were American. It seems to be only in England that such focused minds are called eccentric, and then generally by the non-English. I would agree that they are not your average man-in-the-street, but then no one is. People are different, thank goodness.

Such as these unharassed copers: a husband and wife in a London suburb who bought their first car on their small teaching salaries. There was no garage, and neither room nor money to build one; they didn't want to leave the car outside; they certainly weren't going to move, that most hateful of long-winded chores. So they knocked down the front wall of their little drawing-room cum dining-room to make it into a garage, put up weatherproof curtaining for the car's sake; and sat in the car in the evenings to mark pupils' papers, read, eat dinner on their knees. The black-and-white television was on the bonnet of the car. As the car was a four-seater, they could have a couple to dinner.

The car-owning husband and wife loved Truffaut's films. They had first seen *Jules et Jim* in a cinema; when they saw it on the box, both exclaimed about how perfectly composed the film must be, to reduce with such fitness to TV-screen size. (The husband apologized to me for a technical fault in the set. Quietly, his wife turned off the windscreen wipers.) *La Peau Douce*, *L'Enfant Sauvage*; they caught in all his films a quality of rapt purpose that Truffaut, possessing it, conveyed to his characters. In his *Such a Gorgeous Kid Like Me*, there is a figure they sprang to, without, I think, knowing that they were soul-mates. The figure is an exterminator, as intent on his profession as they were on the living-conditions for their car. The kin spirit is a charming and devout man with the soul of a troubador. His name is Arthur. Nice name for a white mouse. He is played by Charles Denner, whose upright, good, alertly stupid face looks very like an exterminator's when you come to think of it. He drives a large truck with sky-blue sides announcing his Christian name and profession. His chief weapon against the evils of the animal kingdom – the evils of man overwhelm him, and he has decided not to take them on – seems to be a rusting gadget that puffs out fatal gases and looks much like some treadle sewing machine invented by James Watt on his way to arriving at the steam engine.

The exterminator's quiet happiness about his name on the van summons up George Cukor's film for the wonderful Judy Holliday, *It Should Happen to You*, written by Garson Kanin. She is called Gladys Glover, and she wants the name to be everywhere. Judy Holliday's shyness and total femininity – though allied with abiding determination in pursuit of goals that are perfectly normal to her but decidedly offbeam to others – make her the opposite of the nobly sensible and equally witty Katharine Hepburn, who I have heard referred to as Charlemagne's aunt. We first meet Gladys Glover with her shoes off feeding the pigeons in Central Park. She's on the breadline herself, having had the sack as a corset-model for hip measurements an inch and a half off, but to a Judy Holliday character that constitutes no reason to impose food-rationing on pigeons. An advertising space that strikes her as being just the right size to fit her name is up for rent in Columbus Circle, and for $210 a month she gets it. Peter Lawford, as a nice but rich businessman, simply forgot to renew his lease, but no promised dates or offers of lesser sites are going to make her swerve. She doesn't want to be famous herself; she just wants her name to be famous. In that unforgettable soft voice, she talks her way into becoming the owner of a whole chain of hoarding-sites; they are lettered, with nice simplicity, 'Gladys Glover'. The sign-painters begin by making a mistake with the second initial and 'Gladys Clover' nearly rises to fame, but fate saves her: the sign-painters of a 1952 Manhattan, being relatively free of traffic din, are able to hear her make the correction from the street. Jack Lemmon, falling for her, says that a name should stand for something. She says, as wary of syntax as Marilyn saying 'About what we were speaking', 'I don't follow your point.' One could take this sweet-natured film to be a satire of the culture that allows someone to be famous for being famous, but one would be straining things to do it. Gladys Glover simply wants the best for her name, as if it were a luckless child of hers who deserved a break.

Fixity of mind and heart on a goal just slightly out of the line of vision called normal: however much most of us may try to stay in step, anyone's stride is liable to stray, so no wonder these unapologetic mavericks command our allegiance. Monsieur Robert Dhéry first raised our particular spirits to the sky with a revue in Paris called *Ah! Les Belles Bacchantes!* We were at once in a new realm of comedy, the realm of concealed catastrophe. The atmosphere onstage was curious.

Apprehensive, tight-lipped about disasters never voiced, immensely brave in crises beyond explanation. The compère, looking braced, announced the first scene. The creation of the universe was to be depicted. We felt sure he could bring it off. But after the announcement, he simply gazed at a place a few feet in front of him. The dismay that smote him was total and communicable. The ominous space was never explained, but whatever it was, it threw every singer and dancer into terrible disquiet. Nothing, it seemed, could be done. You felt that semaphoring for help to the wings would be to no avail. At last, the trouble was revealed. Gas was escaping from the footlights. But no use worrying about it at this point, for by now a lion was at large backstage and a dressing-room was on fire. An enjoyable film version of the revue, which escorts us backstage, has a persistent narrative thread about a plumber striding about the dressing-room corridors hell-bent on mending a tap. He pays no heed to the mêlée of naked showgirls whose lovely flesh bumps against his plumber's toolbag. Let the ordinary drool. His concentration is on finding the needed size of tap-washer.

M. Dhéry has a singular way of moving his lips away from his teeth as he speaks. He does it suspiciously, as though he were pulling the pin out of a hand-grenade. I noticed it especially in *La Plume de Ma Tante* – a revue imported by London and New York – when he looked balefully at an actor named Christian Duvaleix. He said, 'May I present my brother-in-law, Amsterdam?' The name and relationship don't crop up again. I have never heard an introduction more baleful. Mr Duvaleix, thus introduced to stage society, pays an inexplicable penalty for the début when his electric guitar blows up in his face, provoking no response. The Dhéry tribe does not express surprise. Not even Mme Colette Brosset, Dhéry's wife, when she appears as an understudy ballet-dancer trying to deal simultaneously with an unrehearsed *pas de deux* and an Eton-cropped ballerina making ill-timed love overtures. At the same time, as I remember it, a doleful character in a corner of the stage was interesting himself by munching dog biscuits. Dhéry's gallant platoon, one of a kind, profoundly believes that the dilemmas of other people's daily lives, however startling, should not be reduced to the commonplace status of being questioned.

Much comedy seems to depend on this restraint from questioning. It is a point very much grasped by Philippe de Broca. In *Infidelity*, his characters maintain an insulated self-amusement even *in extremis*, or bed. '*Qu'est-ce que tu bois?*' says a women to her lover, when he is scarcely inside the door; '*Tes lèvres*,' he says, bounding on her with a thrilling guttural. Most of the dialogue is beadily funny, and the scarcely-remarked enthusiasms that possess the characters are intriguingly odd: there is a passing sequence that establishes that Jean-Pierre Cassel is keen on country-dancing in clogs. Moments like this, and the scene in which Micheline Presle importantly mows a square yard of lawn while her miserable lover reads bad verse to her, remind one a little of *Mon Oncle*. The chief differences being that de Broca has none of Tati's lonely poetic eye, and that Monsieur Hulot, unlike the citizens of de Broca's world, is supremely awake.

Some of the laughs seem not so much evoked as extracted: the audience's guffaws over a bursting-collar gag at a swish party, for instance, sounded like the gasps of men in a half-nelson. 'The critic,' said Shaw with a glare, 'soon gets cured of the public's delusion that everything that makes it laugh amuses it.' But the film would justify itself if only by the moment when, standing in a frigid group of deceiving wife, discovered lover and treacherous friend, François Perier sweetly says into a silence choked with vitriol that an angel must be passing.

And de Broca's *Les Jeux de l'Amour*: one of the best gravely funny comedies from France. The two male principals are embalmed in obsession with trivia. The husband-figure (unmarried) is a sprightly faun absorbed in the painting of *trompe l'oeil* roses. The lover (unfulfilled) is a hopelessly square estate agent lost in bachelor housekeeping rituals. Their girl is an endearing calm pragmatist not particularly choosy about which of them is to father the baby she means to have, but intent on having it. The action occurs, or rather picks its way through, a cluttered Parisian antique shop owned by the heroine. I have never seen a film that makes funnier use of furniture; one gets to know the booby traps of witch balls and birdcages as though they were one's own, and there is a nice display of the tactics possible in a double bed that is accessible from only one side.

Jean-Pierre Cassel, who has a nose that one could paint miniatures with, gives a performance of idyllic egocentricity as the hero, prancing alone through the bracken at a picnic and exclaiming after a kiss, lost in self-admiration: 'Very few men would kneel in new trousers.' Geneviève Cluny can express sex in a huff as well as any actresses I have seen; she also gives an exhaustive demonstration of the racket that it is possible to make with cold cream and a Kleenex, and the advantage of possessing the reading-lamp during a row in bed.

Bea Lillie, that unparalleled concentrator on matters clear only to her, gives not a fig for furniture, nor for clothes either. In *Exit Smiling*, which was, so far as I can find out, her only film, she played a girl of all work in a theatrical touring company. Among other things she understudies the heroine, and one night she has to go on. Her key scene – to be played with a cad who has a riding whip – requires her to wear a slinky black evening dress. Getting into it is a nightmare. Any ordinary understudy would be in a state about remembering her lines, but Miss Lillie is no ordinary anything and her struggle is with the dress, which turns out to have the hanger still left inside it. Coolly, she plays the seduction scene with the sneering lout crouching over her. At any minute, his whip will be out. He gets nearer and nearer to her. She, lying on a sofa, declines to cower. The closer his embrace, the more bored she is. After a short time she looks at her watch. He doesn't see, because she does it behind his back, by lifting up one slender leg so the satin dress slips back; her wrist-watch, man-sized, is strapped to her ankle. Miss Lillie's battles among the minefields of women's clothes are famous; evening gloves that won't unbutton, long tight skirts that can be moved in only on roller-skates, ostrich-feather boas that make one feel the endangered species to be women; but this scene marks her triumph in the field.

★ ★ ★

Inspector Clouseau, the unemployable detective, seemed to me to have sprung from fiction until I saw an empty police car double-parked outside a supermarket with the emergency lights whizzing round while the driver and his alert companion were doing their Christmas food shopping. Clouseau would not have been as unprofessional. Even though his attention is often on the wrong thing, it is always on a possibly criminal thing.

In *Inspector Clouseau*, with Alan Arkin as the Inspector, Clouseau is called in to help England over a big robbery case. The Scotland Yard commissioner – Patrick Cargill – commandeers Clouseau under duress from the Prime Minister and clearly loathes doing it. A stuffy man with a knighthood, he obviously feels a great deal better without blasted foreigners round his neck. But Clouseau has a way with Albion. He can disentangle Cockney. A Cockney suspect asserts that he don't know nuffink. Monsieur Holmes says keenly, 'He who knows nothing knows something, eh?'

Clouseau's sublimely messy mind led, in Blake Edwards's hands (as writer and director), to a marvellous foul-up of the classic master–servant relationship of comedy. Even in the hands of the great Wodehouse, its comic basis was to have the victim played by the master and the overlord by the servant, who throws his boss into terror by any threat of quitting. You will remember the Damocles sword that dangled over Bertie Wooster every time Jeeves got wind that Bertie was thinking of wearing a clearly mistaken suit he had had the cheek to order himself. In *The Pink Panther*, of course, Clouseau's failure as a detective is more than made up for by his beastliness to Cato, the Chinese manservant whom he refers to as 'you little yellow devil'. Cato is certainly much better at his job than Clouseau, jumping out of the fridge to surprise the boss as though it were his spiritual home. Clouseau is more accident-prone than man should be expected to bear, for all his baseless confidence in his detecting capacities. As an eavesdropper, for instance, he eventually always finds that there is no one behind the door he is listening at so intently. Objects wait in ambush for him, and his dressing-gown cord goes into a Gordian knot just as he is climbing into the marriage bed. The unknotting immediately takes precedence over his bride. As Clouseau, Peter Sellers mastered the character's flawless sense of mis-timing. He speaks wrong English with unswerving happy emphasis. A man must be apprehended before he does more dommage. He, Clouseau, in order to do his detecting, must have a rheum in a hotel; rheum rhyming with bheumb, a bomb that he happens to be holding for some reason. His self-importance is unruffled and his acquaintance extends to 'the Pop', spoken of as if certainly ready to come to see him from the Vatican, and even the Almighty, who is in the palm of his hand: when a secretary says 'My God,' he instantly says, 'Mine too'. He needs Him. He is wonderfully unobservant of the immediate world and its mundane ordering of cause and effect: of the fact that a banged door will cause bruises, for instance. In an abstract thinker, the attribute might make him break new ground. As it is, Clouseau finds himself in unkind collision with the thingness of things. The sense of the concrete expected of a police inspector is of too mundane a sort for this lofty mooner. It is like asking Simone Weil to bottle gooseberries. His missing of the point is a demonstration of squint-eyed focus at its best. Even when he is simply strolling along a busy French street, with his accustomed look of off-centre purposefulness that always proves so taxing to the fortitude of others, he manages to poke his own baton into his eye before bowing politely to a bank robber. Comedy of displacement with a vengeance. I once saw an over-trained air hostess smile hospitably at an overhead call-light before turning with no expression at all to the passenger. Clouseau in flight-crew uniform.

The uncovetable hard-boiled egg of a diamond that is the prize of Blake Edwards's *The Return of the Pink Panther* has a flaw that conjures up the image of a pink panther when the jewel is held to the light. The French cop who is brought in to find the invaluable ovoid after it has been brilliantly thieved also has a flaw. It is the flaw of being completely unfitted to be a cop. Called Inspector Clouseau, as he was in *The Pink Panther* and

A Shot in the Dark (both 1964), he became rampant again in the subtle comic person of Peter Sellers in *The Return of the Pink Panther.* Sellers refined a beautiful and infant clarity about slapstick humour as he grew older. The detective superficially exudes all the apt professional virtues – grasp, alertness, authority – but the impression turns out to be delusory. Under Clouseau's stoic mask of lofty exemption from fluster, which is much like the expression worn in a honking traffic jam by the one driver who happens not to be in a hurry, his cast of thought is impractical, errant and bashful. He might well turn out to be much gifted in realms not yet dreamed of – composing for a massed band of nose flutes, discovering that cats live outside the space–time continuum – but his career as a cop does not expend his talents, whatever they are. And, whatever they are, they exact much fortitude from others.

Peter Sellers's performances as Clouseau were one of the most delicately cataclysmic studies in accident-proneness since the silents. The detective's politeness to society's sadists in his determination to cleave to being a proud victim is a key and ancestral paradox of comedy. He knows that he is a professional. Keenly alert on the job. Observers of his fixed vision take their pickings when his mind is hell-bent on the peripheral. They think him an ass. We know that he is not. Merely one-minded, and admirably not an oppor tunist. In the way of comedy, how our world of straying minds suffers from such single-mindedness. He is being efficient within such limits, and such a trial to people not one-track.

He tries to convince a begging street musician with a monkey, pronounced minkey, that begging is forbidden without a licence. Typically, edict degenerates into argument, and meanwhile the monkey amiably nibbles the baton. As the dispute goes on, the bank is smoothly robbed behind Clouseau's back. When Clouseau has to explain in higher places why he didn't twig what was going on, he does it in the huffy mood of a waitress saying she hasn't got two pairs of hands. He says he did not nu a bank was being rubed. It is this attitude that drives his superior officer mad. The boss, wittily played by a Herbert Lom newborn in comedy, goes downhill in a swift spiral. He begins suavely, sitting behind a very executive-looking desk. It holds not only a real gun but also an executive-looking joke present, from his wife: a gun-shaped cigarette lighter. We begin to sense that this chief inspector is an executive on the brink, an executive in desperate need of worry beads. The source of the need is the torment of employing Clouseau, a wreaker of havoc about whom the chief inspector says that Attila the Hun is a Red Cross volunteer by comparison. Clouseau's presence in the office gives the chief inspector a nervous tic, and goes on to cause a serious halving of the nose, the chief inspector shooting off the end with his own gun when he is meaning to light a sedating cigarette in aid of recovery from a visit by Clouseau. Before this, Clouseau has brought his enragingly calm powers of disapproval to bear on the deliberate efforts of the chief inspector to get the real gun to work on Clouseau himself. Surveying things with the particular sourness of the mechanically inept watching mechanical ineptitude in others, he is never in any doubt that the weapon is the cigarette lighter. The murder in the chief inspector's heart is quite hidden from his slumberous but testy underling. 'Probably out of fluid,' advises Clouseau expertly, driving the chief inspector beyond his limits. And 'You need a new flint.' Exit. Mania. Bang. Self-inflicted end of a perfectly good half-nose. The chief inspector's mind is eventually so disarrayed by dreams of killing Clouseau that he illustratively strangles a psychoanalyst who has been trying to get him to put his dreams into mere words.

The Pink Panther is very good slapstick; *The Return of the Pink Panther* is slapstick carried to the most shapely and reckless degree. Peter Sellers does some beautiful things in this matured portrait of Clouseau. The detective has become an exquisite study in disgruntlement. When he is summoned to the mythical Arab country of Lugash to inspect the site of the famous diamond's theft – an act we have seen being committed by a darkly disguised burglar equipped with an aerosol spray to detect protective radar equipment, wax to butter a floor so that the burglar can slide in the direction of the Pink Panther's plinth, a mechanism that looks like an astronaut's idea of a Plantagenet longbow, and a couple of pairs of extensible pincers that operate in the questing manner of lobster claws – the Sellers character looks at the scene of the crime in the spirit of some bored and quite unqualified dentist contemplating a foray into the molars. He trudges about in mild discontent, uttering something between a 'Hum' and a 'Tsk', emptying a flurry of what looks like talcum powder to detect fingerprints, and attempting aplomb to override the fact that the lens has fallen out of his Holmes-style magnifying glass. He decides instantly that the culprit is the mysterious Phantom, perhaps because the Phantom is the only criminal this ill-read amateur has heard of. Pouncing as if on an original thought, he arrives at the idea long held by everyone before him in the police force: that the Phantom is Sir Charles Litton, played by Christopher Plummer in this peculiarly well-characterized custard-pie larkiness. Clouseau announces triumphantly that the dastardly job is the work of Sir Sharles Phantom, the notorious Litton. The search for corroborative clues takes the inspector in directions too idiosyncratic for the plot to be troubled with. In this film, as in many of the best comedies, narrative and character live separate lives. The plot here proceeds on its own way while Clouseau proceeds on his. He asks, with a look of intense craftiness, if Sir Sharles has a swimming pull. The question has no bearing on anything, but never mind. Then he dresses up, variously. And then he plunges into another swimming pull twice, at the wheel of a van of one kind or another that has gone out of control because Clouseau has irritably removed any clutch, brake, or accelerator that has got in his way. This is his approach to all engineering questions. When a device offends him, he plucks it out. Disguised as a telephone engineer outside a grand villain Nice, he hygienically pulls out the innards of a severe case of stuck doorbell, and informs a jealous escort of the giggling Lady Litton, as he winds yards of wire around the doorbell plate, 'I have fixed your doorbell from ringing.' Disguised as a hotel cleaner in Lady Litton's hotel suite in Gstaad, he gets waylaid by his own interest in a faulty lamp, which he inspects by the method of putting his finger into the naked socket and getting a colossal electric shock.

For the benefit of children, to whom the picture is joy, some of the best moments include the sticking of a brocaded seat cover to Clouseau's trousers, a sauna-bath sequence that he plays disguised as a towel hook, the ingestion of a know-all parrot into the huge sucking fitment of a hotel-sized vacuum cleaner, and a magnified reaction by the same fitment to the bosom of a very large German-Swiss masseuse. For adults, there is funniness of the most copious and delicately built sort in the temperament of the hero of this screenplay by Frank Waldman and Blake Edwards. Clouseau belongs to the type of the obsessive *manqué*. His job is a detective's, but his real happiness lies in a secret life of speechless practical jokes that he shares with his Oriental manservant, a tongue-tied but spry fanatic of farce who will serve his own surprise Chinese fortune cookies in a Japanese restaurant. Sellers was in a fine period of taking his own low-key time, and he was working here at his best. He seemed to have perfected his gift for depicting minor bureaucratic disaffection in the souls of extraordinary and earnest men. This Clouseau – following from the earlier ones, and from the Indian in *The Party*, the Italian in *After the Fox* and the Los Angeles lawyer in *I Love You, Alice B. Toklas!* – was the funniest, most sober, and most tenderly observed man Sellers had created since his famous Bombay Indian on a gramophone record of long ago, who answered the condescension of a BBC interviewer about an Indian production of *My Fair Lady* with a puzzlement much more august. She asked questions about the cast. He took it, shy and hurt, that she was questioning his caste.

Blake Edwards's *Revenge of the Pink Panther* again had Peter Sellers as Inspector Clouseau. (On hearing his name, an eight-year-old advisor of mine said, 'I know who that man is: he's Robinson Crusoe.') And again there was Herbert Lom as Chief Inspector Dreyfus, the man who is periodically driven into mental institutions by Clouseau's imperviousness to his gaffes. Against such armoured ineptitude Dreyfus is quite defenceless. In this film he is left with a nervous tic: not, as before, in the face, but in the shoulder. Cato (Burt Kwouk), Clouseau's long-suffering Oriental servant, whom the master cheerfully insults, is also carried over from earlier Blake Edwards films that celebrated Clouseau's sublimely messy mind.

There is no plot. It is a string bag: a series of spaces strung together, like long silences between intimates as they talk. All the characters know each other very well, and we ourselves know them very well by now. The biggest space, ill-calculated in comedy, comes at the beginning, when we are left for too long a time simply waiting for Clouseau to appear. But if the picture has no ready story, it certainly has a theme: again, Clouseau's indestructibility. This is the man who has survived sixteen assassination attempts, and now he is the subject of a memorial service at which the Herbert Lom character is forced to read the eulogy. It was written by a sentimental woman who is seen crying in the church at her own words, and it makes the eulogist break up into tears of giggles. We don't often see a film or a play in which a character's laughing is funny – it is one of the famous dangers of comedy acting – but the Dreyfus–Clouseau predicament has been so skilfully built up by Blake Edwards that it works. 'Our loss is surely Heaven's gain,' says Dreyfus, struggling to get the words out, sobbing with laughter.

One of the best things confirmed by this film was Dyan Cannon's gift for comedy. She has an ideal comedienne's face, classically beautiful at the top and curiously pressed around the mouth and chin. She also has the true comic gift of seriousness in adversity, suggesting the dignity of the off-beam. There is a beautifully executed slapstick scene in which, with Peter Sellers, she finds herself dealing with a situation that provides three glasses for two people. The glasses are moved around between them like oranges in the hands of a juggler. Neither can work out the muddle. She ends up clinking a toast to herself, a glass in each hand. The character of Clouseau might well have crowded her to the sidelines, but no. For his part, he has limitless play with disguises adopted for no particular reason, including one of a Swedish fisherman who speaks a Swedish-sounding nonsense and who has a rubber parrot on his shoulder, and a figure modelled on Brando in *The Godfather* who coughs through the cotton wadding in his cheeks and who sports an enormously padded black pin-striped suit, correspondent shoes and a white tie. But Dyan Cannon survives it all with a comic reserve that is admirable and distinct. Clouseau tells her she looks 'ruvishing' tonight. She does indeed, with something absorbed about the set of her mouth which says 'comedy' as firmly as the precision of Buster Keaton's profile.

★ ★ ★

Brutality can be funny if it is directed at someone who we all really agree we must protect, such as children and animals. A covert swipe at a horrible child or someone else's lap-dog makes people laugh because we have often only just managed to stop ourselves doing the same thing. Harry Langdon, whose cheeks always seemed to be full of boiled sweets and whose eyes were made up like a girl who has been crying, has a very satisfying moment in *Smile, Please* in which a sadistic toddler gets unknowingly thwacked by his own besotted mother.

Disproportion is funny: making an effort that is out of scale with the task, such as a strong man losing his temper with a flea, or Einstein training all his intellect on boiling an egg. Or behaving stoically in a situation that would throw most people into a fit. Buster Keaton, the most fastidious comedian there has ever been, played a sequence in which he escapes from a horde of policemen and gets stuck on a paddlesteamer wheel that starts to turn. The thing is that, as he walks rapidly round the inside of the wheel, he looks more like a dapper clerk striding to the station, and what he seems mostly bothered about is his hat.

Blindness to commonly perceived restrictions is funny. Everyone else knows that a telephone receiver is firmly a telephone receiver; Chaplin thinks it is within an ace of being a trumpet. The alarm clock in *The Pawn Shop* strays off into being a failing heart, a yard of drapery ribbon and a can of niffy fish. No one has ever made puns with objects like Chaplin.

The great later Cockney, Tony Hancock, dubious above all, had a bit in common with Chaplin, but only a *bit*. None of your puns, mind you; clichés, that's another thing. Wish I'd said it myself. He did some of the greatest work in comedy about blot painting.

There exists for some comedians the self-set problem of crossing oceans. It exists even about the meaning of the word 'mid-Atlantic' – in English-English it means the middle of the Atlantic, and in America it means the states in the midsection of the Atlantic coast. English comedians, great ones, very great ones, including Tony Hancock, have sometimes destroyed themselves in the effort to be, in the English sense, mid-Atlantic. I can never forget an evening at The Top of the Town in London when Hancock had thrown away his beloved English scriptwriters, Ray Galton and Alan Simpson, because he felt they were preventing him from reaching Las Vegas. He was working on a sadly ill-founded wish. Shortly after, he died.

Don't let's forget his work with Galton and Simpson when he was truly planted. His character of the globally earnest blood donor, pining a bit to get back to his kipper. He whines for a biscuit after giving the first drop of blood to a prissy nurse. He has several hours of affront and then a fainting spell when he discovers the pinprick is only the beginning. She tells him that they need a proper pint of blood. Quite understandably, he complains that losing a pint would leave him with an empty arm. And where's the biscuit?

Like all great comedians, Hancock in his films has the bearing of a solitary. He is a marooned man to whom the rest of the world looks impossibly remote. His distinction is that this does not worry him in the least because, as he yells at the end of *The Rebel*, he regards the world as raving mad. An American in the same position tends to react nervily, remaining apprehensively watchful, like Keaton; a Frenchman will create an inverted dream-life instead, like Tati; but Hancock stares balefully at the distant majority and maintains an unbudging antagonism. Contrary to the legends about

English restraint, a strain of guileful rudeness is a feature of the nation's character, in fiction and in life. The painter whom Hancock creates in *The Rebel* is a brother-in-arms to Joyce Cary's Gulley Jimson. He also has a strange glint of Augustus John.

Without Hancock's presence, the story of *The Rebel* sounds misleadingly mawkish and worked out: a bowler-hatted clerk who is a secret artist suddenly throws away his ledgers and takes off for Paris, leading him into baffling comedy situations about Existentialism, action painting, tycoon art collectors and chi-chi art pundits. If Tony Hancock were a comedian of the little-man sort, sentimentality could hardly be avoided because one would feel that a shy genius was being trodden under. But his scriptwriters knew him inside out, and their judgement was perfectly right; one is in no doubt that he is an appalling painter, and applied to art his lugubrious terseness is marvellously funny.

'Your colour's in the wrong shape,' he says flatly to a fellow painter in Paris. After a brief glare at the canvas, a nude, he strides up to it and unsettles the artist by saying that he likes the sense of humour in the foot. Then suddenly, with curt authority, pointing to a shadow behind the left heel: '*There's* your picture.'

His attitude to his own work is also gustily insulating. Hacking away in his London digs at 'Aphrodite at the Water Hole', a concrete nude wickedly suggestive of an Epstein, he shouts excitedly, 'A little bit more off the old choppers, I fancy,' and knocks a haggish incisor down the throat.

When his landlady (Irene Handl) objects to his representing ducks as beetroot-coloured, he points out severely that she obviously can't ever have tried painting birds getting out of the water. 'They're off in a flash. You just have to thwack on whatever you have on your brush at the time.' This house decorator's view of art, which leads him to look at his canvases as beadily as he once regarded a bubble under the wallpaper during a paper-hanging session on TV, goes down in this film with great *éclat* in Paris, where his way of talking about his work as 'filling in a quick twelve-by-eight' is also much admired.

★ ★ ★

The vacuities of everyday chit-chat gone more than slightly off are the domain of the incomparable N. F. Simpson, an English playwright whose job at the time of his quiet eruption in the theatre was a schoolmaster. The *Observer* first leapt to his work, in a dramatists' competition in 1958; the English Stage Company mounted his works in London and the Jan Hus Theatre off-Broadway. We need revivals. His characters' anxieties are not the ordinary man's. Nor would Oedipus 'identify': nuts to the current idea that a public passionately needs to 'empathize', a word to be handled at a distance with a pair of red-hot tongs before we ceremonially burn it for good. N. F. Simpson's works for the stage include *The Resounding Tinkle*, *One-Way Pendulum*, *The Hole*, and *The Cresta Run*.

In case you are wondering about the titles: *The Resounding Tinkle* was thoughtfully (and by permission) taken by Mr Simpson from the end of a Christmas-holiday essay set to his pupils. One of them had been given a bike, and his essay ended with the remark that he went off on his first ride ringing the bell with a resounding tinkle. The title has nothing to do with the play's content. In Mr Simpson's world that would demean titling to labelling. Some unwise pedant on the BBC asked him why he had called the second of his surrealist works *One-Way Pendulum*. 'Because that's its name.'

The questions that bother Simpson's characters are taken, by them and us, gravely. In *One-Way Pendulum*, the daughter of the deeply ordinary suburban family whose off-centre concerns form the play (which is not to say that they give it *shape*) stands stalemated in front of a mirror. The mother, Mrs Groomkirby, who goes about the place with the weaponry of housework and sees everything as a dust collector, asks testily about the hold-up. Her child says: 'I can't go out with my arms this length.' One immediately sees the arbitrariness. An arm is a limb of flagrantly undecided length. It reaches neither the hip nor the knee. Mrs Groomkirby shrugs off the dilemma and goes on with her feather-duster. She is cleaning up after her husband's regular bout of work, with the help of a Do-It-Yourself kit, on building a replica of the Old Bailey in the parlour. The son of the house can be heard off-stage teaching Speak-Your-Weight machines to sing the Hallelujah Chorus. Every now and then, in what, for want of a better word, one could call the action of the play, 'Ten stone, eleven pounds' flouts an apprentice machine by the second or third Hallelujah, but the son plugs on. The ways of the law, when the Old Bailey is complete, take off into surrealism no more ridiculous than many an actual Old Bailey case. Mr Groomkirby is up for suspected homicide and needs an alibi for the date. September 22nd, say. The prosecuting counsel, a sheep-wigged man whose languorous cross-questioning is done with one foot in élitist position on the seat beside him, asks whether Groomkirby was in Reykjavik that day. No, sir. Were you in Rio that day? No, sir. In Toronto? No, sir. In Torquay? No, sir. And you ask the court to believe that by this amazing coincidence you were not in any of these places, all on the same day?

The Resounding Tinkle starts just after the delivery of an elephant to the lawn of the suburban house of Middie and Bro Paradock. The elephant has come in a size larger than ordered. Size is the only problem they see in the animal. He is swapped for a neighbour's snake, but that turns out to be too small. People drop in. Uncle Ted comes, turning out to be a woman, and is offered a read in the form of a slice of books, which he enjoys, though not too large a slice, thank you. A woman comes in to do not the washing-up but the eating-up. A man knocks at the door and asks Bro Paradock to form a government.

The Hole has appeal to everyone who has ever watched people looking at a hole in the ground. Four men gathered around a manhole, spend an interesting time between furious pauses arguing about what they see at the bottom. A tramp, who describes himself as the nucleus of a queue, is joined by a red-neck authoritarian, a plain gazer, and a student philosopher. The hole contains, they decide, card-players, card-billiard players, golfers, tropical fish, and a prisoner. The prisoner having been done in by a bomb, the four decide that the manhole simply contains an electrical junction-box, whose cables may be either leaving or entering. Simpson is not at all unreal in his surrealism. I remember that, when President Nixon visited China, the TV correspondent covering long gaps of hand-shaking and Chinese-language welcomes had a chat about the road that the motorcade was to take. It was called, said the networks, The Road To the Airport. Translators intervened in Chinese. Eventually it was announced, in English, that the name was The Road To and From the Airport.

One-Way Pendulum has a ratty discussion about a skull on the mantelpiece. To the housewife who would obviously sooner have a nice clock there, thank you very much, her daughter says shortly that it is a *memento mori*: 'It's supposed to remind you of death.' The woman looks at it witheringly. 'And does it?' she says. There is a doughty grip of sense about Simpson that defines the surreal. In *The Cresta Run*, spying turns up in a suburban front room and the housewife here hasn't any time for that either. To her it is self-evident that espionage hasn't any practical use. She sees it as another of these symbol what-nots, supposed in this case to remind you of your country, and what exasperates her is that it doesn't work. Symbols are supposed to work. To remind you of something. Any symbol on the mantelpiece or wherever else that doesn't do its job is yet another chore for the feather duster. The thing is a dud.

When her husband gets roped into helping out MI5, the job obviously makes him think only of his lifelong rule about 'not asking for it', and of how tricky it is to carry on not asking for it if you are a spy. As far as his wife is concerned, knitting in a braced sort of way and foreseeing the mess that espionage is going to make in the house, it makes her think only of men's childishness about games. Women in N. F. Simpson's plays always treat men as pitifully hobby-prone, happy to amuse themselves with the Old Bailey or to make fool lists of Cabinets while housewives work. Leonard in *The Cresta Run* may think he is going off to play out a grim drama, setting off for the West End in his spy get-up one evening, but Lillian looks at him thinly: 'They don't play it out any night of the year, you know.' The author's instinct for the complacencies of language is blisteringly funny: 'a global holocaust of the first water,' says a big shot at the Ministry importantly.

The play advances two pieces of impossible sense about

spying that are much funnier than its details about caviare-plots and bottomless string bags. One of them is that, if one function of spying is to cultivate patriotism, then it is madness not to advertise it as much as possible, which is what a part of the spy's unconscious perilously longs to do anyway. ('I don't suppose you've even put a cross against no publicity,' says Lillian sarcastically while her husband is filling in his spy entry form.)

The other observation is that anyone in MI5 must have trouble keeping up the necessary level of nationalism. A sense of patriotism in this play is an unnatural state that has to be chemically induced. The Ministry big shot suffers from a multiple-allegiance syndrome, and he is said to need naturalizing every three years, with a booster whenever reminded, as though flag-wagging were a sort of cowpox serum needed to keep a man topped up with the right chauvinistic antibodies. Like Bergson, a thinker who developed a mechanistic theory of laughter, Simpson is engrossed by the funniness of a human being who treats his thoughts and feelings as though they were subject to physical laws.

Simpson is unclassifiable, but it may be permissible to say that he is related to the Goons, especially to the Goonery of the great BBC radio show that went on between Peter Sellers and the inspired Irish clown Spike Milligan. Spike Milligan is illogic's poet.

Spike Milligan was in bed, in a version of Goncharov's *Oblomov* on stage in London in 1965. There was a great deal of brilliant improvising. The rest of the cast looked at the bed and found it bedlam. The producers bravely took him to be in his right mind and also in Goncharov's. They closed, and started again. When the curtain went up on *Son of Oblomov* there were mutinous mutterings from under the great fur rug. 'Same old bed,' said Spike Milligan faintly. Not quite. In his transfiguring wreck of the original the bed had moved over a bit to the prompt side in the first scene. 'Same old audience,' the grumbler under the bedclothes went on, bracing himself to be an actor and start the play.

Son of Oblomov took a rebellious technical decision. It acknowledges freely that an audience is present, lodged in a different time-scale to the play and with a limitless capacity for boredom smouldering below its hungry belt; it also states that the actor is not the character but a paid workman trying to look natural under a load of someone else's lines. By this dazzling flash of the obvious, the evening becomes helplessly funny and a liberating theatrical experience.

The candour is all Milligan's. It is the nature of the comedian to acknowledge the obvious. He does it because he isn't capable of anything else, and the only malady for the parent of this *Oblomov I* was that he had to try hard to be capable of avoiding the obvious, lying down obediently in the satin-lined casket of Riccardo Arragno's adaptation and trying to pretend it was natural to be embalmed.

In *Son of Oblomov* they let him rip. The 'Son' springs not really from Goncharov's near-masterpiece of a novel, and certainly not from the Arragno adaptation, but from Spike Milligan's perpetual awareness that here are the three of us in our three corners, the actor, the play and the audience. He points out implicitly that we have three quite separate kinds of existence: a man at work, much more observant of play and audience than anyone thinks; a work of art; and a body of wary ostriches who believe themselves to be invisible. It is out of this battling triangle that theatre emerges, and the important thing about *Son of Oblomov* was that it goosed all three into a much more dynamic life, including the ostriches.

In a commercial theatre now this is something of a revolution, in spite of Brecht influences outside it. The usual pretence is still that the audience doesn't exist and that the actor and his role are one, making total identification the most generally admired kind of acting (this is what Ionesco said exasperated him about the theatre: he found the sight of an actor weeping real tears unbearable). The pretence has nothing to do with the theatre's useful apparatus of illusions: it has more to do with prudery, and we passionately need to be rid of it.

Thanks to Spike Milligan's archivist tendency – liking for pieces of paper – he has kept a letter from the Lord Chamberlain, then England's theatre censor, a position at last abolished after more than three centuries. I quote:

This Licence is issued on the understanding that the following alterations are made to the script:

Act I
Page 1: Omit the name of the Prime Minister: no representation of his voice is allowed.
Page 16: Omit '. . . clockwork Virgin Mary made in Hong Kong, whistles the Twist.' Omit references to the Royal Family, the Queen's Christmas Message, and the Duke's Shooting. . . .
Page 21: The detergent song. Omit 'You get all the dirt off the tail of your shirt.' Substitute 'You get all the dirt off the front of your shirt.'

Act II
Page 8: The mock priest must not wear a crucifix on his snorkel. It must be immediately made clear that the book the priest handles is not the Bible.
Page 10: Omit from 'We've just consummated our marriage' to and inclusive of 'a steaming hot summer's night.'
Page 13: Omit from 'In return they are willing . . .' to and inclusive of 'the Duke of Edinburgh is a wow with Greek dishes.' Substitute 'Hark ye! Hark ye! The Day of Judgment is at hand.'

Act III
Page 12–13: Omit the song 'plastic Mac Man' and substitute 'Oh you dirty young devil, how dare you presume to wet the bed when the po's in the room. I'll wallop your bum with a dirty great broom when I get up in the morning.'
Page 14: Omit 'the perversion of rubber'. Substitute 'the kreurpels and blinges of the rubber'. Omit the chamber-pot under the bed.

As we all know, reality daily outdoes art in surreality. There is a sort of genius at work in the letter, typed by one of the Lord Chamberlain's many lady-like secretaries, who I have often seen at work. By what sublime *non sequitur* process did the monarchical representatives bowdlerizing away in the Offices of Grace and Favour hit on the alternative 'Hark ye'? Who thought of the alternatives to 'perversions' for page 14? I remember once showing the letter to N. F. Simpson in hope of cheering him up about the critics who complained that his plays had no shape, no organized structure. He read the letter, looked better, returned to the critics' complaints about him. 'Of course, they are perfectly right. And I could give the' – small wave of the hand – 'things dramatic shape, I think. But it would be breaking faith with chaos.'

We have drifted much further than we think from the mainstream of the theatre, Greek and Shakespearean and Restoration, in which it was natural for actors to detach themselves from their roles and recognize the audience. Watching most plays now is like watching the telly. It happens behind glass. Have a choc, they can't hear. Try a toffee crunch. Such thoughtful demolitionists as Simpson and Milligan and Hancock break the glass.

* * *

There is a great resource of comedy too, in breaking faith with the established. Mangling the classics, for instance: not always such fine things when you come to re-read them after infancy.

Perhaps Dumas's *The Three Musketeers* exists partly to satisfy adapters who have a sense of didactic horseplay. Years ago, Roger Planchon put an outrageously funny stage production of it into his repertory at Lyons.

And a 1974 film version of the book, shot by Richard Lester from a script by George MacDonald Fraser, cheerfully messed up Dumas in a mixture of BBC period-film language and English-radio *Goon Show* idioms from the Spike Milligan–Peter Sellers days. It has a magnificently mixed cast of the famous. The fighting men exist in obvious danger from duelling bravely undertaken in the midst of hanging laundry, and all the actors have roles that must sometimes have burst up in their faces like jack-in-the-boxes. The three musketeers, varyingly inefficient at their career but nonchalant about the differences, are played by Oliver Reed, Richard Chamberlain and Frank Finlay. They are joined by Michael York as

D'Artagnan, who offers his mother's special ointment for sword wounds to friend and foe alike, and strides about hopefully in unstated need of a hairbrush and something to clothe himself in apart from tattered brown leather. You imagine his mother as having often said desperately, like a troubled nanny, 'There's no warmth in leather,' and worrying perhaps about his underclothes in case he is knocked down, which is an accident that he invites when any dog, horse, swordsman or royal long skirt crosses his path. Charlton Heston plays Cardinal Richelieu, in a purple cap that he somehow manages to make look as secular as Beatrice Lillie's red fez. Geraldine Chaplin is Anne of Austria. Jean-Pierre Cassel, of the quill-shaped nose, is Louis XIII. Roy Kinnear plays a tub-shaped, wobbling Planchet. Spike Milligan is M. Bonancieux, in stocking cap and nightshirt, trying to be sensible in crisis. ('I don't wish to be sent to the Bastille,' he says, 'because it's got very deep dungeons and terrible instruments of torture operated by very unsympathetic men and they snip very important parts off people.') He is married to Raquel Welch, and is obviously amazed by his good fortune in having her to peer at over the sheets. Faye Dunaway is Milady, a classy girl who exercises the full treachery and determination of a bigoted right-wing cabinet minister.

The deadpan, swerving script may reflect the comic guile of the novel in the parts that one generally skips, but it probably owes its larky blitheness more to the original talents of Lester and his cast. The film is faithfully full of the seething mud of the seventeenth century. Great beauties point out that they sorely need baths; sweetmeats are served on trays borne on the heads of midgets; fencing wounds give pain; overdressed fights are conducted in an earnest mood that somersaults quickly into slapstick and then kills. D'Artagnan is acrobatically lethal, even though he is equipped with a sword cut off practically to the handle, like a butter knife, and even though he is filled with the spirit of an eager schoolboy mixing among blasé tourists; Cardinal Richelieu appears to be dragging himself from one sightseeing haunt to another on feet that hurt. David Watkin, a brilliant photographer, takes what is becoming the accustomed aesthetic way of getting round the now accepted convention of photographing in colour (required for TV sales) by using a stylization of near monochrome. If the film sometimes moves by fits and starts, so that it has to keep beginning from square one with each sequence, this may be partly because there are so many equal heroes and heroines, partly because the overwhelmed narrative is allowed no high points, and partly because the invention now and then seems drummed up. But the pratfalls, and the rude turnings taken by antique speech, are very funny. They are readymade for the beady attentiveness of wits and children.

Lester also made a sufficiently splendid mess of a fairly stupid classic in *Robin and Marian*. Robin Hood is getting on. His hair is thinning. Richard the Lion Heart, always a dicey chap, has gone bonkers. Maid Marian, deserted by Robin when he scarpered to the Holy Land with Richard, has failed in suicide and turned to God for the success due to the fulfilled woman. He took her on as Mother Jennet, an abbess. Not everyone knows, though God will, that jennet is allied to a dreadful milk pudding of England's heritage called junket.

Out on a Limb

From Aristophanes' time, political satire has been based in showing by paradox some curbing of liberty, a paradox so exaggerated that it is beyond censors. It is in the nature of great satire to be so simple that no reining-back by officialdom can bridle it. By 'censor', understand nothing merely to do with the Lord Chamberlain, or the mufflers of dictatorships. Censorship is the grip of conservatism. In the capitalist 'Free West', it is the censorship of profit. When censors were clamped by ancient circumstance, think of the objectors to the *Lysistrata*.

When members of the Russian upper class travelled in Europe in the nineteenth century, they were often scandalized by the lack of corruption. In 1897 a nobleman who had had to wait his turn at a German post office, instead of paying the usual Russian bribe to be served first, wrote a letter home saying loftily that the country would never progress until it learnt graft. This is very much the background of Gogol's *The Government Inspector*.

The one-eyed town that the play depicts is deeply impressed by corruption as a political system. The mayor, judge and civil officers sixth-class practise it rather humbly, as though only the *ton* of St Petersburg really know how to do it. The muffin-faced officials seem to think of graft as an accomplishment that properly belongs to the classy, something they are liable to drop clangers about. Their efforts at slipping silence-money to the ravenous young clerk whom they take to be a high-bred Tsarist Inspector are made in a mood of thrilled servility.

Imagine the town of the play to be rather like Gogol's own birthplace, near Poltava in the Ukraine. It is a community that has never before entered anyone's calculations, being a good three years' gallop from any frontier. The Mayor's room is a cluttered one, and is probably loaded with bugs. The contents include an upright piano, a stray stirrup, a vase of sunflowers and a string of onions.

In Peter Hall's production, the floor was raked, and when Paul Scofield as the imagined official, Khlestakov, was most enthralling to the citizens they came downstage and closed up into a tiny space like a crowd against the rails at the Derby. Scofield wore a willow-green suit and a blond wig with a beautiful kisscurl. The inn where he was first seen, trying to get some food out of the landlord without having to flog his ravishing trousers to pay for it, is a stinking hole that made his vowels skid about in agonies of genteelism. When he said 'Niaouw', the negative got as many diphthongs as Eliza Doolittle's. The influences on the accent seemed to include Birmingham, a lot of sermons, and the girls who record nonsensical goodwill on the telephone.

In Khlestakov's room, where he grandly says that the bedbugs bite like wolfhounds, the hungry dandy bolts unspeakable food and complains about it as if he weren't getting a mouthful. As soon as he cottons on to the role that the town has invented for him, his gift for patronizing finds a task. 'I suppose you've always lived round heah?' he says royally to a myopic postmaster who has obviously never set a galosh anywhere else in his life. Transplanted to the Mayor's house, the hero gets slowly and radiantly drunk. 'Shall I compare thee . . . ti tum ti tum . . . One of my sonnets.' He also claims *Romeo and Juliet*, *Don Juan* and *The Marriage of Figaro*. The town swoons.

Khlestakov tells them about a bridge four in St Petersburg: 'The English Ambassador, the Foreign Minister, the French Ambassador, the German Ambassador and . . . me.' After miscalculations like this Scofield tended to leave his mouth ajar for a while. He gave the man a genius for making movements that furniture prevents him from finishing. Patience Collier as the Mayor's wife, wearing blue eye-shadow and a hair-do like a peroxided geisha girl, finds the imposter quite flawless. After he has made a spinning sloshed exit, yelling 'Salted cod!' in the cracked voice of Lear, she says after a polite pause: 'Wha' a fescineh'ing man.'

The characters are dressed and played rather as though they were heavy animals dolled up for a dinner dance. In a state of later religious mania Gogol interpreted his work as a Christian fable, with the town representing the state of men's souls and the final announcement of a real inspector a Day of Judgment, which is only a step beyond the official dismissal of his work as a comedy of humours.

The Slav way of questioning the status quo bravely remains in Czechoslovakia. Kafka's figure of the baffled solitary man is upheld and continued.

He is the hero of *Joseph Kilian*, who hires a cat from a pet shop and, having fulfilled this private and socially useless desire, finds that the shop has mysteriously vanished. And more obviously even than that, he is Joseph K. in Ivan Klima's play *The Castle*, which deals with a youthful idealist thrust into a State-run home for corrupt and privileged intellectuals where his presence so disquiets the inmates that they murder him.

The scalding, questioning play in Prague in 1965 was Vaclav Havel's *The Garden Party*. Absurdist in form but sharply political in content. One of the characters becomes head of the Liquidation Department in order to inaugurate the liquidation of the Inauguration Department. Another is a breezy de-Stalinized bureaucrat who proves by his pronouncements ('I'm glad to see you have contrary opinions: everyone should have from one to three contrary opinions') that a thaw can be regulated just as firmly as a freeze. A third converses in mock-Khrushchev proverbs: 'He who argues with a mosquito net will never dance with a goat near Podmokly.'

If the object of satire is what convention accepts but the mind must be rid of, Czech film-makers find it. The knife meets the bone. A group of serious and gifted Czech people are expressing themselves through film as naturally as, say, the writers of the Spanish Civil War did through poetry. The phenomenon is moving and significant. It possesses as much energy as the Polish cinema's after the great political loosening of 1956, and perhaps it will be fortunate enough to have more staying power. In some of the films, there is a technical vivacity equal to that of the French New Wave, though their content strikes me as a great deal more organic to the state of their country. The intimacy of purpose among the members of the group seems as powerful as Bloomsbury's was, but there is nothing cliquish about it. And there is an air of having scarcely begun.

This isn't the familiar Western use of movies to manufacture other people's fantasies, or the equally familiar bureaucratic use of them to beat audiences over the head with object lessons, but an attempt to shoot into the film-maker's own dark places of poetry and violence and nostalgia for play. Czech directors and screenwriters are trying to find expression for the rock-bottom instincts that are often censored by the self long before a bureaucrat gets near them.

In 1956 the movement hadn't even started to gather. Cinema people spoke affectionately of their best known director, Jiři Weiss, and the famous puppet films of Trnka, and then turned to the satiric theatre and the acts in pocket night clubs, as though forms for minority audiences were the only ones that offered any hope of carrying a man's real voice. The assumption then about film-making in Czechoslovakia matched our own commercial industry's at its most hapless. There was the same despair of speaking eloquently to many people at once, and generalizations of ideology seemed as inescapable an enemy as the generalization of profit guess-work to the particularity of good cinema. The flowering is a triumph of superior nerve, humour, seriousness, wit.

The flavour of Czech films is pungent and distinct. Their point of departure is not the one we are saddled with, which assumes that audiences won't understand the oblique, that they hanker after fantasy fulfilments about face-pulping and after comedies about tax-deductible adultery. Czech films now seem to start from the assumption that everyone is sick to death of public utterance that nibbles round the edges of things as they are, and that there is not a man left in the country who could honestly be deceived. It is a powerful context for film-making. But all Slavs seem to possess some of Chekhov's transfiguring gift of seeing idiosyncrasy without finding it bizarre. The Czechs' ability not to diminish strangeness into quaintness is part of their natural engagement, like their absolute incapacity to shelter in banter. There are a lot of very funny things in their films, but they aren't wisecracks, and no one jokes in an adopted voice. Gags in Prague are obviously a weapon against propagandist pathos. The good boys of Stalinism were coated with a pathos like blubber; jokes work faster than a reinterpretation of history to scrape off the lard.

In Jiři Menzel's *Closely Observed Trains* and in Hynek Bocan's *Nobody Laughs Last*, the bureaucrats indeed follow from Gogol. There are foppish informers, minor officials with bankrolls of fat around the neck, Philistines operating as social moralists, and the conductors of two ludicrous trials by small-fry potentates in an ecstasy of regulations.

Closely Observed Trains is about a shy, whey-faced boy during the war who takes a job at a railway station as a likely opportunity for shirking, coming as he does from a long line of shirkers. His forebears include a hypnotist grandfather who once sufficiently roused himself to try to stop the oncoming German tanks by glaring at them in his professional capacity. He was not successful. His grandson, veins pulsing with the blood of ancestral duds, battles with sexual defeats on many sides while Nazi ammunition trains pass through the station almost unnoticed. The rest of the railway staff seem half-seas-over with lechery. Their irritability about one another's pleasures is very funny, since they feel the utmost placidity about the flamboyance of their own.

Prague and Warsaw generated their own humour of the absurd long before Ionesco was born. Painstaking local apologists accommodate it now politically by explaining it as a protest against the unmanageable logic of the bomb, or, alternatively, as an indictment of itself, though I'm not sure how one indicts depravity of the absurd by being depravingly absurd. Its reason for existence may have more to do with its funniness. Though Vera Chytilova's *The Daisies* is surprisingly analysed by herself as a 'necrologue about a negative way of life', perhaps to repel hostile boarders, it strikes me as a delicately barmy and freewheeling piece of slapstick, dedicated to recording the passing impulses of two ravishing teenagers with the pre-moral interests of infants. The heroines lead lives of hedonism and chat in a world bounded by haircurlers, men, bikini underclothes, and looming, enthralling food. They have a go at an Existential conversation in the bathroom over a piece of bread, and one of them lusts unendurably for marmalade while she is being seduced. In a restaurant scene, with one girl playing fifth wheel and the other enthusiastically enacting grown-up behaviour with an understandably muted man, the redundant girl fills the silence up by remarking intelligently on the heaviness of the spoons. At the end of the film, bearing on their eyelids a good kilo each of mascara, they invade a banquet hall on an eating binge that is weirdly joyful and funny. They pummel steak tartare barehanded, and thwack cream cakes like mud pies. Lofty food in aspic goes down their gullets or on to the floor by the ton. Then they are sorry. The reincarnation scene is shot in remorseful black-and-white after the full-colour blowout, and the soundtrack crackles with self-addressed mutters about doing better. The havoc artists are dressed now in penitential newspaper and string, trotting about quite cheerily and piling back wrecked food on to silver dishes as if it hadn't been turned into pig swill. A fable about depravity? Surely not. The first female Mack Sennett. A dainty hymn to gorging, photographed with energy and taste by the director's husband, Jaroslav Kucera, and played by dolly girls with the voiceboxes of goats and the bodies of succubi.

Hell is not other people, but us, say the brave Czech films that do not roll with the crunch; us, Judases, insufficient lovers, idealists who behave like shabby improvisers, capable at best of puny contact, and fugitive, for which we shall almost certainly be isolated. These films are as witty as any I remember about the difficulty of modern types of courage. With satiric restraint from comment, and the satirist's taste in hyperbole, they catch the nightmare countryside of neurosis in twentieth-century extremity, a land blown through by such fear that even the contours of friendship and love can shift like the dunes of a desert in the night.

★ ★ ★

Without wit of the order that stares out death, the many-times-devastated Poles could not have survived. Wit, and their wit in particular, has the speed that short-circuits the bigots and bureaucrats whom Poles historically have needed to vanquish. Wit is a cipher. Wit is a password. Poles survive by codes. Film may be the youngest art, but Polish films are born old, like many children before school regresses them. The codified movies of Poland seem to carry in them the whole knowledge of their country's history: partitions, carvings-up at peace conference after peace conference, an outlet to the sea, no outlet to the sea, other languages' names for birthplaces Poles have fought for, the dates of Kosciusko and the two battles of Tannenberg, the symbolism of Stanislaus II and Lublin and the Chopin Revolutionary, the double meaning of Poland's Roman Catholicism, the multiple meaning of Danzig-Gdansk.

One of the first times I went to Poland, in 1954, a Polish friend explained the Polish Problem to me in full: 'It is an excellent country, but badly located.' The friend was the great film director Andrzej Munk, who was killed in a car crash in Poland in September 1961. He was a sceptic with a halo of stiff hair that stood up like a sink brush, a thoughtful and laconic man with the wryness that seems to be the bile and blood of Poland. He was driving me somewhere in Poland the summer he died. We were going along a tiny, filthy road full of garbage, like a lane in London before the Great Fire of 1666. It was called Stalin Street. 'When the old man was still in the chair,' said Munk, 'an edict went out from Moscow saying that the main street in every satellite country was to be named

Stalin Street. Luckily', gesturing at the reeking little road, 'this was called Main Street in the sixteenth century.'

Often the work of émigré Poles gives the feeling that Polishness is not to be tampered with: Jerzy Skolimowski's work for one. Long involved with films in Paris and England, he wrote with Roman Polanski the script of *A Knife in the Water* (1961) when both were still in Poland. A fraction of a generation younger than Munk, and so too young to have fought in the Warsaw Rising, Skolimowski wrote and made in London in 1981 a totally Polish comedy, *Moonlighting*. An unskilful liar called Nowak, played by Jeremy Irons, is sent to England with three non-English-speaking co-workers to do a building job on a mews house in London for a well-off boss who commutes between Poland and England. Nowak is presented as being apolitical, though there is no such thing in Poland or anywhere else. Their stingy employer, benefiting from the minute value of the Polish zloty, has paid them in their local currency to finish the conversion in four weeks and doled out £20 as their recreation budget. In a few days, they have blown the lot plus another deviously acquired £20 on a glazingly desirable secondhand colour TV that busts at once. Nowak alone can understand the English headline news of military upheaval in Warsaw, martial law and the confrontation between the government and Solidarity. Under time pressure to keep his dog-tired trio at work, he pretends to them that they have had five hours' sleep when they have had only three, pretends that all is well at home, pretends that they are getting messages from their wives through calls he takes at a public phone box lengthily occupied by an exasperating Englishwoman of the sort who would say 'How dare you' to a vicarage chintz sofa if she had bumped into it. With the four weeks running out fast, he revives his team with a hot bath in plumbing not yet surrounded by any of the *luxe* circumstances ordered from Warsaw. Natural pine panelling, exposed brick walls, the usual posh-primitive mews look of eighties London. Nowak takes to petty crime, returning a second shoplifted turkey for cash when he has already shoplifted a first. English decency sometimes surfaces, but Skolimowski has a beady eye for lofty local nastiness. A nosy neighbour with the bearing of someone retired from a tea station in India enters into combat about stealing *The Times*. And all the while, there beats under this accomplished story of desperation parading as a lark Jeremy Irons's knowledge, kept from his infinitely exhausted colleagues, that the Poland they are longing to go back to is not at all the place they left.

The pang of exile prods the most fond and fierce satire by the lost. It is there in Roman Polanski's *The Tenant* (1975), with Polanski playing a French citizen called Trelkowsky who has repelled people all his life. He seems to be a tenant with a short lease on his own carcass. His very face has the rawness of a quick study for a finished work, marking his big, Cruikshank features and leaving expressiveness to be filled in later. He moves into an apartment left empty after a suicidal girl's recent tenancy. Polanski conveys the sense that the hero is assessing his own activities as if he were a landlord longing to serve an eviction notice. One morning Trelkowsky wakes up in drag, his vacant frame now occupied by the girl suicide's personality; his mental self-banishment has become a physical notice to quit. This is an odd film, marred by Polanski's taste for the double dare, made poignant by Polanski's split between his Polishness and his quest for the Hollywood he was to end up in with such metaphorical exactness. His talent has always roped in the wanton: it seems most coherent in his first (and home-based) feature, *A Knife in the Water*, made in Poland. The film is a scalding original, alert, nettled, about three people in a situation full of lazy dangers. A bored married couple, the sort of people who thrust each other out of the driving seat without speaking, pick up a chillingly self-reliant boy on the way to a sailing weekend. The boy is intrigued by the enterprise of sexually conquering both, partly because he resents the perpetual showing off about sailing. Polanski's amusedly distant view of himself led him in this and later films into endless, brilliant wrangles between his French and his Polish identities, his atheism and his Jewish Catholicism, his sophistication and his valuable lack of guile. Few artists have been more finger-marked by homesickness.

Polanski graduated from the Polish Film School at Łodz, founded in 1947 after a seedling start in Cracow by a group of cineastes trying to put the devastated industry back on its feet. The first generation of graduates included Andrzej Munk and Andrzej Wajda, who have been called the obverse sides of Polishness: Munk the unbudgeable ironist, Wajda the expansive romantic. Munk was trained as an architect, Wajda as a painter. Where Munk broods over the ground plans and palpably spends months in doubt about whether the structure will really stand, Wajda makes flourishes, elated with his dazzling gift, which has developed wonderfully alongside Poland's history.

Munk directed with craft. No one with a less studious sense of nonsense would have jousted as he did with the authorities over *Cross-Eyed Luck* (1960), a bitterly funny parallel to *The Good Soldier Schweik*. Only the ending failed to get through, which he put there in hope that it would be cut, in the old ploy to keep the rest. In the uncut version, the luckless hero is arrested in a lavatory, not because of the man whom he has killed but because he is suspected of having written vulgar seditious messages on the walls. The censors' objection was to the indignity of such a setting for a government arrest. I think Munk misjudged the value of the scene: later censors let it stand, and its sedateness is funny.

In 1957 Munk made *Eroica*, alone in its antiheroic attitude to the Warsaw Rising. In the first half of the film, marked 'Scherzo alla Polacca', a flourishing spiv has joined the Resistance, but his surge of *gloire* soon ebbs and he leaves for the country. His wife is entertaining a Hungarian lieutenant, who sends him back to Warsaw with a message that the Hungarians are ready to quit the Axis in exchange for Russian recognition. Wary though sloshed, seeing a battle through a pastoral haze of stolen tokay, the legate eventually finds the Hungarian offer refused: and to avoid being alone with his wife now that the cuckolding lieutenant has fled, again bravely joins the Resistance.

The comic scherzo is full of glancing blows, but because the protagonist is no soldier, military self-regard could still survive. The second part, marked 'Ostinato Lugubre' and set in a Polish officers' POW camp, is about the copper-bottomed hero class. After the Rising, a fresh batch of natural leaders is sent to the camp, joining the relics of the 1939 campaign and quickly adopting their intricate fiction of not letting oneself go. The myth that keeps backs stiffest is the myth of the courageous Zawistowski, said to have escaped, but in fact ailing in a loft above the washhouse. Only three officers know he is alive: the secret is kept out of shame rather than security, and when he commits suicide the Nazis, in much the same spirit, provide an old boiler to smuggle out his body. Their hunt for him has been too public; their own military dignity is at stake. The legend survives. *Eroica* is comic and searing, full of ungrateful wit and acted with tight, wry style, but what one admires most is the intellectual order beneath it. Munk was a genuine satirist, rash-spirited and level-minded.

Through the code substitutions possible in fiction about the War – Nazis for Russians, loyalty for perfidy – Wajda was a challenger from the first. He began his career with an astonishing trilogy about Warsaw after the war. His codes were all too factually based, with Polish youth shown in division after the 1944 Warsaw Rising. In *A Generation* (1954), *Kanal* (1956), and *Ashes and Diamonds* (1958), he showed us scabrously the split in the young Poles' aims that was nursed with such care by Moscow. Wajda's great trilogy rests for its full irony on historical recall of the already divided Allies' last-gasp expediency. Munk and Wajda show us the close clasp of classic and romantic in Poland's particular satiric comedy. It is, as satire will be, produced in stress. Their films show the same worn energy, a humour that plays dead but always gets up for more, and a scepticism that probably has to do with geography: that 'badly located' country.

Wajda started film work as the great Aleksander Ford's assistant on *Five Boys*. The fact that the influential Ford agreed to act as 'artistic supervisor' on Wajda's projected *A Generation* gave it immediate licence. Wajda himself, and everyone connected with the trilogy, had fought as a young patriot in Warsaw. *A Generation* is set in Wola, a working-class part of the city. There are two protagonists: one a dour proletarian not to be deflected, one a troubled, baffled man switching from one position to another. *A Generation* has to mouth some crass characterizing slogans to fit in with the tenets of the times, but there is no doubt where Wajda's support lies: with the destined man who sees ambiguity. Played by Tadeusz Janczar, on the run from the Germans after a relief operation in the ghetto, he dodges into a stairwell and runs higher and higher up the steps till he is barred by an iron grille. Climbing up it, he jumps to his death. That is not to say that Wajda sold his other head character short. Played by Tadeusz Lomnicki, one of Poland's most varied actors, he becomes heroic through his straightforwardness, his modesty and his gentleness in a love affair. Wajda is one of the very few film-makers who seem never to have seen any reason to divide those two basic energies in humanity, the urge for constancy expressed in loving and the urge for change expressed in revolution, supported in pressed circumstance by the quick cipher of satire. Andrzej Wajda's work uses code with fleetness.

The theme of the Occupation, treated with complexity by Poles because enemy Nazis became enemy Russians in the no-win replacements cruelly common after victory waltzes, has always been a permissible theme for Soviet censors, purblind to double meanings. Munk wasn't interested in the kind of direct narratives about the war that are the commonplace of film production in all Communist countries. He did something quite different in *Eroica*, with its iron-nerved mockery of his country's cherished military romanticism.

'Poland's military romanticism' has been misunderstood for centuries. It lies in a nerve of irony and stamina that is not belligerent, nourished in hungry times only by wit. After the Second World War, with Warsaw razed, and what was left of its people infamously misled and emerging from rubble and sewers with thin faces whitened by stone dust and eyelashes clogged with fatigue, the first thing Poles did was to look for ways of rebuilding the Old Town. There were no architectural plans extant. The teenagers had been in hiding too long ever to have seen the Old Town. But Canaletto had ages ago stayed there on tour from Venice, and his drawings, found after long searches, were precise. Pretty well every old man, old woman and child left in Warsaw rebuilt the Old Town according to the drawings, finding the right small bricks among the rubble.

Now the Old Town has small underground cafés in it where some of Poland's many matchlight dissidents can be heard, the hour and place given by word of mouth. This being Warsaw, there are many doubles, and you have to have the courageous trust of a local to tell the real from a decoy. The *boîtes* are tiny, and the performers braced to change track if they sense an intruder.

There can have been no printed notices. Historically, countries in less tight straits can afford the 'unofficial' ordinary sort of what England used to call broadsheets, or broadsides. Poland depends on an 'unofficial' printing business that allows only nineteen copies at a time of anything, including wedding invitations. So word of mouth has to take over. A survivor of Auschwitz on crutches will meet a student in some dim part of a lamplit street and give him or her details of the next lecture in 'The Flying University': the underground version of the 'official' university. The schedule is orderly but secret. In the Writers' Union where writers and academics of hostile stripe try to keep things going by sharing a cafeteria table, there is a sting of danger. I was having lunch (potatoes and cauliflower) with two old friends who taught Shakespeare in the Flying University: someone else joined us at the communal table, and my friends went silent. The stranger, uncomfortable, asked about the translation of a line in *Lear.* We talked as best could be, went silent, and he upped and left. My friends held their hush and simply said, when he had gone, 'A party hack.'

That night I saw them again: they were on stage in a night club, academics playing Lear and Fool, Lear wearing a Times-Square-looking button-badge with an image of the Moscow-endowed Ministry of Arts and Culture on it, the loathed wedding-cake building that smugly surveys Warsaw. This is where all play and film scripts have to be submitted. My chum playing Lear gave meaning to 'Pray you, undo this button.'

Another courageous Polish film director told me in Warsaw that he was making a comedy about a man who, like Munk's hero, chalked up Solidarity slogans. I asked him how he had got the slogans past the censor; he too said that it was a matter of diverting the eye to the wrong thing. He too made his hero a lavatory attendant, and the Ministry had been so concerned to ban any shot of the graffiti which might involve naked plumbing that the wording got by unscathed.

For years a writer called Slawomir Mrozek has been producing plays and stories whose existence in what the West sees as the censored part of the world seems almost magically mistaken. Most of them are openly political; they are cast as fables, but they are as obviously rooted in the reality of Poland as a political cartoon in the reality of a face.

'Why did we torture our poor poets and abstract painters?' says a character in *Police*, a short play about a totalitarian Utopia where the police have been so successful in quelling criticism that they have to take off their uniforms and behave as *agents provocateurs* in the hope of creating someone to arrest. One defrocked policeman, totally undermined by plain clothes, gets his wife to sew some official braid on to his underpants, which in a police state must be a fairly frightening idea as well as a funny one.

Mrozek is tartly undeluded about the universal authoritarian practice of giving the rebel a little harmless rope; even in prison, the insurgent is still allowed his revolutionary outlets. 'He can stand on a bucket on the bed and look out of the window, which is forbidden . . .'

Before Professor Jan Kott's production of *Police* – the first piece of directing by the witty author of *Shakespeare, Our Contemporary* – Mrozek's only available work in English was a book of short stories called *The Elephant.* The stories are short and swiftly drawn, like Japanese hieroglyphs, with a pernicious alertness to self-deception on the Right and on the Left. There is one story about a man so keen on the required political virtue of optimism that he paints himself in the colours of the rainbow, bends himself into a hoop on a balcony and falls to his death, but goes on spreading the right spirit even as a corpse because he has instructed that his coffin should be covered with a flag reading 'Three Cheers'. It was for these stories that the *Polish State Cultural Review* blandly awarded Mrozek the annual literary prize in 1957.

Out at Sea is a fable about capitalism and totalitarianism in one. A fat man, a medium man and a thin man on a raft are conducting free elections that can have only one outcome, which is that the two of them who are well endowed in flesh will eat the one made of skin and bones and brainwash him into a state of euphoric belief in his freedom of choice. Both this play and *Police* are drawn in one ribald, doodling line. The bravery of Mrozek's mood is hard to resist, like his humour.

He has also written a prankish full-length play called *Tango*, not yet produced outside Poland and Yugoslavia. It is an enormously funny piece of writing that I would love to see done in the 'free West', staged by someone who has the wit to do it flat as a pancake. Mrozek knows himself that eccentric people are funny on stage only if they are intensely boring to one another. The verbal texture of *Tango* is wonderfully irritable, a fabric of the lectures and insults of a family of libertarians who have sent one another into a stupor with their theories.

Like *Police*, *Tango* is about a group of dejected Utopians, and the question that it sweetly asks them is why Utopia should have turned out so lousily. The freethinkers have degenerated into a coma of disgruntlement about one another's liberties; what is more, they seem to have spawned a copper-bottomed right-wing bigot for a son. Their central achievement, still rejoiced in, is that they have escaped from a convention that long ago prevented them from dancing the tango. Dad has won the freedom not to button his trousers; Mum, 'in the flower of middle age', is unenthusiastically promiscuous with an exceptionally sordid freethinker called Eddie. The rebel reactionary son stages a sniffily old-fashioned wedding for himself and becomes a sort of domestic Fascist. The implications about political nostalgia and wet liberalism are as recognizable in England and America as in Poland, like the surreal rudeness of the humour.

* * *

Under the reign of Nicholas I of Tsarist Russia, it was said by an unusually liberal censor: 'Ideas are being treated like thieves or the leprous.' It was not until Alexander II that ideas in Russia were treated as any friends to society. It is axiomatic of thought that ideas should march alongside us, made staunch by humour and the ability of satire to extend a chill arm against commandments hostile to humankind. This is the great achievement of satire; its conspiracy with common benefit and its upholding of speculation by a singular man free of the stranglehold of general opinion. Satire will always lead us to singularity, to messages of cheek and danger that break the ranks and allow new liberties. A Romanian cartoon called *Homo Sapiens* has a glabrous and pear-shaped representative of our species proceed briskly from flint-rubbing to atom-splitting. Warily peeking into the next frame of the film to learn whether he is going to destroy himself, and horrified by what he sees, he then beetles off by rocket to another planet, there finding a small incipient *homo sapiens* and sadly breaking off its tail.

Much has followed, from brave occupants of the planet living in spaces called, by the 'free West', hostile.

* * *

Japanese films are gifted at a sort of inturned quiet satire that we haven't quite recognized. As long ago as 1961, long before Itami's deserved salute from all over for *The Funeral* and *Tampopo* and *The Taxing Woman*, political self-whitewashing was raised to the level of a slapstick vaudeville turn in Manao Horiuchi's *Women Behind Barbed Wire*, about an alleged Japanese war criminal responsible for a women's internment camp that was later described by its grateful inmates as 'literally a Garden of Eden in the tropics'. The hero, who never stopped worrying about his charges' protein intake, morale and underclothes ('Really? No undergarments left?' he asks anxiously), is condemned to death by the Allies after the war on the scant grounds that one of the prisoners tripped and might have been thought to have been pushed. Ex-prisoners rebel in a body and establish through flashbacks that he was probity itself, providing them with a swimming pool and sewing-machines, helping them to set up cooking committees and severely punishing an orderly who peered at a prisoner taking a shower.

The orderly had his excuses, since he was drunk – 'Inquiries reveal that he imbibed at the Macassar Service Quarters and returned via the shower-hut,' says a subtitle, in the exquisite Thurber-Japanese that is the mollifying element in the film; but no such justification can be made for the women prisoners, who were merely crazed with passion for the commandant on no alcoholic basis at all, one of them going so far as to creep through his mosquito net one night when he was asleep. Repelling her sadly, the hero naturally manages to save his own neck in the end, along with the national face, including its other cheek.

* * *

We were there. We all have been, and are, through the generosity of comedy. Comedy restores to us our past, in a way that is outside the unfortunate commitment of journalism and television journalism to the immediate. Through comedy, we know for sure what it is to have been in Molière's house, in the house of Congreve, having dinner with da Ponte when he had been hounded from Europe after his friend Mozart's death. He sailed to America to found a knowledge of Latin and was obstructed by not getting a visa. Non-Americans trying to do something about what Betty Comden and Adolph Green called the unmelted pot will know the line of descent.

1968 was one of America's many endless years. The spring of deaths, the Fascist August of the Windy City, and the autumn of half measures and tragic farce, when possible heads of state turned up on television with smiles cut out of orange pith.

In that year, there was a minor flummox and furore at the New York Film Festival about some satiric political comedies being élitist (non-box office). Plenty of good and important work has appealed only to small audiences; plenty more could be theorized about as being both highbrow and popular: Shakespeare, Swift, Buster Keaton, the Beatles. Geniuses who have flung pontoon bridges of gaiety and point.

One of the films at issue was Jan Nemeč's *A Report on the Party and the Guests*. Was. *Is*. Comedy work of this sort doesn't rest in peace, it rests in arousal.

The film was made in Czechoslovakia, from a screenplay by Nemeč and Ester Krumbachová. Satire's adherents outside Czechoslovakia today were lucky to have seen it when they did. The Czechs had to wait nearly two years, until the Dubček regime lifted the ban.

The film is a sophisticated comic fable. With satire's compassion, it shows us people who suppose themselves to be happy and, through lack of thinking, relinquish balm. It begins, under the titles, with the sound of running water in the country. A brook somewhere. People are at ease, having a picnic. They eat and joke. Life is sweet. There is a rat squeak of danger when a girl says gaily that she could never bear to be alone. Then strangers are about in the forest – perfectly benign, it seems, but they begin to hustle the picnickers by the arm as they make friends, and edge them into a dell, where they play enigmatic games that have a kindergarten character with a twinge of malignity. The picnickers queue up in front of a table, trying to question nothing. They do what they can to sustain the old mood: it is a day off, after all, and nothing much has altered, apart from the influx of cheerful enough strangers behaving on the eerily playful assumption that they are in command. Here and there, the picnickers show a chink of worry ('I thought they were guests.' 'So did I'). Still, the sun shines. 'We'll line up here.' 'Perhaps alphabetically, if that's what they want.' 'Men on one side, women on the other.' A man facing the jovial playmate behind the table finds himself offering his papers. Suddenly, there is mugging, pleasantly done. A girl says, 'But that wasn't a nice welcome, beating a man up.' Her tactless moment passes, and a white-costumed dictator-host comes tripping along, to lead everyone to a formal banquet in the sun beside a lake. There are candelabras, waiters, the appearance of goodwill; also henchmen, yes-men, and the host smiling and keeping his hands clean. The original picnickers are mixed indistinguishably with the chubby invaders. They are dragooned into enjoyment: people who might be schoolteachers or foremen, and an ordinarily obedient wife who is too keen on the party (the tacit pun seems bitterly meant) to follow her husband when he leaves to go for a walk. Without a word, the group scents an escape. Places are suddenly shuffled. No one feels himself to be sitting in the right seat. The dictator-host figure asks a clever-looking man to make a speech: 'People know your name. Your word has weight.' A funster who is adept at voicing the line of the moment cries merrily, 'One for all, all for one!' Though no one quite says so, the husband's empty chair is troubling now in a different way, for unanimity has set in, and if one has gone, all should go, surely? 'Maybe he likes to be alone,' says someone polite, visibly trying to imagine such a thing and failing in the sunny herd. The guests eat daintily, pretending that the travesty banquet in the company of unknown fellow-eaters who may be informers or murderers is a lucky improvement on their picnic. At the end of the picture, the dogs are after the man who left the table; there is a sound of barking under the final frames, and the candles in the daylight are snuffed out. Satiric comedy at its highest. Oh, Prague.

Stance in Protocol's Chaos

Comedy has everything to do with order. In an ordered time, it can afford to raise tumult. In this scatty time of ours, its common sense can uniquely convey a longer memory. In epochs of caution, it raises hackles and questioning. Questioning, happily, blinds etiquette.

Many the books on etiquette. They seem, with some comic poignancy but no less courage, to arise at the moment when the species is bracing itself for the next step into an ungentle time. When things are about to slide over the cliff, hang on to the nearest tree and say 'Thank you'.

Mark Twain's *An Unfinished Burlesque of Books of Etiquette* inspired Scott Fitzgerald, according to his friend Edmund Wilson, to say that he had once looked into Emily Post and been inspired with the idea of writing a play in which all the motivations should consist of trying to do the right thing. 'Dramatic conflict,' reported Wilson, 'would be produced by setting people at cross-purposes through stalemates of good form, from which the only possible rescue would be the intervention of some bounder as *deus ex machina* to put an end to the sufferings of the gentlefolk who had been paralyzed by Mrs Post's principles.' The 'considerate guest' is his dramatic heroine: the woman who is sweet to everyone and lets children and pets scramble all over her with exclamations of joy. Wilson suggests that she could as easily be shown as a menace from whom any gathering would have to be saved: Mrs Post's hideous villain, 'The Guest No One Invites Again'.

Historically it seems that etiquette can expect to be observed when there is some strong need, sensed but not comprehended, for society to hang together. It ruled in Jane Austen's world because social tenets about wealth, revolution, the rules of women's conduct, the caste system, were about to be questioned. It ruled in Proust's world because of the assumption in it that each character wanted to enter society.

Mark Twain saw satiric comedy implicit in that assumption. His book of etiquette is unfinished perhaps because he guessed that only a society secretly fearful of being socially 'unfinished' (not a graduate of finishing school) could ever need such cribs to politesse. Manners – observation of other people – has slithered in his book into blind protocol unstripped as cruelty:

> At the funeral: Do not criticize the person in whose honor the entertainment is being given.
> At a fire: *Form of Tender of Rescue from Strange Young Gentleman to Strange Young Lady at a Fire.*
> 'Although through the fiat of cruel fate, I have been debarred the gracious privilege of your acquaintance, permit me, Miss [*here insert name, if known*], the inestimable honor of offering you the aid of a true and loyal arm against the fiery doom which now o'ershadows you with its crimson wing.' [This form to be memorized, and practiced in private.]

To amend this formula of concern, one is given careful comparative notes about how to rescue a chambermaid in the case of the same fire.

> MEM. In rescuing a chambermaid, presentation of card is not necessary, neither should one say 'Permit me'. The form of tender of service should also be changed. Example:

> *Form of Tender of Rescue from Young Gentleman to Chambermaid at a Fire.*
>
> 'There is no occasion for alarm, Mary [*insertion of surname not permissible*]; keep cool, do everything just as I tell you, and, D.V., I will save you.'

And then there is the question of the order in which people are to be rescued.

> Partiality, in the matter of rescue, to be shown to:
> 1. Fiancées.
> 2. Persons toward whom the operator feels a tender sentiment, but has not yet declared himself.
> 3. Sisters.
> 4. Stepsisters.
> 5. Nieces.
> 6. First cousins.
> 7. Cripples.
> 8. Second cousins.
> 9. Invalids.
> 10. Young-lady relations by marriage.
> 11. Third cousins, and young-lady friends of the family.
> 12. The Unclassified.
>
> Parties belonging to these twelve divisions should be saved in the order in which they are named.

Again and again, Mark Twain hits notes that remind me of Buñuel, with his agog sense of decorum preserved in impossible circumstances; and of Tati, who observes the true mannerliness of heroes upholding the hospitable circumstances of permitted singularity in a regulated world of technology. Twain, Buñuel, Tati: masters whose work may well be at its most cogent, and certainly its wittiest, when it touches on undermining of manners grown mechanical. Any child, thus any adult, knows the festivity of holding a silence while fuss and pomp declare themselves with no notion of being out of scale. Buñuel and Tati share an observant sense of humour in etiquette without proportion. They are comic masters of watching the pretty ways of politesse when it is attendant on conditions of large chaos.

★ ★ ★

Buñuel's *The Exterminating Angel* is a hallucinatorily funny film that dredges up in all of us the suspicion that coveted social occasions are rimmed by the dark edge of nightmare. A dinner party for twenty is about to begin. Slap-up gatherings of the rich and bored, savaging each other with the affability usual in the circumstances, start making offhand passes that would lead to *crimes passionnels* if passion here were felt to be anything but the consuming bourgeois goal of Not Making a Flap.

In the kitchen, servants putting glasses on trays and shovelling caviare on to a swan of solid ice start to sniff trouble and quit the place with the instinct of rats on a ship about to draw away from the quay. The party nevertheless proceeds on its mummified way, with little clicks of cutlery and squeaks of meaningless pleasantries that sometimes boil over into exhilarated savagery. Something is happening that hasn't anything to do with the strapless satin dresses, nor with the party faces, which begin to look like the heads of suckling pigs glazed in aspic. There is a concert – 'I beg of you, something from Scarlatti' – and then people speak of getting their coats, but no one actually manages to leave.

Gradually the food runs out. The guests, arriving back to the throng from more or less adulterous naps on the drawing-room floor, wander around looking for a glass of anything. Life grows more medieval. A fire is made in the middle of the carpet, fuelled with a splintered cello, to roast a lamb; an elderly guest dies, and all that anyone minds about is the smell of the corpse. The men loosen their ties, and shave their legs with an electric razor. The women begin holding cabbalistic services with the help of a couple of hens' feet that one of them has in her evening bag; another promises faithfully to buy a Virgin at Lourdes in washable rubber if she is ever released. In the end they bed down for the night. They are trapped inextricably in the envied room. 'This is the hour of maximum depression,' says someone at dawn; the lamps are still on, and the milkman doesn't call.

The hostess, managing on her last one cylinder of a butler, gathers together a semblance of coping and asks for cold cuts. Soon the guests are hacking at a water pipe with an axe to find something to drink. Now the women in satin have bare feet. One has hair clips stuck into the top of her strapless dress. The butler is eating a plate of paper frills to fill his stomach, maybe Buñuel's mind being on the holy wafers pressed by priests on the starving in the Latin America he lived in so long. A man complains sharply to a lady that she smells like a hyena; there are sessions of palmistry; and the civilized start looking like bundles of laundry on the floor. 'Hell is other people.' Well, yes; Hell is a *lot* of other people: people who won't go. These people start to repeat some of the things they said when the party was still apparently normal, desperately trying to get back to the point where they went wrong. 'I beg you, something from Scarlatti,' the same woman says again, sounding quite wild. An occult woman continues to play games with chicken claws. Beyond the gates, a priest with a nose for the newsy carts along a tour of children to see the now renowned hermetic house. Sealed off by what? Superstition? Conventionality? The habits of pretence with which the human personality can wall itself up and finally suffocate? Buñuel's prefatory note to the film declines in advance to spell anything out. No master ever does. Back at the purgatorial party, the guests are now walking round and round in their mysterious confinement, like attempted suicides being forced to move in order to keep alive. Next door, a brown bear skids up a column. A small flock of sheep skelter up the handsome staircase. The occult woman has been doing battle with a disembodied hand, trying to stub it out as if it were a seething vestige of a wasp.

A thousand ferociously accurate details of custom survive under the stress of this exterminating night of politesse, seen at a quizzical bias that could be only Buñuel's. Nothing is trapping these sophisticates but their own collective hysteria. But all the same the chains of conformity are real enough. *The Exterminating Angel* is about panic and suggestibility, about the unconscious, about the comic reassurance that people feel in the steel grip of class and superstition. When the guests are finally giving thanks for their release at Mass, three twittering priests are glued to the ground in the vestry in exactly the same way as the thankful were; like them, the priests don't quite care to try to make a move before everyone else. They can find, of course, no words for their predicament. The lopped hand that behaved so badly to the occult dinner-guest seems to have moved in to grip their throats. Like all Buñuel's films, *The Exterminating Angel* is thrillingly made, written by him with iron humour, and as universal as dreaming.

⋆ ⋆ ⋆

This incomparable Luis Buñuel was a film-maker of so many prophetic talents that his wit often gets pushed aside if film buffs do the counting. The academics of film history are a sombre lot. He is honoured as a Surrealist, and perhaps that lumping together with Dali accounts for the scholarly inattention to his recklessly funny undermining of the ways of the bourgeoisie. Especially in the late, great films of his return from Mexico to his native Spain in his eighties, he was made rapt by the misplaced decorum of people in unnegotiable circumstances.

A while before he died, Buñuel showed me a still of himself directing a scene in *El*. In the old photograph he looked interested and amused, as he generally did in the later days when I came to know him. The scene he was directing showed a valet polishing his bicycle. Certain shapes seem to make Buñuel laugh; bicycles, cellos. In *L'Age d'Or*, fragments of Beethoven symphonies and Wagner operas are made startling and comic by being re-scored for string-quartet scale, with the reiterative Beethoven final cadence or the emphatic Wagnerian mezzo given to the cello. And who can forget the mysteriously funny solemn lady cellist in *The Discreet Charm of the Bourgeoisie*? Buñuel sees life pencilled in with mystery. Cinema is wonderful when it's handled by a wry comic spirit. I once heard Buñuel say, 'What is the good of the cinema when it apes everything conformist and sentimental in us? It is a curious thing that a film can create such moments of compressed ritual.' Maybe all humour, too, has an essence in compression and ritual.

* * *

And Jacques Tati. The courtly modern master, spokesman, our observer of technology's absurdities, a man of thought cooling his forehead against the pane of the future.

Jacques Tati was protocol's convivial wrecker. It was also in his nature to extend to technology's unmindful world of artifice the genuine good manners of not howling at its chaos. He merely observes, and shares with us his quizzicality. The great inventor and player of Monsieur Hulot, who may be the one all-round master of cinema today who is Keaton's equal, must be accounted a sage who is modernity's unrivalled wit. He began his career as a magnificently funny mime. He can seem to be an air hostess; a rugby player; a dancer; a tennis player conjoined mysteriously with a racquet; a stuffy English diplomat; a French workman testing the *plat du jour*. He is a fine observer of national characteristics. He said to me seriously in a French bistro, '*Le snack* is a flop in France. It is like a bad direction of the actors. The Frenchmen who are the players are not good at *le snack*. They eat like this.' He did a mime of a French lorry driver tasting a mouthful of the *coquilles* he himself was eating, raising his eyes to the ceiling, adding pepper, munching critically. '*Le snack* is a little disaster partly because it tastes the same everywhere and partly because of the effect it has on people who serve it. In a nice restaurant like this, for instance, the waiter will come to you and whisper advice.' He got up, hung a napkin over his arm, bent down and said to me conspiratorially, 'The *plat du jour* today is not so good. You have time, yes? We make a little *béarnaise* and I find two good *tournedos* as good as last Friday when you came with Pierre.' He sat down again.

Tati's eye for physical gesture is vigilant. He can change in a second from an English policeman expressing, he says, 'subservience and order and dignity', to a French gendarme with his hands on his hips whistling as he writes down the number of a wilful car, his face first expressing melodramatic despair and finally complying with a courtly bow when the car turns out to have a Diplomatic Corps number-plate.

Tati's gift for mime expresses his passion for everything native and natural. It also conveys a lifelong attraction to people's blessed gift for fun, and for silliness in circumstances that are upholstered with fussed gentility. This unique talent makes his films a mixture of painting and burlesque. *Jour de fête*, *Mon Oncle*, *Les Vacances de Monsieur Hulot*, *Traffic*, *Playtime*, the unparaded *Parade*, all have something stylized and balletic to them as well as being eagle-eyed about the commonplace. The real and the imaginative blend. The delicate little fish of a girl becomes a mermaid; the practical also has a Janus face that looks at the mysterious.

'The first rule of burlesque,' he said, 'is that illogicality is logical, its strangeness rational and familiar to the people of its world. Its absurdity obeys a meaning to which its followers are the only ones who seem to hold the key.' His beautifully funny films happen in bizarre weather. He engraves a comic nuance with the seriousness of his peculiar echo of sadness and questioning. There are no judges here. There never are in Tati's work. His famous Monsieur Hulot merely observes, like Tati himself. All the same, it is not a godless world. 'We are on an earth ruled by a deity which is the conscience of its inhabitants,' he said to me once, starting with relief on a topic that interested him after an interminable telephone interruption about some sedate social arrangements during which he had been, as usual, entirely polite and patient, amusing himself by sitting on a sofa arm and pretending to be a switch board operator doing complicated knitting things with telephone wires whenever a new event was added to his itinerary (an admiral's party, an Embassy lunch, a press conference, two hours in the editing room, a meeting with a Mayor).

This sage man was notably well-mannered and decorous. He has 'never wanted to film in a bedroom'. On the other hand, no one is quicker to pick out false courtesies, including the perky politeness of unfortunate dogs dressed up in tartan coats and led on leads by tripping women. He is always on the side of mongrels and muddle. His world is one of composure, children playing tricks, cheerful urchin dogs beating modernity, ordinary people somehow effecting a truce with unknown surroundings.

But one makes a mistake to suppose that Tati is at war with progress. Never with real progress. And even towards plastic his films extend an amnesty. Tati is like the nineteenth-century educated man wise enough to cope with the twentieth. He has no demons. His films are the work of an unpossessed man. Russians say that he is very Russian. Long ago Colette wrote of him that in music hall he had invented a way of being everything at once. One sees why she would have responded to his beneficent earthliness. Of his sport mimes, she wrote that he was both the player and the ball, 'the football and the goalkeeper, the boxer and his opponent, the bicycle and its rider. He makes you see invisible partners, and objects in his empty hands. He plays on your imagination with the talent of a great artist . . . When Jacques Tati imitates horse and rider, Paris sees a psychological creature come to life, the centaur.'

In life, Tati seemed to regard his own face as a trodden-on mishmash. He was not particularly for it, partly because it belonged to him and he was not too much in favour of himself, though otherwise his loyalty was indeed to mess. Apart from Renoir, he is about the only man I have ever known who has not complained about the calibre of busy women's washing-up.

Like Mozart, whose prodigal character he shared, he died a pauper. Keaton, too, died at the edge. Not Chaplin, though. Perhaps the yapping-dog sentimentality of some of Chaplin's work has to do with his canniness about lucre and the fine print of contracts. The world has not repaid Tati for the present to us of his work. The pirates of film-buffery made money out of showing his films and gave him nothing. He mortgaged his house outside Paris and lost it, but never lost a friend or his own delight in perfection.

To go back to washing-up, he expressed from the beginning a hatred of fuss. He was an ally of ill-fitting clothes, whistling, jumping on car bumpers to provoke lady-like drivers in a traffic jam, solutions to the rule of any generalized discipline. In his early *Jour de fête*, when he plays a postman on a bicycle, a cross-eyed man is hammering in the tent-peg of a circus tent; on account of the eyes, sometimes his hammer hits the target and sometimes it misses. Tati is on the side of both hits and misses.

And among things his films despise: cruelty about individuality (like that of the cross-eyed); furious hygiene; small people put at a loss by tall gadgets; empty merriments; almost all social gatherings of more than two.

There is a particular mutinous mumble in the ordinary course of events which can suddenly sound like W. C. Fields; there are debonair acts of stoicism which evoke Keaton; and there is an overweening electronic buzz which reminds you of the films of Jacques Tati as strongly as a particular kind of starched lope summons up Tati himself. When Monsieur Hulot's author balances a soundtrack, the human voice plays a small and outclassed part in the din of the inanimate. A while ago, at some stiff dinner party in California, where the outdoor ping-pong table was made of marble ('Because marble doesn't warp in the sea air,' said the owner gravely), I remember a nearly unnegotiable ten minutes when the roar of twenty-four people's chicken bones being ground up by the garbage disposal unit in the grandly enlightened open-plan living-room was entirely victorious over the twenty-four brave souls who went on pretending to be able to hear each other. The soundtrack was unmistakably Tati's, and so was the politely-programmed lunacy of people ignoring the racket. No other director has ever pitted the still, small voice of human contact so delicately against the nerveless dominion of modern conveniences. Some noisy hot-water pipes become a major character in *Jour de fête*. In *Mon Oncle* the buzzings and hissings and gulpings of peremptory gadgets are prodigious.

Jacques Tati was born on 9 October 1908 at Le Pecq, near Saint-Germain-en-Laye, a suburb of Paris. One grandfather, Count Dimitri Tatischeff, an attaché of the Russian Embassy in Paris, married a Frenchwoman. His other grandfather was Dutch, called van Hoof; he ran a picture-framing shop in Paris. The customers included Toulouse-Lautrec and van Gogh. Van Gogh more than once offered to pay his bills with a painting, but van Hoof, who sounds even less commercially crafty than his grandson – who mortgaged his own house to make his masterpiece, *Playtime*, in 1968 – insisted on cash, not canvases. Later on, Tati's father took over the business. The young Tati was sent to a college of arts and engineering to prepare him for a future of picture-framing. Then he came to England as an apprentice to an English farmer called Spillers. He stayed as a boarder with a family who had a seventeen-year-old son with a passion for rugby. Tati became fascinated by the conventions of the sport and picked, very early, on the husks of politesse that have intrigued and amused him in his feature films. In his great lifetime he would do one a mime of the false friendliness that goes on in football changing-rooms 'to make up for hurting one another quite badly'. He became an amateur mimic of the etiquette of various sports, and eventually told his father he wanted to go into music hall.

'You can imagine his fury,' said Tati in Paris. 'I would be cut off without a sou, he said, if I wanted to do such a thing. Well, I am without a sou still and I am perfectly happy. In those days, the days when I was first cut off without his sou, I would sit in cafés and talk. When I needed to eat I would go to a certain cabaret and imitate a sloshed waiter who is always making mistakes. For an evening of sloshed waiting I would be given dinner and fifty francs.'

It would have been fine to see him on the field; six feet two of him, apparently always with a way of being able to lean alertly in any direction. The tilt is generally forward, exposing an eager five or six inches of striped sock, but it has been known to go just as far to the side. There is a sweet minute in *Mon Oncle* when, without interrupting the talk he is having with someone ahead of him, he keels neatly to the side to hear his four-foot nephew mutter something into his ear, and then quickly straightens up again to get some money out of his pockets so that the boy can buy a supply of crullers. The famous figure with the umbrella makes the stances of other and more ordinary people – and indeed, of other and more ordinary umbrellas – look rather peculiar after a time. The umbrella, which he sometimes holds like a low-slung rifle, can also suggest the upward pull of an invisible helium balloon or the company of a thin aunt sprinting ahead. Now and again he will hold it by the ferrule and seem to have to tug against it, as if it were a leash with a hidden dog straining on the end. For himself, he seems to have learned nothing from the gait and posture of others. He is not one of the upright bipeds, because he slants; he doesn't so much walk as get ready to dive. And he hardly ever seems to sit. There is too much leg around, perhaps. Or maybe his hip joints have never taken to the suggestion of the right angle. Sometimes – very occasionally – he will lie down, and the effect is spectacular. He tends to do it wearing his hat, with the jutting pipe remaining in his mouth. To my recollection, none of his films show him lying on anything so commonplace as a bed, although he has been seen supine on a road in *Les Vacances de Monsieur Hulot*, and curved amazingly along the serpentine front of a tormenting modern sofa tipped over on to its back in *Mon Oncle*. This is no ordinary man. He can make asphalt look quite like an air mattress; he can also make it clear that a modern piece of furniture feels uncommonly like asphalt.

I spent a fine spread of time with Tati and his work. Notebooks bring him to the immediate present. His tall body is as expressive as his voice, which he can switch in a second from French patois to French diplomatic talk, or from French spoken by an upper-class Englishman to something like ticker-tape gibberish. 'I learnt English quite well when I was in England,' he said. 'But then, when I was in Paris during the Occupation, I got a German accent. Then the Americans came and I got an American accent. Perhaps it was lucky the Russians didn't come and I didn't get a Russian accent. Or perhaps I have one.' (He hasn't. But his Russianness is strong. His uncle was shot in the same room as the Tsar.) He can do a beautiful mime of tennis played by a Frenchman of 1910, moving almost in slow motion towards lordly defeat, with a habit of hunching his shoulders, furrowing his brow, holding the racquet close to his body for a backhand stroke, and ending gallantly with a handshake given almost as though he were saluting a victorious general on behalf of a nation with a history of antique military glories. 'It is like when I make pictures,' he said. 'In the case of a film, I don't want people to say "What a wonderful picture" but to notice details and enjoy themselves. Everyone has a right to laugh and whistle. Of course, one should also be able to be a showman.'

He was looking closely at three people in the street at the time. They were arguing about the price of a cabbage. 'What are you doing?' I said. 'Working,' he said, without thinking about the answer: by 'work' here he meant 'look', which is what must have made him such a great music-hall mime, and next a master film director. Tati sees and hears phenomenally, except that he lacks much self-absorption. One evening he left his glasses behind twice, without making any fuss about finding them, but he jumped like a shot rabbit when he heard a whistle outside in the street. He responds a lot to whistles, as to all noises that speak for language or overrule it. He is moved by the antithesis between what people say and what goes on within and between the actual and possible worlds. Sometimes Tati's work has the wild humour of Dostoyevsky. He is compassionately drawn to the times when people make fools of themselves, often out of loneliness in modern surroundings. 'The more décor, the more people are alone,' he said. He notices even the funniest and silliest signals of solitude in the midst of alarming contemporaneity. A waiter does his hair in the kitchen in *Playtime* before taking in the fish; a woman puts a hat on to come into the Motor Exhibition in *Traffic*.

Tati left English music hall on an impulse. 'I was in London rehearsing a floor show. I arrived at 9:30. The director said the performance was going to be for one man and his secretary but he made the conductor get dressed up. In tails. At 9:30 in the morning. He changed the order of performance and I am number nine, which is a terrible place to be. So at 10:30 in the morning I am taking off my make-up, and feeling sad, and thinking that the worst choice I could have made was to be in music hall. Then I take off my costume and I go out into Finsbury Market. Fish, meat, quite an important market. And I start to find everyone funny except me. Who knows? Who looks at these people and says to them that they are funny? That is why they are funny, of course. I decide to try to make films about people like this. They are quite the opposite of a performer in music hall who starves his spirit if he doesn't get one little clap from the audience.

'For young entertainers now, without the music-hall tradition, it is even more difficult. By the time they record, the singers start to be stars. That is the sad thing. It was such an important school, music hall. However, don't think we have made a new generation that has no talent.' Tati has always got on with the young, perhaps because he always feels disconcertingly young himself, especially when he is making a film. 'When I go to the studio every morning, I feel like a soldier without a sweetheart going to the front.'

In 1932 he made a short called *Oscar, Champion de tennis*, and two years later one called *On Demande une brute*. In 1935 he wrote *Gai Dimanche*, which was to grow into *Les Vacances de Monsieur Hulot* (1953), and in 1938 he wrote and made *Retour à la terre*. He insists that all his early shorts are awful and that he laughs at them now for the wrong reasons. 1933 and 1934 were the years of his Paris theatrical breakthrough. After appearing in a cabaret called Gerby's, he performed at the Ritz with Chevalier and Mistinguett, then at the Théâtre Michel, and finally at the ABC. By 1935 he was regularly in music hall, doing pantomimes of football, tennis, fishing, and was the mime in René Clément's first film, *Soigne ton gauche*. His comic genius was already becoming clear. It lies partly in being a lightning conductor for unforeseeable happenings. He was scheduled to appear at Radio City Music Hall in 1939 and the American trip gave him a promising glimpse of baseball, but he finished up in the French Army in the Dragoons. In 1944 he made a short called *School for Postmen*, which is a sort of study for his exquisitely sober first full-length feature comedy, *Jour de fête* (1949), a hymn to the virtue of the bicycle as a means of speedier transport for postal delivery. Tati rides the bicycle with gentlemanly panache and a stiff back, legs alert for making quick stops and arms ready for doorbell-ringing, envelope-throwing and other techniques of modern communication.

He married his adored wife in 1944. He calls her 'Madame Teetai', and when he has to leave her to go abroad to work, he tends to kiss her goodbye tenderly and say, 'You see, I have to go; you are *trop utilisée.*' They have two children, full-grown, called Sophie and Pierre, photographs of whom he carries in bulk in his wallet. He takes being a parent seriously and once said to me in a rare and typically uncoquettish moment of anger at the world, 'When a young boy or girl goes to prison the parents perhaps should go to prison too, for two weeks.' Generally he is a more easy-going man. 'How I got into show business I don't understand. Unlike Keaton, for instance, my family had nothing to do with show business. But I came to have a very good visual memory. Not a word memory. I can never remember the name of a hotel. Very often I take the train I don't want. But I could shoot my first communion even now . . .

'I'm not sure that I believe in exactness,' he said, and then repeated himself in English for the pleasure of saying that he didn't believe in 'exactness, *exactly*', using the voice of the most over-precise upper-class Englishman. (As he said, he learnt English when he was first in London, and his ear for class accents stayed as piquant as his eye for the movements that are the physical deposits of human character.) 'Not exactness in painting, for example. Before the Barbizon school you had everything marked. This is a house, this is a cow. Then came the Impressionists. At the start people found them not their cup of tea, but then they began to say, if you watch carefully, a cow seems more naturally drawn with three lines than the "real" finished kind of painting.' He has tended more and more to this kind of stylization in film-making. In *Playtime* and *Traffic* he never shows a completed cow.

His observation of people's gait is as supra-real as the way he signs his own name, with the two 't's looking like top hats and the 'i' a beaming candle. 'When people don't know each other they follow right angles,' he said to me, tracing 90 degrees on a brick wall. 'When they are intimate they go in curves.' He has followed this rule in *Playtime* in its spry comic nightmare of office workers living in a building like a glass egg-box, and a woman with a trolley of office elevenses wheeling it about in neat turns. He seems much interested in people's sense of physical geometry. His great M. Hulot, whipping off his hat, bows at an angle of 45 degrees and smokes a long pipe at a raffish jut, so that the pipe has the look of a thin Italian cigar. Hulot carries his perfectly rolled umbrella as if it were a billiard cue, or tucked under his arm like an officer's military stick.

Hulot's walk in his elevated trousers and his short check-lined mackintosh is wary but polite, with something of the dandy in its spring-heeled activity and its tacit sympathy for other people's cream-pie accidents. Tati himself, who wore trousers nearly down to the ground in reaction, along with two sweaters and no tie, was as debonair in his comprehension of pratfalls as Keaton was. His famous creation is a character of elegant simplicity, with an inner sense of rhythm of the way things should be. This sense is nothing that Hulot ever insists or expounds. 'He promenades, that's all,' said Tati. 'He takes a walk, innocent and tranquil. He simply looks at things. Is it his fault if we have baptised him with our invented desires and needs? And if, believing ourselves to be serious, we have insisted on being solemn?'

Mon Oncle is an attack of blistering docility on the generally unadmitted discomfort dealt out by house pride, contemporary design and high standards of dusting. Hulot's sister, called Mme Arpel, who is seldom seen without a duster, lives in a balefully mechanized and hygienic house, where a speck of dirt would be like an oath in the Vatican. Her husband, who is in plastics, is a quail-shaped man who wears thick clothes however bright the sun. They live a life of unvarying merriness and pep. The front gates open by remote-control buzzer, and at the same time, if the company merits it, a sculptured fish in the middle of the unnatural little garden starts spouting water. For trade deliveries, and for her brother, the fountain subsides with a dejected final spout. The Arpels live in a world of ceremony but no actual fun, of regal bother with two convoluted chairs that are placed in throne positions for the Arpels to watch mere television, of flavourless steaks cooked in two seconds by infra-red rays, of high heels clicking on polished floors. Clothes are like the poor in the New Testament: always with them and quite a trial. A severe-looking guest whom Mme Arpel casts as a splendid possible wife for Hulot, and as a certain admirer of the house, is dressed in a sort of horse rug or tablerunner. A dog leash then gets impossibly tangled in one of her long earrings. The women in the Arpels' world are perpetually harassed by their bags and stoles and hobble skirts, and M. Arpel throws his wife into a panic by nearly forgetting his gloves when he drives to work.

Hulot, on the other hand, is curiously absented from his clothes, which regularly include the familiar short raincoat and ancient hat whatever the weather. He also seems agreeably unemployable. His natural allies are mongrel dogs and dirty children, who follow him in droves. His nephew, Gérard, adores him. Gérard's chirpy mother tends to sterilize the boy out of existence; Hulot is a comrade, being muddle's natural kin. The uncle lives on the top floor of a charming, ramshackle house in an old part of Paris, with windows that he arranges carefully before leaving every day so that his aged canary will get the sun's reflection. Until the last shot of the film, one never sees the inside of this house. All one catches are glimpses through half-open stairways and hall windows of people's heads and feet, or a segment of a girl lodger in a bath towel waiting to scuttle across a corridor when Hulot's legs have disappeared downstairs. Tati is visually very interested in bits of people. If he were playing the game of pinning the tail on the donkey, he would tend to find the dissociated tail too engrossing to go any further.

Maybe all funniness has a tendency to throw settled things

into doubt. Where most people will automatically complete an action, a great comedian will stop in the middle to have a think about the point of it, and the point will often vanish before our eyes. In *Mon Oncle* Hulot has this effect very strongly about the importance of holding down a job. His sister, who is bothered by his life as if it were a piece of grit in her eye, has him put to work in her husband's plastics factory. The place produces miles of red plastic piping, for some reason or other. Various machines pump out rivers of it. Hulot is mildly interested. 'Keep an eye on number five,' says a workmate mystifyingly, wrapped up in a piece of cellophane like a sandwich in an automat, and taking no notice of the fact that Hulot is slumped over a table and half-moribund because of a gas leak. Number five, a rebel machine, starts to produce piping with occasional strange swellings in it, like a furlong of boa constrictor that has slowly eaten its way through a flock of sheep. The thing then takes it into its head to start tying off the piping every few inches, as if it were a sausage machine. Hulot goes on manfully keeping an eye on it, which is all he has been told to do, and quite right. Care for the plastic can go too far.

His sister is a living witness to that. For her wedding anniversary, she has given her husband an automatic and doubtless plastic garage door that opens when his car goes past an electric eye. M. Arpel is overjoyed in his plastic way. 'No more keys. Happy?' his wife chirrups. Their dachsund then sniffs the electric eye and shuts them in the garage, yapping amiably while they try to persuade him to sniff again. The new door, like the bedroom floor of the house, has two round windows near the top; the Arpels' disembodied faces appear, yelling inaudibly for help, and bobbing about behind the windows like air bubbles in a bricklayer's level.

Husband and wife in Tati's films are content, mostly. They represent a new system of vapid happiness. Hulot represents the old disorder. The Arpels, who rather grow on you, are funny partly because they treat themselves as if they were machines and partly because they have lost the defining human sense of relative importance. Trotting around with their gadgets and their dusters and planning tea parties, they have no grasp of their scale in the universe; they are a counterpart of the endearing Great Danes who will try to fit all four legs on to a lap, deludedly thinking themselves the size of Pekes. These proud owners of the awful model house, tripping around on an artistic but farcically unwalkable pattern of paving stones and being careful not to put a toe to the grass, conduct themselves with a sober sense of import and duty. When they entertain, they might be the President of the Republic and his wife welcoming the signatories of a peace treaty. The difference is that they are only having some neighbours to a paralysingly difficult tea party at which everyone is spattered by a minor débâcle with the spouting fish; but this destroys no one's aplomb and no one's sense of occasion. It is part of Tati's humour that the Arpels' perception of things is fastidiously concentrated and only a trifle off the point. Who is to say, in fact, that their absorption is not the norm, even if it does screen out what seems more fascinating to the casual observer? In *Jour de fête* the postman, played by Jacques Tati, is entranced by the idea of Americanization of the mails through speedier transport. Speedier transport means, to him, bicycling instead of walking. The bicycle suits Tati. He uses one in *Mon Oncle* – a rather dashing one, with a puttering little motor. The shape of the thing fits his legs, which are long enough to turn the bike at will into a quadruped. Bicycles also meet a certain stateliness in his style and a certain disinclination for any vehicle that outsizes the human frame. You feel that he much detests the shiny cars in *Mon Oncle*. He prefers doughnut carts and horse-drawn wagons. The failed plastic piping is hurriedly taken away in a cart drawn by a strong-minded grey horse that exerts a will of its own about going to the right when the driver wants the left; its mood is not so unlike the recalcitrance of the plastic machine, after all.

Hulot has his own rules about mess. He is the eternal ally of dust, though himself neat. He pauses, for instance, in passing from the old quarter to the hygienic new, to replace a brick in a pile of débris, and marches with a sprightly distinctness that gives his gait a peculiar pecking motion, like a housewifely flamingo in a hurry. This neatness often reaches soldierly proportions. Tati himself is interested by modern people's predilection for parking cars in military file. *Mon Oncle*'s shot of Hulot going upstairs to his flat is as orderly as any drill-sergeant could wish. Hulot appears in window after window in his progress upward, always moving with the same springy, mathematical grace. Outside, when he leans forward to shake hands, always quite undeterred by his umbrella, he angles his stance like a bird drinking water, to catch words that are often either incoherent or inane. Of inanity he is politely uncritical, though very watchful. About his modernized sister and her fusspot husband his view is also mild: that they spend too much time turning on and off their fish fountain in the garden, and on following the swirls of crazy paving laid to keep them off their own grass, a habit that allows Tati to exploit to the full his interest in the oddities of convention-bound walking. His own wife, when she is in a hurry, produces an unconscious mime of the scurrying Mme Arpel; perhaps something about Mme Tati's way of making haste even suggested Mme Arpel's walk to the doting, hawk-eyed Tati.

The birth of Hulot himself is more clear and also lies in gait: 'I thought of him because I knew an architect who walked like him. He merged with a simple man I had known in the military. The way this soldier answered the colonel's insults made it quite impossible for the colonel to be cross. Hulot is not really a hero character, however. He is just a man who walks in the road. He is not the cause of funny situations, he is in the middle of them. When people say "go right", he goes left, because his mind is a little on the moon at the time.'

Again this interest in the expressiveness of the directions people take with their limbs. There is a splendid man in *Playtime*, a happy drunk thrown out of a half-built but posh nightclub, who follows the neon arrow outside, which happens to take a curve from the place where he lands after ejection and to lead straight back into the club, an invitation that he blandly follows. *Traffic* is also much absorbed by contradictory signals leading to mishap. The film is a graphic havoc. Pairs of arrows point equally dictatorially at right angles to one another. Signs painted on the road in the Sanskrit of traffic departments tell people either to stop or to proceed, to park or not to park, the reading depending on your mood. The signs are anyway mostly invisible, as they are painted on roads perpetually covered by honking cars squeezed bumper to bumper in perfectly stationary positions, attended by owners who walk understandingly up and down beside their immobilized charges. Man is the horseless carriage that can actually move. The film is a quiet political remark about the evil futility of a society economically based on pouring out quickly-obsolescent cars that overfill the roads, pollute the atmosphere and represent the desirable while retracting at the same time the whole point of their desirability, which lies in travelling.

Tati's first feature, *Jour de fête*, was seen first in black-and-white and then, some twenty years later, in a version with some details hand-coloured by Tati himself (in later movies he went on to use colour as beautifully and symbolically as any painter, rare in film comedy). About *Jour de fête*, a chronicle of small-town life on fête-day, he said, 'I would have dearly liked to have shown the fun-fair in colour, and the streets in black and white for sadness.' The film opens with a shot of balloons. Early morning. The tent poles are being erected. The fair builds up. Merry-go-round horses spin past real horses. A child skips behind the merry-go-round. Tati as the postman, walking at a stalled long-legged rush, flees the teetering flagpole. Even a horse is frightened by the garlands. The postman bravely manoeuvres his way past a donkey and carries on.

There are many of Tati's typically small occurrences in this film, in which people have the lonely intentness of the best film comedy. A man playing the cymbals in the village brass band is shown trying to swat a fly. The postman gets tied up in streamers. His bike runs into trouble: wheeled in shreds, it is taken by its master to the funfair, where Tati peers through a tent at a promotion film about communications. He is told by the screen that the postman is the modern helicopter. Buoyant thought. When his bicycle is repaired, he goes back to it with dignity and the straight-backed aplomb of a futuristic executive, sometimes riding it like a desk chair at an important conference. But there are wasps to bother him. Intrusively pastoral note. Their buzzing looms on the soundtrack. As the day goes by, the fête limpingly continues. Horses get tired. An old crone with a goat suddenly appears. The postman is enthralled by a man on a motor bicycle mounting a ladder on the merry-go-round. Much excited by his rôle as the village helicopter, our hero on his bicycle hangs on to the back of a lorry and stamps letters on the lowered tailgate at breakneck speed, using it as a desk. We have seen him muttering 'Rapidité, rapidité' to himself as a slogan, racing about with his letter pouch efficiently whizzing round one shoulder. The recipients of his modern deliveries are not up to standard. The baker can't take his letters because his hands are covered with flour. A busy bell-ringer visited by the postman, manic but still stately, hands on the rope to the priest while he disappears to read his letter. Another letter gets caught in a grain machine.

It is all very difficult, to be obsessed by speed and a recalcitrant bicycle in a slumbering village where the inhabitants are opiately slow to write signatures on receipts. Even sheep stand in the path of progress: the postman takes a short cut over a hill to catch his run-away bike, which is following the road curving round the hill, but amicable sheep slow him up. The retrieved bike is eventually carefully padlocked and then forgotten until the postman's energy returns and the rider, revived, careers onwards on his vicar's-wife bicycle and triumphantly passes a group of vehement racing cyclists.

Jour de fête is Tati's first near-abstract film. It uses sound surreally. He has resurrected slapstick and made it as gentle as Keaton's was, though he would deny it. 'You won't find another Chaplin, you won't find another Keaton, because the school is closed,' he said to me; but there couldn't be another Tati, either. He was a poetic original with the mysterious gift of bringing balm to modern chaos and of creating conditions in which the warring opposites of standardization and individuality can live in reconciliation.

In an irredeemably modern tropical town, American-speaking when things came to lost luggage (as they did) and to form-filling (as they did), Tati was presented at a solemn ceremony with a key to the city. It would, of course, open nothing. It must have represented the blend of kindliness and idiotic empty symbolism that Tati detects in the world and demonstrates in his films with a unique style of compassion, seriousness and uproariousness. 'It is funny, this presenting of the key,' he told me after the ceremony, 'but I am also full of fear.' He badly wanted things to go well and people to be at their best. He is the ally of all such attempts. But the endeavour of air-conditioning puzzles him: 'You take off your coat to come in, yes, in order to be cold enough to warm up outside without it?' Yet he sees the effort, just as he goes along with the modern world's opaque sense of priorities. When he happens to be submerged in officialdom, he gives one the feeling of trying to keep indistinct but no doubt crucial appointments, and of trying to learn an arcane tongue.

The luggage lost in flight meant filling in something called an 'irregularity report'. Tati struggled so because the form had a box saying firmly 'Write nothing in this box'. In his films, he has a delicate way of suggesting the chaos of the natural in the collision with the manmade. The great slapstick scene of the restaurant in *Playtime* is full of lamp bulbs fusing in the midst of party conviviality, and noses that seem to be being broken on plate-glass doors. The glass entrance of the half-finished restaurant is lost, but the doorman struggles on with his job and simply opens the door handle with a flourish. New-glued tiles stick to customers' shoes, a clip-on bow tie is retrieved from a dish drenched with mayonnaise, the harassed architect rushes around with a ruler re-measuring a serving hatch too small to take the ornately decorated fish that hapless cooks are trying to force through the gap. In *Jour de fête*, a cross-eyed man armed with a hammer drives in tent stakes that have to be moved sideways to suit his squint so that he can aim. No assault of the random, however, prevents the proud enterprise of *Jour de fête*'s sublime postman with his hearth-brush moustache promoting efficiency on his sedate bicycle.

Tati has a great affection for vehicles of character. Hulot

possesses a home-made sports roadster that rides on what seem to be bicycle wheels. Tati said to me in France, 'Now, a new car: maybe the old one has more memories. *Souvenirs.* When my old car came back from the repair shop I was so happy. At the benzine station, well-modernized men throw away everything because it doesn't work. But they start to be friends with my old car. You can come in with a new car that is no problem of theirs. It is a doll. In the case of my car, they start to be on its side. When I come in with my forty-year-old Renault they feel that is their relation. They see every morning someone who is quite sick but it still goes.' He raised his head and sniffed with a look of family ease.

Les Vacances de Monsieur Hulot is about the seriousness of people taking a holiday. Like every other feature film that Tati has made, *Les Vacances* has a moral theme. He is concerned to show the straits of people who underestimate the superiority of instinct and humour compared to codes of etiquette and fuss. (In 1953 it justly won the International Critics' Prize at the Cannes Festival.) Formality keeps on wrecking fun. Suntanners work away as hard as at the office. A game of ping-pong is constantly disrupted by two bridge foursomes. Monsieur Hulot, lying on his back mending his beloved car, finds a spare wheel whipped from him, covered with autumn leaves, and treated as a wreath at a funeral. One remembers the concentration of Monsieur Hulot about everything. About painting a kayak from a pot that moves in and out with the tide. He works away in unwitting rhythm with the oceanic movements of the paint pot, not noticing a thing, modestly attuned to the whims of the inhuman, just as he is in the scene in which he tries to deal with the garden sprinkler. The sprinkler has drenching bursts of sudden energy and a watery life of its own.

'Our world becomes every day more anonymous,' Tati said, talking not about his films but about life, as good film-makers and all real artists do. 'In other times, the butcher was a man with a coloured shirt. Now he puts on a white overall like a male nurse. The world is in the process of becoming an enormous clinic. But if, at the beginning, the inhabitants know themselves to be at sea and then force themselves to change their new city to suit their idiosyncrasies, then they will come to arriving at humanizing modern décor, little by little. Accidents will happen. People will laugh.' Chairs in the shape of Henry Moore sculptures will be felt to be uncomfortable for sitting in. Tati builds monuments to the common sense of human nature, so believing that it transcends the mechanisms of modernity that spectacles of the humdrum are transformed into a dream. The cars in *Traffic*, locked in a traffic jam, seem to be going at the pace of men walking on the moon. The cars near the end of *Playtime* go in a slow circle, while concrete mixers and cranes gyrate. Imagery of fun: some beautiful Catherine-wheel.

Fun. Even plastic yields to Tati's sunny and peculiarly studious temperament. In *Mon Oncle*, M. Hulot invades his sister's resistibly hygienic kitchen and finds in it a horrible plastic jar that is magically bounceable, though when this concentrated man tries the same thing with a glass jar it shivers into fragments and he considers the virtue of skulking away from the mess and denying any connection with it.

The world of Hulot's little house is far removed from the nearby hygiene of the new quarter, which Tati the film-maker shows us as filled with the modern squeaks and buzzers and bells that obviously strike him as one of the funnier characteristics of progress. The Arpel fish-fountain is turned on whenever the doorbell outside her blank steel garden door emits its own particular officious squeak. The fountain works hardest for one of Mme Arpel's dreadful tea parties. The party is attended by, among others, a thin woman with a face that is all equine features, under a coolie hat that seems to be a lampshade. There are squeals of excitement about the steak machine in the impeccable kitchen, where the Arpel child sits alone and morose in front of an egg that has been boiled by infra-red heat and put on to a plate surgically sprayed by his mother, wearing gloves and using a pair of forceps on the egg; perhaps fearing the intrusion of germs through the shell, perhaps expressing distaste for other people's food. You feel she must be the world's worst cook, and the least convivial wife on earth. In the evenings she and her husband sit apart at a sterilized distance in Martian-looking chairs, gazing proudly at nothing through plate-glass.

There are, again, few natural sounds in the film: mostly hisses from unsittable-on cushions, tinkles of trolleys, the bird-cries of politeness from her tea-party guests. The child is entirely silent, even when he is scrubbed as hard as if he were a surgeon's hands before an appendectomy, his small frame poignant and dim behind a shower curtain while his mother has a ferocious go at his skin, which already glows pink with the mark of scrubbing-brush bristles and a thousand bouts of rubbing. There is a sorry contrast between his life and the blitheness of the filthy urchins in the old quarter, taking turns jumping down from a hill to make dust every time a man with a broom thinks he has swept it up, and whistling invisibly at passers-by so that they turn their heads on the point of bumping into a lamp-post. The street kids may be poor, but they obviously have a much better time than the ever-polished child.

In New Orleans, when *Mon Oncle* was about to be shown, a father wanted to be photographed with his pint-sized little boy. Tati bent down from his six-foot-two height to the child's level to fit into the photograph before going into the cinema with me. 'I was thinking, when I made *Mon Oncle* seventeen years ago, "It's a very nice little picture about people, and this is maybe what's going to happen to your children." I didn't know how true it would turn out to be.' Tati feels very protectively towards children: almost religiously, much as he hates false religiosity and the idiot people who accused him, over the hilarious funeral wreath scene in *Les Vacances de Monsieur Hulot*, of having no respect for death. On the contrary. He still has the highest respect for the courage with which one of his grandmothers died.

'My father had a very strong will. I wish he could have been more like the uncle in *Mon Oncle*. My father's mother was married to someone Russian Orthodox. As I have told you, she was a great influence on my life. Everyone loved her. She was very religious and a heroine in my eyes, even though I never went to church. We have agreed that it may be an ersatz show. We don't know, do we? Who does? It's stupid, at any rate, to give money to be blessed by God. If you believe in something you have to do it yourself, yes? You have to stop in a big forest and make your own mind up and decide about your own conscience in front of a tree.'

He had already told me a story about the death of his beloved grandmother, when an altar-boy tripped over with a lighted candle and started burning a rug that took everyone's attention away from the funeral rites. Comedy. Riot. Tati's watchfulness for happenings off-stage. As he said, 'One has to go to a cinema to see a movie but one doesn't have to go to a church to have an ethic.' I imagine that death alarms him as much as it does anyone, even more than deaths of impulse, which he dreads. He is always on the side of hurtless mischief and of improvisation.

He obviously likes, for instance, the old woman's method of attracting Hulot's attention in his broken-down, pretty house in *Mon Oncle*. She lives on the floor below him, and she simply bangs on her ceiling with the end of a long-handled broom. Why use a bell or waste steps if you are an old lady? He believes in simple ways of doing things. But if people want to be complicated: well, there's space for it, if they insist.

For instance: On his way to rehearse a New Orleans screening of *Playtime* when the projection worried him, because the film is in 70mm and he thought the projectionist might have trouble with the masking of the frame, he found himself in a radio taxi with a woman's voice blabbering on the radio. He had the attention for the other things to say with concern to the driver, 'Does she do that all the time?'

'Yes. She rattles on without stopping,' the driver said.

'You poor chap,' said Tati.

In the empty cinema he whirled about, looking at things anxiously, and found the projectionist. As Tati had dreaded the print of the film hadn't even arrived. It was to come from Los Angeles by plane at the last minute. 'Two very important policemen on motorcycles will escort it,' Tati told the projectionist. 'But it makes me sorry that you should have to wait. The curtains will close at the end of the picture? No? Oh?' He looked at the gold curtains suspiciously. 'Now you see,' he said, 'at the end of the picture I have no end, so it is essential that the curtains close.'

'Is *Monsieur Hulot* without an end, too?' said the projectionist, already charmed, but a little desperate.

'No. *Monsieur Hulot* has an end. I tell you what. I'll sit here, in my old trousers and my sweater and my black tie if we are in a hurry and there is no time to put on full fig, and I will pull the curtains myself, because I know when there is no end,' said Tati, struggling efficiently in the wings with defunct switches. 'The curtains used to run on electricity, but it's cut off, eh? Never mind. I'll do it.'

He practised.

'You can't work the things from the projection booth?' he said.

'No,' said the projectionist.

'You people have a little bit of French blood,' said Tati calmingly.

Tati seems good at not imparting rattle. Several people in France who have worked with him say that. He is very practical, and uncertain about what other people will find funny, though he knows exactly what makes him laugh. 'With *Playtime*, you find it too long? Or no? Or perhaps?' he asked me, amused by his own doubt. 'Of course, one can fall asleep in a wonderful concert, or one's shoes can hurt in a wonderful painting exhibition. I don't like to say to people "This is funny," because they may find it only a little bit funny.

'Comedians speak with their legs. I spent years in music hall, you know, and I realize therefore especially that you need legs. Music hall has also taught me that it is often difficult to be funny without an accompanist or a nice girl waiting to catch you, because being funny is like being on the high wire or juggling.'

Tati himself generally seems to believe that there is a way out of problems, given a little lack of constraining dignity. It is one of the things that make him technically a joy to work with, his film crews say, even though he appears at the beginning of shooting to want the impossible. *Playtime* is his most ambitious film technically. It is made in four movements, so to speak. In the first, groups of tourists leaving New York – its concrete, its chrome, its glass – smile at the foreign but identical concrete, chrome and glass of Paris. Orly Airport enchants them with its Europeanness. It would spoil the adventure of Abroad to admit that its look strikes them as exactly the same as the airports they have made such enthusiastic efforts to leave. 'This dear old city,' they say fondly to the airport. In the same section of the film, M. Hulot briefly appears in an arrival at an office where the dozens of floors are identically inhabited.

In the second movement we are at an International Trade Fair. A German is proudly demonstrating a door that shuts in golden silence, frustrating all efforts at bad-tempered slamming. It is the effigy of wrong-headed architectural achievement: a door that the makers have deprived of the age-long expressiveness of an exit made in a huff. A potential modern-age enthusiast, suddenly cross, finds himself thwarted in his tracks by the vaunted hush.

The third movement is one of the great set-pieces in the history of slapstick, taking place in the shambles of Tati's now famous inspiration about an unusable grand nightclub. It is christened 'the Royal Garden'. The architect, fussy but unfunctional, is still checking his insanely impractical measurements; the wet paint of chairs regally imprints the words 'Royal Garden' on the backs of dancers; imperiously elegant women wear identically chic little black dresses with shoe-string shoulder straps; a drunk Englishman repeatedly falls off a bar-stool. When the ceiling finally caves in, the battle against impractical formality has been won. The guests improvise their own boozy party with their own amateur pianist at the piano. A characteristic Tati triumph has occurred; a stately restaurant has been transformed into a chaotic and entirely personal bistro. In the kitchen we have seen a waiter with trousers ripped by a dining-room chair that has pointed crowns on the back. Another waiter has come in with a ripped jacket. They exchange jackets to make one unripped waiter. The ripped one then has to cede his shoes because another waiter has lost a shoe sole on the tacky tiles of the new floor outside. He is even stripped of his tie by the waiter whose clip-on bow tie fell into the sauce. Formality is always the loser with Tati. It lost earlier on in the film, in the scenes laid in the modern glass nightmare of an office building, where a dilapidated old porter calculated that he had just enough time for another drag on a forbidden cigarette when he heard high heels clicking towards him from far away along the passage. Nothing in this building is made for the human frame. A smallish liftman has to stand on tiptoe to speak into some contraption so as to announce M. Hulot, who is waiting politely for an appointment that is never actually consummated until long afterwards, when he and the man he wants to see meet by accident in the street.

And the fourth movement of the film is the departure of the tourists: not at all disappointed by having seen the great buildings of Paris only in reflections in plate-glass doors, feeling happily sated with trophies and snapshots, showing one another tourist-market memento scarves and exclaiming over them with delight. Everything has been fine.

Playtime shows Tati as a master of finding small pleasures in the overwhelmingly standardized. A tiny, stuffed functionary of some sort carries a briefcase with a tag on it that twirls like a child's toy in the wind. A woman in the customs hall pats a case meaningfully, as if there were something immensely valuable to her inside it. As indeed there is. A dog, to judge from the whimpering noise on the soundtrack. And in the restaurant scene, a lady joyfully gets stuck in the crack between two bits of modern floor. *Playtime* is the nearest Tati has come to making a film without dialogue. He employs mutters almost abstractly, and switches from French to American to German without subtitles, because lack of verbal comprehension between colleagues or intimates is part of the point he is making. No wonder children adore this film, and no wonder adults are exhilarated by Tati's unique feeling for the wondrous funniness of things and the charm of accident. The characters in the nightclub adore the chaos in spite of a few jets of anger that spout from the strait-laced. And no wonder, in Tati's universe, that the gluey crowd throws up a spirited American girl who takes over the piano and plays convivial waltzes after the regulation mood music for three-foot-apart dancing that the management provided.

The tourists are never mocked. Tati finds few people foolish, because he sees few people as being finally incapable of bending. One of his American visitors asks softly, 'How do you say "drugstore" in French?', a little ashamed of her ignorance and sweetly ignoring the signs reading 'drugstore' everywhere. Tati even feels kindly to the dandy master architect, who is himself a prisoner of the grand jail he has built in this nightclub at the back of a building that may represent, heaven help us, the future: and he likes the office workers who earnestly telephone one another from next- door box-rooms for folders of indubitably needless records. The official scenes are conducted in careful privacy, through scurrying confidential secretaries; the scenes of intimacy and friendship and chance are carried on in full view, out in the street. Tati is on the side of the people in the street, of course, but that is not to say that his film doesn't imply feeling for the nightclub women with their careful hairdos and bouffant bosoms. *Playtime* is an achievement of mischief and magic and prophecy, with touching powers of observation. Tati is not of the laugh-track age of entertainers. In this satire of the glass and plastic age he finds poetry and undying moments of music hall. The film made me remember that one of his avowed heroes is Little Tich, the famous entertainer who worked the music halls in England.

Playtime also epitomizes Tati's politics. They could be described, perhaps, as populist-anarchist-comical-lyrical. 'Hulot is not the hero of *Playtime*,' he says. The main character is the décor and the heroes are the people who break it up. 'I am not a communist. I could have been, if communist history was not so sad. It makes me sound old-fashioned, but I think I am an anarchist. Great things were done by the historic anarchists . . . The students of May 1968 seemed very good at the beginning. But when they came to the workers at Renault, the workers say, what do you propose? They say, we have fought for years to have a bigger apartment. You see, revolution has always come from intellectuals, but it has to have a popular impulse. I would like to make films for everybody, though this doesn't mean that every film I make is alike. In the Hulot films or *Playtime* there is not a shot I have made that I can put in another picture. A film is like a person. Picasso has nothing to do with Renoir or Michel St Denis, and students want to see what is personal. They mostly don't like to live in a society where manufacturers make money by distributing electric guitars. This is true capitalist society. I am on the side of the students, I have to say. They ask, how can you be honest if a government stuffed with scientific people doesn't say that the water from the Seine is about to smell terrible? The government budget, for instance, is based on cars and petrol. Now, how can one speak nostalgically about trees if each day you bring into the city thousands of cars polluting the air? That's where the students are right. I feel sad for them that they weren't as successful in 1968 as they are in taking dope. You can't have a good talk with a man who lies down and goes to sleep in the middle of a sentence. Finish. On the whole, though, as I said, I salute the students. They have proved that girls often have silly make-up. If they don't want to wear shoes, fine. Though they are unfortunately also showing that they live in a ghetto, and I don't like that. They have done something far more wonderful when they have managed to cross frontiers. In one American city, for instance, I asked why there was only one black in a thousand whites at college. I didn't mean to be asking a political question, because I am not American. I shall not judge. None of the professors answered me. It was the students who all responded. They agreed, of course, and this was in the South, where it is not so easy. Students and children are interested in change and they give me courage to continue. The older people are not so good. I met a woman from Mississippi. She said, "No, the times have not much changed, and now we have these horrible machines."

'Hulot begins to disappear in *Playtime* because everyone is the hero,' said Tati. In fact, every now and then in the film, there are glimpses of a back view, hoisted trousers, a furled umbrella, angles of posture that look like Hulot's and turn out to be someone else's. 'A lot of people think I am Monsieur Hulot, but

I am really quite different,' said Tati. 'I can't always walk head in air. I'd crack up. The expression wouldn't stay. Monsieur Hulot is out of the moon, as I said. But today there is no moon.'

We were leaning together on the reception desk of an old-fashioned hotel in Paris. I thought of the exchange in Brecht: 'Unhappy the land without a hero'; 'No, unhappy the land that needs a hero.' Tati respects people who find the humdrum enough, much as he despises their moments of nonsensicality. 'In *Les Vacances de Monsieur Hulot*, why do the holiday-makers treat a holiday as a job? They aren't very gay. They don't like stopping working. The financiers in the sand go on talking about finance. The dishy girls are breaking their necks not to look like other dishy girls. Monsieur Hulot is from another universe. He won't plan things. This causes chaos when he plays tennis, of course.'

In *Mon Oncle* Monsieur Hulot is his nephew's co-conspirator in liking the old quarter of the city better than the scrubbed, gadgety new one: a taste that, in the child, amounts to mutiny. Hulot is a good friend. He is the child's safety valve. He is concerned about him because the boy's mother sees the greatest fruit of a good upbringing in respect for Monsieur Arpel's car. She lives a life in which gadgets, not the frail human race, need doctors and nannies. Tati's Hulot, by bringing the child into the disruptive old part of the city and by even managing to play an interesting kind of havoc with the gadgetry of the new, uniquely becomes an adult signpost into a world of fun.

'I should like to make films that are not lowering to the spirit. A new building can be very harrowing. I should like to give people a chance to whistle.' Tati himself whistles a lot. His own tunes. He believes that transistor radios stop people making up their own tunes, just as portentous décor does. 'I mean décor that is self-important. That was the reason I wrote *Playtime*, which is maybe the smallest picture in 70mm ever made.' His film is a salute to decorous characters raised to the rare level of non-conformists.

We were in Paris when there was a garbage strike. He was on the side of the strikers, as one would expect, though not so silly as to ignore the complexity of the economic issues. 'People are okay. They take time. That's what I like.' He glared at a lorry full of the military who had come in as strike-breakers and then spread his hands, looking at the pile of mess outside every house and shop. 'What's that?' I said, walking over to a heap of what seemed to be ticker-tape or blank film-strips. 'Telex,' he said, picking up a metre or two of it and pretending to read, shaking with laughter. 'All those important messages. Gold is up! Gold is down! Buy into aluminium! I expect the office boy threw it away before the vice-president had had a chance to read it. What a scandal!' He stirred the heap as if it were an enormous plate of noodles. Children gathered, watching solemnly, and then started to bounce in the tape as if it were a feather-bed. 'You see, they are like engaged couples trying out a mattress, only they are having more fun than if you were a bed-salesman protecting the springs.'

He called his film *Playtime* even in France, not only because he has a genuine political feeling for universality, but also because he savours the intrusion of Anglicisms that the Académie tries to stave off at the barbed-wire gate. 'People live in "buildings",' he said thoughtfully in Paris, looking round at the city. 'We eat "sandwiches" or "self-serve", or we park at "parking". I hope that the word "playtime" will give a new day to the French language. I thought of calling the film *Recréation*, but then I thought of the housewives shopping at the "super-market". There's a magazine called *Twenty* and a brand of drinks called "Verigoud".' He denies vivaciously that the film is an attack on modern architecture. 'It is a comedy about our time. No one important notices that things have changed. For instance, dogs and children don't. Dogs are very natural. For dogs in New York, it is still the old New York.

'About grown-ups, I would like to make a film called *Confusion*. It would take place in the new tunnel in the Concorde and it would be about tourists and a guide. Every time the guide says "There is so and so" the tourist bus goes down another tunnel before the passengers see anything except the walls of the new tunnel. The idea of the film is that a lot of clever grown-ups don't know what they are doing.'

The clowns in *Parade* represent anyone who is so insulated that he doesn't know what he is doing. Parents with no taste for the absurd and spirited, for instance. Tati made the film for television in 1973. It is a semi-documentary of the circus, with an enchanting epilogue about small children and balloons, about a rose being painted behind the scenery, about painters juggling paint brushes, about *haute école* (played by Tati as rider and horse), about audience and cast behaving as one, about a member of the orchestra sitting on someone else's coat-tails, about a joyously broken radio. The film gives you Tati's characteristic feeling that there is no age limit, high or low, for being possessed with the genius for rightness of rhythm and sense of creativity. It is also full of Tati's particular way of imparting an infant bliss about being in on things going wrong during a public spectacle. 'For the first time, the audience itself is in an arena watching a circus. The glass is broken. People talk . . . I am happy if people talk in a cinema. I am happy if a little boy asks a question of his father.'

Tati knows what cheers people up, what depresses them. The airport lounge in *Playtime* is like a crypt. The small asides of natural chaos buoy them up. They grasp at straws, as they do in the scene in the nitery-eatery so grandly called a nightclub. Catastrophe on this scale has always saved the day in film comedy, but never more beautifully. At the end of *Playtime*, the modern lights at the approaches to Orly Airport bend as gracefully and as wistfully as a girl tourist's memento flowers given to her by Hulot. Tati has an acute aesthetic sense. The bilious green neon of the drugstores in *Playtime* makes Hulot think he is going to be sick. By the spell of connections, Tati growingly makes his films both a political comment on the way life is going and also a bow to a planet that has inspired moments of circus.

Tati's ideals for life obviously come from more than music hall, but they still stem from it. He talked to me about his heroes, about jugglers, comic acrobats, comic family scenes, and most of all about Keaton. 'Music hall is one of the reasons why I like to shoot from far away. On the legs, Keaton for me is Number One. You could have a soundtrack through the means of his legs. A dialogue. Interrogation. Then decision.

Finally fear. Chaplin, on the other hand, has been very clever all the time. He's a great comedian. He creates very good situations, but they are a little too much for me. Too much is done on purpose. He says too clearly, "I'm a poor man. I'm cold. I'm hungry."

'When Chaplin made *The Gold Rush*, people could actually go off into the mountains to look for gold. Now they go winter-sporting. Chaplin's boots and bowler would be unfortunately out of place in the snow . . . Not that I don't like the new times, as I said. I'm saying nothing against the marvellous new sunny schools for children. I'm only trying to bring a little humour to – say – Orly Airport. People would have liked me to continue with Hulot in the old way, of course: *Hulot Goes Skiing*, *Hulot at St Tropez* . . . And if I had, I'd have all the money I need and my wife and children would be living in a castle. If I had continued to make small-budget successes in black-and-white, everyone would be happy.' *Playtime* is made in a size that gives a doubled physical dimension to comedy, entirely characteristic of Tati. Whole vistas can be seen. People can choose.

'So far as actors are concerned,' said Tati himself, acting in an American hotel while he was waiting for a call to come through, leaning against a fake Louis Quinze wallpaper, stroking it as if it were mink, and carefully putting straight a dreadful expensive example of sub-Dufy hotel art, 'I like to use real professionals. Professionals at their particular job in the film, that is to say. To show a piece of meat being properly cut at its best, call in a butcher. For *Playtime*, the producers offered me a big budget on décor or Sophia Loren. I chose the décor. Not that I have anything against Sophia Loren, you understand. A beautiful woman, very nice.' He walked like Sophia Loren, and agreed that she is also a born comedienne, even about her own beauty. 'But I dislike star names. In *Les Vacances de Monsieur Hulot*, if I'd put a star into one of the beach huts it would only have made people wonder why the star was on holiday at the same time as Monsieur Hulot.

'People complain that I have made only five or six features, but that is quite a lot if you have a family life, and holidays, and promotion [face], and telephone calls [face], and so on, isn't it? It's perhaps a good thing that *Playtime* didn't make much money because I am always in the position of a new director. I feel young inside, so I feel like a student when I start a new picture. I am not making money for banks, not killing myself for a mortgage repayment; I make films.' Perhaps this is why he is the greatest film comedian since Keaton and the greatest French comedian since Max Linder. He thinks always of audiences. 'That's one of the reasons I don't like to shoot in close-up,' he says. 'I have no right to bang anyone's nose against the screen. I would like to give them an alternative. Something else to watch. In life outside, when people are told that they have to live in such and such a region to go to the factory to get to work, they have no alternative and get sad.

'About influences. Ah, well, it is probably better for audiences to judge whom someone they are watching has admired. For me, I think, Kubrick is now the Number One technically. W. C. Fields makes me laugh and now, for comedy, Woody Allen.' He was speaking to me in the lunch-break at an American school seminar. Watching some smaller children confused by film-buff talk, he suddenly swung into a swift imitation of the way a highly bred Englishman may insist on speaking French when he doesn't know it. The imitation was perfect. 'The man will know three or four very important words and he will get them into a sentence whatever you yourself are trying to talk about.

'I began with a copy of old slapstick. Mistake,' he said to me later, ignoring his own genius for slapstick. 'Then I thought I should find a new sort of visual comedy. Not made by the ordinary kind of technicians, you see. They are like civil servants. It is not their fault. It is the fault of the studios and the backers. Left to themselves, all people are creative. You will get a certain genius from the men in the sound lorries, a certain genius in a moustache from the wardrobe, etcetera, etcetera. It's a big building, the *cinéma comique*. Everyone has brought his stone. If people wonder why I made *Playtime* in 70mm, which is generally for super productions of cavalry charges or undressed stars: well, the comic effect is the change of dimension. The comedy of observation is supported by stereophonic sound which adds to "le gag visuel", "le gag sonore".

'What I've tried to do since *Jour de fête* and ever since the first short I made with René Clément has been to give the comic personality more truth. There was a school of bearing that said silently to the public, "I am the amazing star of the evening. I can do a terrific number of things. I can juggle, I can dance, I'm a great man, I'm a gag man." That was the old school of the circus and the music hall, the one I came from. What I've been trying to show is that the whole world is funny. There's no need to be a comic to make a gag.'

Tati brings back to outscaled man his own measurement. He puts décor in its place and shows that the absurd lies not in the film universe but in the consciousness of the spectator. His gags are never one-liners detached from character, how ever much the characters are detached from one another. The tail of each gag follows the original burst of light, like a comet.

Tati likes asking us to look for signs of people half-obscured by the housing we covet. There are beautiful gradual upward views of Tati's house in *Mon Oncle* that show through windows scraps of inhabitants about their business: all doing things as interesting as the people glimpsed unknown in their apartments in Hitchcock's great *Rear Window*. One sees in *Mon Oncle* fragments of Hulot – his hat, his umbrella, his legs, his ankles – as he goes up the flights of staircases. In *Playtime* there is a vision of the bottom third of a man's legs twiddling around adroitly behind what must be a flight map, moving like a skater on what would seem to be an invisible chair on very oiled ball bearings; the man glides from one position to another, swivelling his ankles. There is a matching style of interrupted composition, off-the-topic and elegantly curious, in the shot of the car crash in *Traffic* when a woman who has nothing to do with the car crash is seen in long-shot doing her exercises.

At lunch with Tati in a neighbourhood bistro, I grew fascinated by the continuing brief sights of a man through constantly opening swing-doors leading to a telephone, or maybe to a cloakroom. The fugitive glimpses showed him helplessly dabbing at a spot of food on his jacket. The on–off glimpsed concentration had a lot of Tati's editing style. He notices everything, except himself, whom he treats with an offhand humour that is the reverse of the analysts' dictum about the rectitude of having a healthy ego.

Tati works with an eye that is both resigned and regenerative, and his film-making technique reflects it. His methods are painstaking and entirely his own. *Playtime* often looks as if it was shot all on location, at Orly and in modern offices, but Tati chose to use a studio. The real steel walls first intended for the film, for instance, were not as cold as he wanted them to be when built, especially when a character in a red hat passed by and made a red reflection: so Tati had them carefully re-built out of non-reflecting steel-like paper. There is another device in *Playtime*, not pressed home, when three identical-looking fashion model kinds of women are standing in front of a plate-glass window in motionless elegance. Tati is saying something quite political here about the standard ization of smart modernity. But only one of the women is real: the other two are photographer paper dummies in the same clothes. It takes a quick eye to tell the wittily small difference.

The designer of *Playtime* was Eugène Roman, who built the enormous sets at Joinville where nearly all of the film was made. Tati seems almost as sad to see the sets disused and dismantled as he was to think of the withering away of the imperial city of Fatehpur Sikri, the ancient grandiloquent Muslim Indian city that was evacuated after a generation. 'Why did the Emperor leave such a place?' asked Tati, looking at the draughtsboard sketch I had drawn of Fatehpur Sikri to show him the plan of the harem quarters where the sumptuous royal wives played a sort of human draughts on squares of red sandstone. 'Because there was no water. The architect had made a mistake. So the games died out,' I said. 'Ah,' he said, 'people must have these things.'

Tati had friends in every shop in Paris, at every street corner:

bistros, butchers, florists, even policemen. His habits are reflected in the sense of companionship that his films have. He liked describing cinematically the idiosyncrasies of people. Any people. 'I want to show who's who. Not like the book called *Who's Who*. That says what school you went to, what club you belong to. I want to show who's who in other ways. What's what. Then I have a chance to look at the big businessman opposite me behind his enormous desk and his telephones, you know [tie-straightening gesture, buzzing gesture, leaning-back-in-expensive-chair gesture], and to let audiences say for themselves, "Well, maybe you're not so important." That's one of the things I like about young people. They like to show what it is to be dressed or undressed. It is a good exercise to say to yourself, "What would those big businessmen be like nude?" When I see them travelling, I see them suffering for their expensive leather luggage. The conveyor belts throwing their cases as if they were hurling baskets of fruit at the fruit market. Except, of course, that actual men at the fruit market are more careful. I believe I like the secondary characters in a film best. They breathe the truth.'

'I suppose it was all those years in music hall that made me realize actors like to have their legs showing. To cut off an actor's legs is like cutting off a swan's neck.' I remember again Buster Keaton's telling me that, when he was doing a leap across the stage, he treated his head as the rudder and his legs as the wind that filled the sails. Tati nodded, asked more, and spoke of Keaton's technical care. 'I am trying to do something that I hope he would have liked with his knotty problem of sound-tracks in comedy. For instance, when people are in strange surroundings, natural sounds always sound louder. He would have understood that.' You can practically hear the creaking rigging in Keaton's great silent film *The Navigator*, about an engaged couple marooned on an otherwise uninhabited and unmanned liner. For Tati, much interest lies in the magnification of the sound of zips, of bells, of electronic devices to open doors, of strangers uneasily shuffling chairs in a waiting room where the chair cushions rise like yeasty bread.

Voices and tantrums drown in gadgets. A universally courteous and universally dopey advisor at a trade fair speaks in four or five unintelligible languages. What difference does the particular language make? Drowned by the noise of over-stuffed cushions when people are nimbly waiting, they are all the same. Remarks made in the human tongue ascend and disappear; the loudest human sounds in his films are ones like the child's hiccups after his devastating overhaul by soap (*Mon Oncle*); or *Playtime*'s unintelligible kitchen row about an omelette in which the words are overshadowed by the banging of swing-doors; or the ritual squawks of *Playtime*'s restaurant guests making vacuous conversation that recedes in importance compared to the din of the *maître d'hôtel*'s turning of his giant pepper mill. Sometimes one catches people being abruptly audible because they are speaking in chat: a woman tourist's 'I didn't know they had a parking problem in Paris'; another tourist's 'My feet are killing me.' On the whole, though, in Tati's films, mechanisms designed for mortal comfort overrule the comfort of being able to mutter and be heard. His camera tends to follow the sounds of these mechanisms rather than do anything so hallowed in conventional sound picture-making as to show the source of dialogue-lines. Tati's camera shows people's heads turning to follow sound. We see bafflement and loneliness in them. What was the whistle? Was that buzz for me? Who is there to interpret it for me? Do I get up, sit down, pretend to enjoy myself, pretend that this noisy dress is comfortable, pretend that this din called an upholstered chair is anywhere to sit in peace?

To Tati, I suspect that all human speech composed of fake politeness, excuses, obsequiousness is genuinely unintelligible. It is the language of a modern Ice Age, no louder or more comprehensible than the squeaks of a computer at work, and he therefore makes it defer on his own beautifully composed soundtracks to his occasional interpolation of some ordinary domestic remark.

Tati said, 'I have spent a fortune to have magnetic sound. No distributor wants it. But optical is out. I am not speaking about making a Chevrolet. That I can't do. But a man less happy than I am takes a salary. He is in charge of Sony, say. He is very important, but he is not allowed to have a small idea. He says, for instance, paint the lift blue. There is immediately a conference. If you want to have an idea, a better idea, it is not permitted.'

The self-important silent imperatives of modern city living – **Push/Pull** on supermarket doors, **Walk/Don't Walk** on traffic lights – distress Tati on the part of humankind. But with any luck, he hopes, we will find them at least amusing, as he does. For Tati, to be able to laugh is like being able to hum. 'When I am directing actors,' he says, 'I try to have a tune in my head for them because it is difficult to be funny without music. In music hall, as you know, we always had a rhythm.' I told him that both Chaplin and Keaton, when they were making their silent films, had found it an immense help to the actors and themselves to have the regular cranking noise of the camera running. He didn't know about that. 'Music hall is difficult without music because it is like dance,' he said, and thought about it, lying on his elbow in a hotel room where a waiter had just brought us tea-time coffee that turned out, to Tati's delight, to be unadulterated hot water (poured out with a flourish) because the wrong urn-tap must have been pushed somewhere. The same thing had happened to us once before. Tati was interested that in neither case – which happened to have been in different countries: America and France – had the waiter hesitated to hang around for a tip. When he had gone, Tati said, 'You see, if he had actually been the man who had made the coffee and poured it into the urn he would have been proud of it and he would have been humiliated to have made even a bad cup of coffee, let alone water.'

He thought and laughed to himself. 'It is this question of departmentalization. It has a lot to do with films. Many actors are interested in lighting, for instance, or scenery, or music, but they can't get near the electrical equipment, or the scene painters' rooms, or the orchestra, or even the microphones or the sound crew's ears, because of the unions. About editing, which intelligent actors know to be important, there is something I have noticed: that the more you cut a film, the longer it seems. When you are not interested, a quarter of an hour passes very slowly. When you are interested, half an hour passes very quickly. I mean, interested in details.'

Detail is the thing that most interests Tati, which is true of almost every artist, in film, acting, writing, painting, or anything else, including the playing of games by children. 'Anyway,' said Tati, 'it is because of this phenomenon of cut-down films seeming endless that *Playtime* is 2 hours 20 minutes. Any shorter, it would have seemed very long. Any longer, of course, I have to say to you [conspiratorial voice], there is the grave danger that it would have seemed too, er, how shall we say? [yawning critic's voice, fingers typing after thought] very, very long. Ah. *Le mot juste. Un peu trop longue.* [Mime with dialogue of over-extended critical mind concentrating on one testy point.] *C'est mieux qu'il y a des longueurs? Eh bien. Maintenant un petit café pour penser. Comment choisir, c'est une question. "Longue." "Longueurs".* I don't suppose critics are really like that, are they? It is only the way a bad actor would do it to get a laugh. Writers of fiction crumple up pieces of paper into the fire. I am not sure about critics, but I dare say that they are the same.' I said I wasn't sure about sociologists or acoustic experts or economists, but that I expected that they crumple up pieces of paper into the fire, too. I told him that some famous English intellectual had called economics 'the gloomy science'. Actors, we agreed, are less gloomy than most people, especially actors who are not stars. Tati gets on with them, loves casting, loves the time-consuming process of perfecting his soundtrack. He always post-synchs his scripts after he shoots, with a deliberately enormous proportion of doctored noises and post-synched scraps of dialogue to any simultaneously recorded 'natural' sound. This is how he gets his characteristic emphasis on the drowning sonic importance of clasps closing on briefcases and burring inter-office telephone contraptions.

He likes his films to be 'about everybody but also about

nobody big'. Before he started *Traffic*, Tati went to a highway and just sat watching. 'People going away for the weekend. Not a smile. A dog looked out of the back of one car, staring at a field where he could have run about.' Again this amused horror, as in *Les Vacances de Monsieur Hulot*, on behalf of people behaving as if play were a hard job. Something here about modern life is not true for them, but they don't know that. 'It is like television commercials. Everyone knows they are not honest but no one stops looking at them. The companies should at least have a quarter of an hour programme to show that the commercials are not to be taken as seriously as the advertisers would like them to be. Of course, this would be anarchy, wouldn't it? We wouldn't know what brand of toothpaste to buy.'

'You see,' said Tati, 'I think there is something wrong with what is made to seem important, who is made to seem important, and *vice versa*. In America there was some big reason why I had to ask to see the man who is practically in charge of painting in America. I will not tell you his name because that would not be nice and anyway it doesn't matter. He had dyed the colour of his hair to look younger. We had a coffee together in his office. Afterwards an old black man came into the office to clean the important man's shoes while we were talking. Then the important man said [impressive wave of the hand], "Clean the shoes of Monsieur Tati." So of course I say no. All I could say in a low voice was, "Would you give him a good tip and ask him not to clean my shoes?" The important man was very offended and I think the black man believed I thought he would wreck my shoes. So everything was wrong from the beginning because everything was about class. About dividing people. This is bad for the sense of humour, for one thing. For example, the first time I came to New York the taxi drivers had a very good sense of humour. Not so much now, and I believe it is because of the glass partition between the driver and the passenger, and because the driver is so frightened of not being paid before the passenger gets out that he locks the passengers' doors with his little gadget from the front. Now he can't be heard and all he does is yell at the other cars and shout at you about how hard he works and how his ulcer is.' This division between work and play is something that troubles Tati almost as much as the divisions of the class system. It worries him about the way things are going; about the world we are going to leave, if any, for our children to inhabit.

'All right, I bore you with another very little story. It is about something that might have come out of an African tribal day that I saw happening at a rehearsal. The cast, very tired, was told, "Finish the song. Finish the scenes. *D'accord?*" "*D'accord, d'accord,*" they begin to chant and clap, making up a song and dance of their own. The work turned into play because they were inventing it, you see?'

Tati worships invention and thinks that everyone is blessedly capable of it, given a little room to move. I was reminded of the benedictive ending of the chaotic nightclub scene in *Playtime*, when the switch from sedate nitery-eatery to boozy, noisy bistro has been completed in its surroundings of mangled tiles and fallen ceiling. The change has been made, people are having fun, the dawn comes up, a cock crows.

'About snobbery, it can take some very funny forms.' Tati's shoulders started to shake. 'I was in hospital. No, don't look like that.' He lowered his voice. 'Something very important, very masculine, you understand,' beating his breast. 'Well, I was waiting patiently under a sheet on a trolley in a corridor, and another trolley that seemed full of worry passed me. The nurses tell me that the patient has had one ball removed. The worry was not the pain, but his wife. She behaved as if the husband's balls were the bank and she was a banker. She had lost her investment, see. The stocks and shares had gone down. Poor man, in pain, and his value gone down to nothing. Or no, I tell you what she was also like. She was like a very important lady of noble rank playing golf, having to use a caddy who was no good. "I can't play with one ball," she said to the caddy, stamping her foot and throwing her club on to the grass. "I may lose it behind the bushes." This is not a nice story to tell you when you aren't a man, so we will lower our voices.

'The other night I was in a bar that had lost its licence so everything was liberated, quite different from the offended wife. Everyone had five drinks. The police came in very late and I think they were going to arrest the proprietor because they didn't believe he had been giving free drinks. Not until I told them, that is, because they could tell from the face that I put on that I was stingy [miser's face] and that I was telling the truth. So then the policemen started having free drinks too. By two in the morning everyone was so drunk they could hardly walk. It was very cheerful. The policemen offered to drive me home because they knew Monsieur Hulot. Drunk policemen driving . . .' Tati's shoulders began to shake again and he wiped his eyes on a dinner napkin and sipped a glass of wine with spinsterish lips. 'Well, we were not in the right *arrondissement* for my home. Policemen here – we were in Paris – are not allowed to cross into another *arrondissement*. But they were very brave. When they crossed over the line, which of course is invisible to us but very visible if you are a policeman, they took great care, being so drunk. They looked to right and left for another police car and then drove me home very fast with their hats off.' Tati had been miming all this. He must have been a joy to his children when they were small. 'I hope the cops got home safely,' he said. 'Of course, the question of the *arrondissements* is absurd, but the cops were very nice and this is a serious story.'

'You know what I should do, of course,' he said, walking about Paris one brilliant late winter afternoon. 'I should like to film a little the differences individuals can make. Because, you understand, in this super-mechanized organization, there will always be a lad who will be fortified with a minute screwdriver and break down an elegant automatic lift that has muzak playing in it as you go up to the thirty-second floor. In the meantime, the screwdriver is doing its work and the lad is whistling a tune of his own. There are two universes now, you see. That is what I am always trying to show.' In Tati's films, more and more, there is the universe that is stupid and standardized and cautious and depressed, and there is the one we would like to live in. It is apparently the same as the other – the same buildings, even – but it is born in the originating mind. It is not stupid, not standardized, but brave, more supple and light-hearted, with zig-zag roads, pavements without crowds paying no heed, sun on the table and time to waste. A gap of sensibility amounting to a moral abyss separates the two worlds, but Jacques Tati sees it as not unbridgeable. The bridge, of all that he designed, stands with his own strength in *Playtime*. It cost him personally about every franc he had, but what a bequest. This wonderful film is the apex of his attack on modern architecture and the way it ignores the scale of the human figure.

The 70mm ratio of the film serves to dignify human beings in surroundings whose size Tati mistrusts as much as he mistrusts fish platters, fish fountains, and rulers in the hands of professional measurers. Tati understood the size of us; there is never a flaw of misjudgment about mortal dimension in his work.

This Vital Sign Has A Malfunction

The unintentionally funny.

The Billy Graham streak that runs in mogul screen-entertainment has long been apt to ask one to step forward for something: for de Mille's Bible, or family life, or Doris Day, or the miracle work of psychiatrists. Some of the 'independent' pictures of the 1980s ask of audiences, or congregations, much the same witless evangelism as the old-time moguls' films that project on a giant scale the tenets of mawkish millionaire accountants. Agnosticism is a gift of comedy.

Some time ago, there was a spate in America of films about psychiatrically deranged people who were cured by holding hands: *David and Lisa* was one of them. Then there was another spate of films about the go-it-alone vigilante who cured the ills of big-city America single-handed. Now there is a run of Hollywood and Broadway comedies about the ineptness of a middle-class man domestically on his own, a notion of obligatory comedy that is presumably booted into life by hefty feminism. Men managing households, cooking, tending babies. Such comedies ask an effort of faith in the funniness of gender-reversal that is just as tough on the spirit as the pictures in which Louis B. Mayer indulged his feelings of the numinous about mothers. Greer Garson once said – I quote from memory, but this is close – that Mr Mayer didn't like art that tilted its mirrors downward toward the gutter and people's problems; he thought it should look upward toward better things. In MGM pictures, many of these things were mothers. Mr Mayer could have turned *The Bacchae* into *Mrs Miniver*.

What do the proselytizers of expense-account comedy want us to believe in now? Still in mothers, of course. And in happy marriage. Also in happy divorce; in the salvationist possibilities of doctors and surgeons, never shown to be scared out of their minds by malpractice suits and thinking self-protectively, as the present system forces them to in America. To counteract this unfortunate reflection of capitalist reality, we are also handed out fables of democracy. Such comic feats, adept in social acrobatics, show us the triumph of the shy at kinds of work that actually deal in push; and the impact that one man can have on conglomerates far beyond the influence of isolated decency. This conviction of the power of the individual, an original Constitutional clause recycled to serve bigotry organizations, gives driving power to a lot of capitalism's popular comic forms. To vigilante rah-rah farces. To man-as-housewife prevailing over nappies, which quickly dwindles into the Jerry Lewis comedy of dither.

* * *

There are some things that perhaps no one but a genius should ever include in an 'experimental' movie. They include:

all tense duologues in which one can see only the actors' shoulder-blades while they trudge along in a mood;
all scenes in which the characters talk back-to-back throughout;
all long-shots of corridors showing a girl running down them photographed from the back throughout;
all urgent close-ups of dripping taps, windscreen-wipers, and feet.

In theatre and film, as in cartoons, some things seem to have intrinsic funniness. The great, late Charles Addams agreed at once about monks' sandals, and even more so about showbiz's use of nuns. We touched on the topic over a newsstand and, over a number of meetings snatched from picking up our entirely respective dry-cleaning and shoe repairing, discussed the matter at length. Obviously Hitchcock, in the straight-faced shot of a spy in a nun's habit but with high-heeled shoes in *The Lady Vanishes*, concurred about nuns' tangles with fashion.

An ex-nun years ago wrote a bestseller called *I Leap Over the Wall*. The Rodgers and Hammerstein musical, *The Sound of Music*, which concerns a postulant who commutes between a fairly chirpy life in a convent and a profane career as a governess, is enough to suggest climbing up the wall. One can take it, I think, that this was the most awful musical we had seen since the war; it made the nadir touched by a Swiss thing called *Oh! My Papa!* look like a zenith. There is a good deal in *The Sound of Music* that suggests Ivor Novello. Some of this resemblance, of course, can be traced to the presence of that endearing pillar of Novello's works, Olive Gilbert. During any of the many sluggish tracts of the action, people could wonder what Olive Gilbert looks like in mini-skirt-length, a thought one doesn't ordinarily have about Church servers. In Novello's days we habitually saw her in evening gowns; in *The Sound of Music*, cast as Mistress of Postulants, she wears a nun's habit. For the moment, nuns and lady cellists are the only major groups I can think of that remain open to actresses who prefer formal dress on stage. In these slapdash days the number of theatrical excuses for full fig are shrinking fast.

There is something distinctly Novello-ish, too, about Oscar Hammerstein's lyrics. One can gauge their sentiments from a few of the titles: 'Do-Re-Mi', 'The Lonely Goatherd', 'My Favourite Things', and 'Climb Ev'ry Mountain'. 'Climb Ev'ry Mountain' was first boomed in London at full blast by the proud-bosomed Mother Abbess as played by Constance Shacklock: 'Climb ev'ry mountain, Ford ev'ry stream, Follow ev'ry rainbow, Till you find your dream.' At the end of the hortatory ode, as the curtain slowly fell and the audience quickly forded, the young postulant-heroine reverently took off her little religious hat and saluted. Not a deity, it seemed; perhaps one of the choices listed in the song 'These are a few of my favourite things'. Rhyme makes two of these favourites brown paper and string.

In *Two Mules for Sister Sara*, with Shirley MacLaine as a particularly sporting nun, Clint Eastwood, as a Texan, saves her in the nick of time from triple rape in Mexico, and only discovers that she is a nun when she puts her clothes on. She leaps up a tree in her black habit to escape from a possible lion, dazzles hostile Indians with the sun's reflection from her upheld crucifix, clambers up a railway bridge to plant a bundle of dynamite, and rather maddens Clint by her habit of wasting water in the desert by blessing things. She looks perfectly gorgeous, and she deals wonderfully with the moment when Clint has been wounded in the chest by an arrow. Throughout the picture, the man's frustration is frightful. 'I sure would have liked to have met up with you before you took up with them clothes and them vows,' he says as they trudge. In the end – and I don't think this is to give anything away, because her language has been quite demotic for a nun – she turns out to be a whore, thus resolving the romantic interest without sacrilege and relieving Clint no end.

And irreversibly funny in what are named, by some, the antic arts: lady cellists, as suggested. The absurdity may have something to do with the manliness needed in playing the instrument while wearing the sort of evening clothes that are called 'dressy'. There is a costume problem here. A woman in a long skirt has to attack the cello between her legs and attend to musicality. There would be a solution in Cherubino breeches.

In the other corner to lady cellists, and well matched in import: Hollywood male stars attempting to play diplomats. There was an outstanding example in a film called *The Omen*. Gregory Peck, called Mr Thorn, looking better-dressed and sounding more sonorous than ever, surprises Lee Remick (playing his wife) by telling her that she is talking to the future

'Ambassador to the Court of St James's.' In case anyone doesn't know what this is, he adds that she is talking to the 'Ambassador to Great Britain'. Earlier they had a stillborn child. The future Ambassador to the Court of St James's, looking as officially concerned as if a Communist film had crept into the Academy Awards ceremony, is told that there is another baby available, just born, whose mother has died and who has no other relatives. A sultry priest lurks. The orphan baby is offered. He is the child of Satan. The Ambassador to the Court of St James's has more than enough evidence to make him suspicious, and you'd think he would astutely object, but motherhood wins. Mrs Thorn happily cuddles the child, who she thinks is her own.

The origin of the film is a poem said to be based on the Book of Revelation:

> When the Jews return to Zion, and
> A comet rips the sky;
> And the Holy Roman Empire rises,
> Then you and I must die.
>
> From the eternal sea he rises,
> Creating armies on either shore;
> Turning man against his brother,
> 'Til man exists no more.

The poet seems to be in a muddle about the Roman Empire and the Holy Roman Empire. However. A batty nurse (Billie Whitelaw) arrives 'from the agency' to replace a suicide. The Ambassador's country place is virtually taken over by a dog who obviously gets his meat from Satan. The baby grows into a grinning ally of the dog and the nurse. His Excellency, in serious lack of his wits, goes on a dangerous expedition in Italy with a blanch-faced English photographer (David Warner) who has developed some warning photographs revealing Satan's rod reaching down to several people who are soon to depart this world in variously horrid ways. His Excellency, who has demonstrated himself to be remarkably incompetent at conducting diplomacy, climbing gates, raising tombstones, fighting off dogs, and informing Scotland Yard what he is up to, distinguishes himself by swallowing whole the photographer's remark that 'As for the rise of the Roman Empire, scholars think that could well be interpreted as the formation of the Common Market.'

And all films about geniuses. As the preface to this, I have to say that in India I gladly received, by rowing boat, an unsolicited, carefully-typed script of an unstaged drama about the harvest. It was to run six hours, more or less. At about five hours, there was the plain nicest stage direction I have ever read. An outburst of the unproduced playwright's stout hope in his genius. The direction read: 'The audience spontaneously stands up and applauds.'

* * *

Films, especially dreadful ones, are dead keen on geniuses, or geniae, though geniae, apart from Mme Curie, come in for little attention unless they have had a love life that allows for the casting of big male stars. There was a Herbert Wilcox movie about Nurse Cavell, with Anna Neagle (singing 'Abide with Me'), who was earlier said to have looked thoroughly well brought up as Queen Victoria, and who certainly looked just as well brought up as Nurse Cavell. I can imagine a film in the geniae lineage about George Sand (though not about George Eliot, until women's liberation insisted that G. H. Lewes was perfectly happy playing second fiddle; and certainly not one about Jane Austen). The greatest genius of all in the eyes of the movie industry appears to be Jesus, if the number of films in the genre is anything to go by. One of the more rotten was Nicholas Ray's *King of Kings*, which was so like a musical that when someone in the multitude said piously 'Give us a sign,' I misheard him and thought Christ was being asked 'Give us a song.' And there was, by the director's mortified admission, John Huston's *Moulin Rouge*, about Toulouse-Lautrec, in which someone identified the carefully crawling José Ferrer – being saddled with playing a genius on his knees – by saying cheerfully at the door, 'So long, Toulouse.' And *The Agony and the Ecstasy*, about Michelangelo, when Michelangelo was taking a snooze in the Sistine Chapel and his outraged countess, with the full flurry of a woman in love, said tartly, 'Michelangelo, are you or are you not going to finish that ceiling?'

What is it about music which leads popular film-makers to produce such drivel about composers? Handel, Mozart, Beethoven, Schubert, Berlioz, Chopin, Schumann, Liszt, Wagner, Johann Strauss II, Brahms, Tchaikovsky, Rimsky-Korsakov, Victor Herbert, Sigmund Romberg, George Gershwin, Irving Berlin, Cole Porter: it has always been the same. There was an Austrian film about Beethoven in which Schubert's stepmother came to him and said distractedly, 'Ludwig, I'm very worried about Franz. He can't finish his symphony.' 'What?' said the growingly deaf Beethoven, hand to ear.

Apart from his handsome, scornful nose and the way his hair springs off his forehead, Carl Boehm in *The Magnificent Rebel* is not recognizably like the real Beethoven. On the other hand he is the spitting image of every other composer that there has ever been in the movies. He has all the traits that this sort of film traditionally uses to indicate artistic genius: he is rude to waiters, he stalks about with his hands behind his back growling at the pavement, and he sleeps late in the mornings.

One of the cinema's most treasured legends about artists is that their masterpieces are directly and instantly inspired by real incidents. In this Beethoven film the young Ludwig refuses to talk to the landlord, who is knocking on the door for the rent, because he is already furiously writing the knocks into the Fifth Symphony. 'Come in or go away,' he bawls, 'but quit that knocking.'

The dialogue is studded with abrupt colloquialisms like this. Beethoven is 'married to a demanding, lovely creature – music'. Out in the woods while the birds are singing, the lovely creature hits him over the head and he sits down under a tree to write a few more great themes. Just as he needs a strong one, the weather breaks, but he goes on writing implacably in the downpour while the raindrops spatter on to his manuscript paper. So we have the Pastoral. When the Countess Giulini is sitting with Beethoven at a café table the orchestra plays a vamped-up version of the Moonlight Sonata in homage: as she appreciatively yells into his ear, 'one of your loveliest'.

And writers as geniuses. Youngblood Hawke, an American farm lad besocked in mud and writing like fury, gives us the primal connection to soil that lends authenticity to art.

Youngblood isn't a Westerner. The film is the first to bring the atmosphere of the prairies into the life of the intellect, with Dmitri Tiomkin gallop-themes going on in carpeted offices and novels being pumped out to chase-music. Youngblood is a coal-truck driver in Kentucky. Between trucking he writes four or five thousand words a night, and after shipping off a caseful to a New York publisher he gets a call to fly East. The plane goes past a breathless close-up of the figure of the Statue of Liberty, whose dignity collapses in the context so that she looks oddly like the lady who stands around with a torch at the beginning of Columbia films; then the hero lands in New York to the sound of 'Yankee Doodle Dandy' and 'Adeste Fideles', with the orchestra crashing out the *dominum* beat as he steps up to his publisher.

The suitcaseful of words turns out to be a best-seller, after a bit of work on it in a garret with a girl. In Hollywood films novels are never written in the usual way because there is no love interest between a man and a desk. Youngblood has the help of a piece of love-interest who is called his stylist. She is the nice girl in the picture: that is to say, the one he doesn't make a pass at and whom he marries in the end. The bad girl, the Awful Warning character, is a married woman who bewitches him with a life of white carpets and a critic friend of hers in evening dress who keeps making speeches about literature at parties. 'All I want is a good story told in an unaffected way.'

By then Youngblood's book has been a best-seller for what a TV interviewer in the film calls 'Lo these many months'. But success begins to spoil his art. Underneath Youngblood's pseudonym he happens to be called Arthur, so when people say Art, or art, he and it become mystically one. I thought the

Awful Warning character was going to have to pay for shacking up with him by becoming a cripple, which is what usually happens to Hollywood mistresses, but the one who goes is actually her son, or what she biblically calls her first-born. He *hangs* himself, because he has heard the people in the next room talking about his mother as 'Youngblood's harlot'.

The style of the dialogue is ornate and unafraid, a flamboyant mixture of Beverly Hills Teutonic and the Book of Ruth. Mary Astor has a fine part as a famous millionaire actress who invites Youngblood down to her considerable little place in the country because she wants to turn his book into a play, sprinting around the swimming pool in evening dress in broad daylight and asking if she's violating his intentions.

* * *

The Swarm must be the most costly B picture ever made. It also happens to be a bee picture. A picture about bees. We have had mouse pictures and pony pictures and dog pictures, and even rat pictures. This is a long and colossal disaster picture about African killer bees, which are said to secrete a toxin even more virulent than the toxin of some Australian jellyfish, and that is apparently very virulent. In some heavily computerized time these African killer bees arrive in swarms to attack America. They cause death by the hundred and then by the thousand. The manner of death is to fall in slow motion. In fact, everything in the film happens very, very slowly. The actors speak with desperate deliberateness, often stabbing the air with their index fingers, and often redundantly using one another's names or titles ('General', 'But, Doctor', 'Paul, Paul') to spin things out even though people are as often saying that 'every minute now is precious' (Michael Caine) or that 'we've got to move fast' (Henry Fonda). You will see from the cast that this is no ordinary bee picture. It also stars Olivia de Havilland as a gracious schoolmistress with enough lacquer on her hair to kill any normal insect. And Fred MacMurray as a suitor for her hand, Ben Johnson as another suitor for her hand, Katharine Ross as a doctor in love with Michael Caine (she sees the image of a bee in one of his eyeballs when she has been stung), José Ferrer as another doctor, Richard Chamberlain as still another doctor, and Richard Widmark as a terrifically bemedalled general whose reactions, like everyone else's, seem to be dangerously retarded for somebody in an emergency. No effort, no star has been spared. The key parts are Michael Caine's as Brad Crane, a farsighted entomologist who has always feared something like this, and Henry Fonda's as Dr Krim, a world-famous immunologist in a wheelchair. After a struggle – getting in touch with the President of the United States and so on – Crane goes into action. He has never dreamed that bees would turn out to be the villains in the disaster he has been fretting about: 'They've always been our friends.' The villainous bees are unfortunately quite often referred to as just 'the Africans' ('We must kill those Africans'), and human characteristics are attributed to them. There is said to be a danger that the whole bang lot of them will return in revenge if they find that some of their fellows have been killed. But, in the main, these bees do not look like candidates for a disaster picture. They are not even disgusting, as a plague of toxic worms would be. Dr Krim refers to them as 'pesky little devils'. The whole atmosphere is really very mild. People are always saying 'your damn bees' or 'your damn poison pellets'. Dr Krim and Brad Crane know all about bees. When Katharine Ross and Michael Caine are for some reason in a freezer for shelter – a *freezer* – Michael Caine looks alertly at the thermometer and says, 'Forty degrees. We'll be all right for a while. Bees don't function well in temperatures under fifty.' There is a scene in an airtight experiment room in which eager scientists have bees all over their white protective clothing: such is the nature of the picture that the clusters of bees look as wasteful of money and as harmless as couture hand-embroidery of beads on an evening dress. The making of this film, which involved, it is calculated, twenty-two million bees, also involved the credited aid of the Department of Defense, the

United States Air Force, and two 'bee technical advisors'. In its own way, this is considerable political satire.

Patient Ulcer

The great comedians of rage are introverts who hardly move a muscle. Like John Cleese, the English actor who looks like a Grenadier Guard, they may be a mass of involuntary and non-mankindlike tics, giving you no sense of any ordinary motor-function sending out legible messages from the brain. Or, like W. C. Fields, they may appear barely to move, except toward a full glass. But they share a sulphurous indifference to the world at large, a planet that does obviously strike them as being 'at large' in the policeman's sense. So they roam the cosmos that kicks up such mayhem while they keep irritably sane behind their own front doors.

'Do the silly walk,' passers-by shout to John Cleese. He stands six feet five and sits like a collapsible ruler in, indeed, collapse. The right-angled walk he resorts to instinctively in some of his best-loved performances raises his legs at ninety degrees to the pelvis and ignores the knee joints. Cleese first did the silly walk in a 1970 episode of *Monty Python's Flying Circus* – the legendary show that he created in 1969 with five of his friends – and by now the walk's onlie begetter is fed up to the teeth with people calling for a demonstration. Time has passed, and the *Monty Python* authors have gone on to other things. But the silly walk remains intact, thank heaven, in *Python* reruns and in *Fawlty Towers*, the recklessly splendid 1975 TV series with John Cleese and Prunella Scales at bay in a dreadful seaside-resort hotel that they are trying to run in Torquay.

Though Cleese gives short shrift to any request for a repeat performance of the famous gait, the instinctive muscular tendency seems to be unquenchable. In London in his 1850s house north of Hyde Park, I noticed that he will try to suppress the twitch of the amazing reflex by relaxing in any easy chair, say, with his legs over one of its arms, but as soon as there is some native domestic emergency, such as hunting for the coffee grinder in the fridge ('My wife, Barbara, is American, so she puts everything in the fridge: Hoover bags, sticking plaster'), his limbs stiffen and the silly walk does its damnedest to be activated in the resister's own terrain. When performed, the walk is the furious vault of a character pretending command over predicaments of his own making that exasperate and obsess him. Its inventor has thought a great deal about anger in the world: in public affairs, in his own life and work – and, indeed, in the decline of civilization as manifested by the state of public telephone booths. 'Someone telephonically knowledgeable and I had a bit of an argument about that. He said that telephone booths didn't work because they were vandalized. I said they were vandalized because they didn't work.'

When we emerged from the kitchen after the coffee-grinder search, Cleese's younger daughter, Camilla, three and three-quarters, was sitting down on the dining-room carpet to take off her red shoes and her white socks. The left sock went into the left shoe, the right sock into the right shoe, and the pair were set together ready for action under the dining-room dresser. John Cleese watched with a respect that, to go by her glances backward to him, she knew she could count on. His life – and not only where children are concerned – bears not the faintest resemblance to his writing, which has some of Molière's dramatic use of misanthropy. Basil Fawlty, along with most of Cleese's *Monty Python* fictions, is fuelled by rage, and Cleese has made of rage or tantrum another humour. It rules his figments' lives, stiffens their spines, unites them in the infuriated intentness that is a key attribute of Cleese's farce. Rage so personified makes Basil's eyes bulge, mesmerized, out of their deep sockets and brings to his face expressions of resolve which memorialize his endless efforts to impose his own sense of nutty order on the lounging disarray he sees about him. When Cleese shows us anger pure, it is not only funny but is also quietly saying that any passion unalloyed is a threat to have around. His fuming characters vividly illustrate the farcical constant of the fanatic in the grip of unmixed feeling, and also the farce of anyone locked in mortal battle with a problem that bothers no one else.

Anger is John Cleese's familiar. He struggled for years in private life with the middle-class embargo on expressing. 'Full permission to get repressed or heavily sarcastic. But to release anger, not on your life.' His ex-wife, Connie Booth, who plays Polly, the assistant manager and waitress in *Fawlty Towers*, collaborated both in the writing of the first episodes in this study of pent-up tantrum and in his private combat with anger. They divorced, but their lasting friendship led smoothly into professional collaboration on the post-divorce episodes of *Fawlty Towers*, as splendid in the study of rage as ever; the two writers know the territory. 'It's the people who try desperately to put a measured surface over secret anger seething away underneath who give you the sense of most violence,' Cleese says. 'The wonderful thing about a sense of humour is that the moment you laugh at obsessive behaviour you've got a bit of space to look at it and defuse it, if you'll forgive the military stuff. I'm also rather keen on anxiety.'

Open anger and hidden anxiety are natural collaborators in the tetchy characters invented by John Cleese. It is the exasperatingly barmy rest of the world that these characters treat as the abnormality. The existence of others takes toll. The effort to suffer hotel guests more or less gladly shows in the lines of determination round Cleese-as-Basil's jaw. He pauses and adds, 'Apart from my Basil Fawlty side, there's my bank-manager side. Urbane, courteous, kind . . .'

John Cleese was born in 1939, in Weston-super-Mare, in Somerset. 'Childhood was very low-key. Dad was forty-six and Mum was forty when I was born. Extremely little happened. I was an only child. Content and solitary, though never *lonely*.' I have never heard a man use emphasis as unemphatically as Cleese does.

'The Germans used to bomb Bristol, just up the Bristol Channel, and if they had any bombs left they dropped them on Weston. Inhabitants used to say, "Who says the Germans haven't got a sense of humour?" Apart from the leftover bombs, nothing violent has happened in Weston. Life there is, of course, entirely free of sex. Occasionally, people are born in Weston by parthenogenesis. Speaking for myself, I was a very slow developer sexually. I lost my virginity very late in life, at the Station Hotel in Auckland, New Zealand. I was in my mid-fifties. As to learning: well, there wasn't much inducement in Weston. It used to have a field-hockey festival, but that was stopped, as people were becoming too excited.'

The family name was Cheese until 1915, when his father amended it because he was going into the army. Cheese lingers in the son's mind. 'The nice thing about cheese is thinking of all those people all over the world doing different things to milk. You could do a sketch about it. "Try hitting the milk with a stick," someone would say. Then an argument. "No, don't hit it, go round and round in the milk with the stick and then see what happens. Don't give up. Something unpredictable might happen." ' And, in the Python film *The Life of Brian*, 'Blessed are the cheesemakers' is one of the Beatitudes heard by the chatty bunch straining to pick up the words from the next-door Mount. The mishearing gives rise to consternation, even though it is studiously explained as probably referring to all manufacturers of dairy produce.

The famous cheese-shop sketch may be the all-time favourite Python invention, though some dissenters will plump for the sketch about the parrot, sold as live but by any description plain dead. 'It's bleedin' demised! This is a late parrot! It's joined the Choir Invisible,' says John Cleese as a pet-shop customer wrangling with the shopkeeper, who argues that it is a Norwegian parrot merely pining for the fjords. Returning as he does to cheese, 'Well, the problem in this cheese shop is that the man says he has some cheese. I go through Wensleydale, Brie, the lot. "No, sir, the mice have got it . . . No, sir, it's not ripe . . . No, sir, it's coming in tomorrow." "Look," I say, "I asked you if you had any cheese. And you said you had. And if you were lying to me I'm going to shoot you," And I do. And I say, "What a senseless waste of human life," or whatever it is that religious leaders say on these occasions. Interesting, really. I wonder what would make a sensible waste of human life.'

I ask whether he has matching thoughts about 'needless violence', and he says 'Ha!' As much exclamation as a laugh: a hooting noise of accord.

Reginald Cheese had 'a marvellous sense of cliché', says the heir. 'He was an insurance salesman and the son of a solicitor's clerk, and the family hoped like anything I'd do something in the same line.' I can't think they were disappointed in the end: the bequeathed knowledge of the bureaucratic is actually very much present in the figures of the thwarted regimen that Cleese excels in writing and playing. His father's savouring of clichés expands into the son's passion for words: for euphemisms that no one uncloaks, for language's unheeded strangenesses. Cleese says that he learned how to silence cricket expertise by uttering the words 'With this cloud cover and a bit of a green top, the seamers should make it move around a bit for the first hour.' He goes on, 'I once wanted to do a character who spoke in clichés completely. "Uncharted waters." "Now, there's a pretty kettle of fish, or should I say a horse of a different colour?" ' He ponders. 'What do we all mean? Amazing, the way we don't listen to ourselves.'

A tireless listener to himself and to others, Cleese has a love affair with words not unlike P. G. Wodehouse's. He starts to list some that beguile him: 'Plummet. Lurk. Ululate. Berserk. Unhinged, as in deranged. Pique. Amok. Akimbo.' That leads him to the possibility of Legs Akimbo, identified as a famous Zulu courtesan.

The Monty Python lot was made up of John Cleese, Graham Chapman, Terry Gilliam, Eric Idle, Terry Jones, and Michael Palin. Their aide-de-camp in New York said that the way the members came together was in a fight over a banana in the BBC canteen.

'Ah, that's the seventh version,' Cleese says. 'There were already six, because there were six Pythons. It could be right about the banana, because we've always been keenly aware of the need for combat training against assault by fresh fruit.' There is a fine sketch in their first film, *And Now for Something Completely Different*, with Cleese as an edgy martinet teaching defence against homicidal attack by people armed with loganberries. Those shows grew into *Monty Python's Flying Circus* (1969–70). There followed, in 1975, a new chaos, called *Monty Python and the Holy Grail*: a loused-up version of the Grail tale, in which King Arthur's obnoxious public-school knights are, as Cleese says, 'extremely mercenary, violent, and untrustworthy – early Thatcherites, really'. One of the parts Cleese plays is an Anglophobic Frenchman who hurls at Arthur and his band some singular oaths. ('English kniggets! . . . You empty-headed animal-food-trough-wiper.') My favourite Python film remains *The Life of Brian* (1979), about a Nazareth naïf born in the stable next to Jesus's. One of the characters played by Cleese makes every effort to bring the spirit of school games to the religious punishings going on: 'Now, look, no one is to stone anyone until I blow this whistle. Is that clear?' Anger seethes under the schoolmasterly lid.

We are in the centre of a studio for his group's ventures now being built. Cleese gazes knowledgeably at the complicated geometry of the room's octagonal ceiling, which is a mirror image of the floor. By some technical miracle that he claims to understand, the room's architecture, although fairly small-scale – some twenty feet across – can achieve improbabilities of volume as astonishing as those in the whispering gallery of St Paul's Cathedral. In the centre sound is loud, and every strand of it distinct. Cleese illustrates by saying, 'Cardinal Richelieu died in 1642,' and then strides to one side to repeat himself at the same volume. The words now register as no more than a whisper. 'Very nice. Yes. The design cuts down the etherostochastic imbulations, you see.'

Back in the centre of the room, he is in forte voice again and says, 'When I saw *Beyond the Fringe*, I think I decided against depression for good. That extraordinary explosion of creativity. I was struck by the fact that there were four people all being equally funny, so twenty-five years later I set out to write four equally funny roles for *Wanda*. My part isn't as funny as the three others, but I'm hugely charming to make up for it.' Another room holds a computer keyboard that can produce a sneeze or a glug or any other sound at any pitch once it has been fed the original. Cleese asks some informed questions of a sound-man colleague and then switches back cheerfully to the topic of low spirits: 'Most people feel guilty about being depressed. I used to feel that if someone in the room was down, in a spirit of pure decency you had to be more down. Wrong.' He sometimes seems to swat at his own thoughts as if they were bees. Like the *Beyond the Fringe* quartet in their time, and the Beatles, the Python lot seem to be conjoined as some enviable band of brothers. Cleese makes running affectionate references to his Python siblings. He interrupts himself in some musings about the hazards of humour that tries to straddle the Atlantic, and says, 'Graham Chapman and the rest of us were touring with the Cambridge Footlights thing in New Zealand. He asked for an omelette, and said, "With three eggs." The waitress gave him an omelette with three fried eggs on the top of it. A lot of things go wrong in New Zealand. That's a xenophobic remark, isn't it? I did a sort of investigation about which country laughs at which, and I've come across only one that doesn't seem to make jokes about another, and that's Denmark. Why, I've no idea. Except that the smallest countries always seem to be the most international in outlook. If Danish people make jokes about stupidity – which is what xenophobic jokes always seem to be about – they make them about the people from Arhus. A Danish city. The French make their insult jokes about the Belgians. The Swedes do them about the Norwegians, and vice versa. The Portuguese do them about the Spanish. I discovered that the Upper Egyptians do them about the Lower Egyptians, and that's pretty deep-running bigotry, because it's been going for five thousand years.'

It amazes Cleese that the character Manuel in *Fawlty Towers* had drawn accusations of prejudice because of the portrayal of Manuel's Spanishness. An inept but willing man of all work with a hysteria tamped down to the calm of total fog, Manuel has a way of trudging doggedly through the foothills surrounding *haute cuisine*. He is a man with larger things on his mind than food presentation: his mother, for instance; health inspectors; the Cockney colleague who overrules him linguistically by making eel pie when what has been asked for is paella; the loss of his beloved rat Basil (a fickle creature sold to the doting Manuel as a Filigree Siberian hamster); and his longing to learn English well enough to understand the insults of the Basil Fawlty he serves with such dignified love in the hotel's continuum of crisis. 'Nitwit!' roars Basil. 'Whit is a witnit?' Manuel asks courageously. He draws off a lot of the pressure that builds up in his boss, who will readily pack Manuel under his arm at speed and use him as a battering ram against the swing-door into the kitchen. 'Dago bird-brain. God knows how they put the Armada together,' says Basil, milk-tooth chauvinist but no less magisterial. The protesters miss the fact that Basil is drawn as the clearest bigot, while his victim has a character of sweetly reliable pessimism against all odds of prejudice.

The character of Basil Fawlty, as of nearly all Cleese's obsessives, is rooted in a particular sort of English testiness made worse by its stabbing politeness. Cleese sees the type as 'the sort of man who says, "I'm awfully sorry, but I think you've mistaken me for someone who gives a damn." ' The type is not at all unt,rue to Basil Fawlty, a man of ranting protocol who overrides pleasure. 'Look! My wife *enjoys* herself. I *worry*!' he yells to his hotel in general. 'A fair summing-up,' Cleese says, 'of the way your average professional neurotic will see his marriage.'

Counteract Basil by thinking of the kind of gentle manners that can be elusive to outsiders in Oxbridge people: people among whom I include, and very much so, John Cleese and his friend Michael Frayn. Frayn wrote the feature film *Clockwise*. Cleese plays an English headmaster with punctuality on the brain and the accompanying characteristic of being consistently late. Frayn's wit and considerateness have a lot in common with John Cleese's. 'He's the sort of man who stands up if you're making him a cup of tea, because he doesn't want to take advantage of you,' Cleese says.

The lurking historian in John Cleese longs to write a history book starting from the year 893. 'A nice insignificant year,' he says. 'Nothing much going on, just people sitting around quietly. No one with sweeping ideas of how to put the world straight.' He is bothered by the self-righteousness of politicians. 'Humour's the God-given mechanism for spotting egotistical behaviour. Look at what we laugh at: greed, lust, rage, envy, self-righteousness. Show me a sitcom about St Francis of Assisi and I'll show you a turkey. Denis Norden' – one of the longest-loved TV wits in England, country of such people, a deft, pondering man tuned in to by a vast constituency – 'says the most important moment in world politics is the moment when someone at a conference gets a raspberry seed between his teeth. The moment of vital concession.'

A pause, of course. He bends down in his study, despite his painful back, to look carefully at some watercolours in his workroom. 'Democracy's a good idea, naturally. Doesn't work, but worth exploring. Like marriage.' He breaks his own silence again to say, with the passionate temperance that is peculiarly his, 'Standing in the middle of the road politically, I'd love to do a stinging satiric show on behalf of standing in the middle of the road politically. A really immoderate attack on immoderates by outstandingly moderate people.'

This extreme moderate is troubled by most organized religion, because of its excesses, but he says its failure obviously matters to people. 'I got interested in it after doing *The Life of Brian*. And there's something I did in a Python book. It's an interview with Vice-Pope Eric. He'd been elected on the same slate as Pope Paul, and he was asked about Christ's teaching and whether there was any conflict between that and the Catholic Church. He explained that if you are propagating a creed of poverty, humility, and tolerance you'd better have a very rich and powerful and authoritarian organization to do it. That seemed to me to catch absolutely the unanswerable paradox in organized religion.'

Cleese clears his throat and starts to talk about the Great Headmaster in the Sky. Schoolmasters loom in the mind of John Cleese. 'I was nervous about being a schoolmaster with a name like mine.'

'Cleese?'

'Cleese, yes.' Sigh. Some burdens can't be explained. The inability is a comic facet.

'But it turned out all right in the end.' A silent survey, leading to a change of angle in the mind: 'I had support from ancient Greek relations, of course. Sophocleese, Pericleese . . .'

I ask about all the psychotherapy. Obviously anxious not to break faith with malady, he says, 'I used to have a recurring anxiety dream. An exam-anxiety dream.' He begins to look eased by telling it. 'I'd dream that I'd suddenly discovered I had to take an exam the very next day in a subject completely unknown to me. So I'd rush round all the Cambridge bookshops looking for the key textbook. They'd be all out of it. "The cat just ate it." It was terrible. I had this dream till I was about thirty-five. Then I started saying to myself, "Wait a moment. I already have a degree from Cambridge. What am I so worried about?" '

Cleese treats the components of himself from a distance, as though they had simply happened to him. A great many of his characters are built on strenuousness spent on the tangential. Maybe this is a comic staple. In *Clockwise*, when the headmaster, hellbent on punctuality, misses his train to a vital, snooty conference because of his hymns to being on time ('Does the sun ever appear late over the horizon saying "Please, sir, the train was on strike"?'), Cleese's course to the goal is sabotaged by every irrelevance imaginable. But dignity sees him through. Yes, a car will be acceptable as a substitute for the missed train, though the idea entails re-courting an ex-girlfriend who left him because of his perpetual lateness. She's needed as a chauffeur in the eventually heavily wounded car. He manages to give his seat belt the appearance of a monarch's sash. The car then gets stuck in the mud of a field unfairly parading as a shortcut. Cleese strides with purpose to a monastery. 'I say, I'm terribly sorry,' he says to an obviously head monk, 'but do you happen to have a tractor?' The monk keeps quiet: not because he is a Trappist but because he is silenced by the manic calm of the man.

Cleese himself is laconic. He cherishes the silence of, for

instance, snooker on television. 'You don't have to have the sound on at all. It's all calmness and skill and good manners. To make snooker work on American television, they'd have to make it a contact sport. And the way they shoot the game gives you this lovely sense of geography. Long shots. I'm very keen on them.'

Every film comedian I've ever known likes working full-figure, and as a film-maker Cleese prefers using master shots as often as he dares, for the sake of letting audiences choose what to watch. John Cleese thinks courteously. 'I'm very fond of good manners, especially those of Italians running restaurants,' he says. 'They make you feel at once that you are one of the cognoscenti, whatever you order. "Osso buco and the house wine, please." "*Perfetto, Signore.*" I once went to a place and ordered veal scaloppine and asked where the Gents' was. "*Perfetto, Signore.*" The waiter made you feel that those were the only two things that any man of genuine taste could possibly have wanted.' A John Cleese character likewise manages, whatever plot predicament he is coping with, or however much mayhem his wild strivings for order create, to seem to be in polite and majestic control. It is very seldom that he cracks under the conditions that try him, and even then he conveys a flash of feeling that all might yet work out. 'I can stand the despair – it's the *hope*,' the hero of *Clockwise* says, sitting in a country lane waiting for the next setback. Enough energy spent to kill a man. But farce doesn't know exhaustion. This actor is a piercing, true-blue technician and the line soars.

* * *

In *Jabberwocky* – cheerfully announced as 'at last, a film for the squeamish' – we are in the Middle Ages, which is to say that we are in the middle of demolition, muddle, and what might well be thought of as a right old mess of pottage. It is a world very like the world of the films of the inspired Monty Python lot, starring one of the same actors – Michael Palin playing a dim-looking youth – and directed by Python's Terry Gilliam. The havoc of a kingdom we are in is ruled by King Bruno the Questionable, played by that great old English music-hall comedian Max Wall. His voice is like something being drawn up and down a nutmeg grater; he carries his orb as if he were about to lob it, and he appears to be dressed in a handmade patchwork horse blanket. Possibly the monarchical robe was made by the nuns living with his daughter, who are all eternally stitching away, and who are named the Sisters of Misery.

Outside, medieval chaos runs amok. Slops are flung from every window. A voice rather like a muezzin's calls 'Rush hour!' and the streets immediately give way to even more push and shove than usual. Dust reigns. The place is powdered with it. Nobody can set foot anywhere, or sneeze, without raising a cloud of it. People irritably get words wrong. The incomparably sniffy John Le Mesurier, playing the Chamberlain, calls the King 'sire' and, receiving no thanks for his manners, lapses into calling him 'darling'. The King has attacks of fury with the mayhem of his realm which seize him like bouts of hay fever. Having graciously congratulated his fragile daughter on how beautiful she looks, he sits with her and the Chamberlain at a tournament that spatters their finery with blood. There must be some better way of choosing a champion than all this carnage, the Chamberlain feels. Someone suggests hide-and-seek. So the knights, still clanking in their armour, but on foot, creep around *Henry V*-style tents and play a game of surprise with each other. This is a world of prayers chanted to flying hogfish; of beggars who smilingly flourish bits and pieces of amputated limbs for a gracefully accepted coin; of filthy, overcrowded battlements; of a wild red-headed fanatic preaching in a smithy that may well be a production line for the most up-to-date in Middle Age torture instruments; of a reputedly brilliant master cooper who hasn't the faintest idea of how to keep the staves of his barrels together. In the midst of this buoyant shambles, a peculiar decorum reigns. Dennis Cooper, in a dreadful fight, protects himself with a painted shield that looks like a papier-mâché knick-knack from a crafts shop. A knight sent out to kill the Jabberwock wears a lobster on his helmet. The monster is a cobwebby creature who, carrying out the crustacean motif, has an upper torso that seems to be definitely in the seafood line. Lower down, he gives the impression of a dilapidated bat, but he has the face of a pair of lobster crackers that has spent centuries on the top floor of the house of the Madwoman of Chaillot.

Dennis is besotted for the moment with a girl called Griselda Fishfinger. (Fishfingers are an unappealing sort of frozen food, often fed to cats, though they are advertised happily on commercial TV as the ideal TV-watching nourishment for the family.) Griselda, known as The Lovely Griselda and cast for her very large size, is a tightly corseted wench who keeps a potato in her bulging upper lacing. She speaks little but munches the potato hungrily. Dennis manages to get the potato and treats it as if it were a golden apple. Like him, everyone else in the film seems to be contentedly misled. A character will tug a door pull, and behind the door a man on the other end of the bell rope will be abruptly jerked up by the neck, screaming blue murder. 'Someone at the door, dear,' a nice-looking wife will then say domestically to her husband at the fireside. The film's citizens – even the King – put up with severe difficulties. The monarch's trumpeter plays paeans that are impossibly out of tune, and the monarch's drummer has an instinct for drumming interruptions to everything the royal herald is trying to say. While the Bishop is in full flood, a dustpan is being used, as it well should be, though it is not the medieval filth that mostly bothers people but the monster, which is said to have once so scared a man that the man's teeth turned white overnight – as, again, they well should do, the general colour of teeth in the Middle Ages being rust-brown according to this film. Still, the characters survive on the whole with amazing good temper. They are only occasionally pettish. There is a nasty moment when Dennis and the Princess are married. 'I pronounce you man and wife,' says the officiating clergyman. '*Princess*,' corrects H.R.H., on her high horse. *Jabberwocky* deserves its Lewis Carroll association; he would have rejoiced in its nincompoop wit and the blue-sky reaches of its nonsense. Not often has the rude been so recklessly funny.

High Hearts

One long accomplice of comedy was called, for a long time, the melancholy humour. Malvolio's wan and crumpled tights are the expression of his being, spreading no grumps. The modern equivalent of this festive capacity of comedy to transform must be the hypochondriacal humour. The unique Woody Allen pertains. Not readily forgotten, his scene in a New York telephone box frantically asking for a third opinion about his headache. The doctors say it's a headache. Pressed for worse, the third opinionator says, 'Yes, we should think of brain tumours. We have to look at the dark side of the spectrum.' Woody Allen makes of hypochondria a great comic substitute for anxiety about the state of mankind, as in *Le Médecin malgré lui*. And then there is the question of angst about loot. Mr Allen would not forget the noble pause of Jack Benny when he is held up and told 'your money or your life', the growing impatience of the robbers about the wait, and his answer, 'I'm thinking.'

Woody Allen: On the closed set of *Hannah and her Sisters* (1987), he asked me anxiously – as he had on the closed set of *Stardust Memories* (1980) – 'You won't give away the plot, will you?' I said that I couldn't anyway, because I didn't know it.

'That makes two of us,' he said, both times. When he keeps plots secret, he is not being wayward. They are secreted even from him, he says. 'Whatever you've planned it's nothing like what you get on the footage, so you're making it up all the time.'

He thinks on his feet. In the earlier days he had great trouble with endings as well as with plots. On both counts *Take the Money and Run* (1969) was apparently near the point of being ditched when the producers and Woody saw the rough-cut. An admirable editor named Ralph Rosenblum, called in to advise, found it 'an astonishing mixture of highs as high as the Marx Brothers, and lows as low as a slapped-together home movie'. The hero, Virgil Starkwell, played by Woody, is a timid desperado hellbent on a life of crime that he is supremely unfitted for. Any man planning to rob a bank by slipping a threat-note to a bank-teller must surely be able to write legibly, let alone to spell. 'This is a gub' will not do, not for a bank-teller. Virgil says that is the way he writes his 'n's. Another teller reads out, 'Please put $50,000 in this bag and abt natural. What's "abt"?' Violence thwarted by exasperation, a major crime hitting the dust through an academic fury that Virgil finds off to the side: comedy has a lot to do with things being out of whack.

The film is introduced in trad documentary style gone skew-whiff. Jackson Beck, Paramount's original newsreel commentator, tells us that Virgil was born in a New Jersey tenement. With the bygone grim urgency of newsreels – a grimness and urgency now taken over in America by TV commercials about products to ward off 'musty odours' in your house and 'ugly wax build-up' on the floor – Beck tells us that the new-born Virgil is 'an exceptionally cute baby . . . Before he is twenty-five years old he will be known to police in six states for assault, armed robbery and illegal possession of a wart.' The rhythm of the list is a lasting part of Woody's comic style. The technique works best when it ends, clonk, on a monosyllable. Woody agrees that monosyllable would be a better word if it were monosyllabic.

Words, music and God are lasting preoccupations. Woody will often approach language as though he had just stubbed his toe on it after thinking for millennia about some other mode (sex, maybe, for which he confesses keenness). In *Sleeper* (1973) he wakes up in the year 2173 as a defrosted robot faced with doing an unqualified operation to reconstruct a dead Big Brother from his only vestige, a nose; his fake-doctor colleague (Diane Keaton) whispers to him about getting on with the croning. 'Cloning, you idiot,' he says, though none the wiser. And as to the music (he faithfully practises the clarinet every day – 'or else your lip goes' – and plays on Mondays at Michael's Pub in New York), it crops up wonderfully in *Take the Money and Run* in interviews that attempt to disentangle Virgil's failed-criminal problem. Virgil's ex-music-teacher is questioned. She taught him the cello. A hopeless pupil. 'He *blew* into it. He had no conception of the instrument.' And God. Virgil's father whines that the boy was an atheist: 'I tried to beat God into him, but it was very tough.'

Before his young stint on the nightclub circuit as a monologuist, Woody was a very young gag-writer, which can make a man an automaton: but as soon as he was on the circuit, he started to use his own particular and distinct self as his material. The sketches were recklessly witty and already full of encouraging signs of the gift of going too far, from which his later and greater gift of reining back follows. He referred to his first wife, an unnamed chill factor he uncharacteristically loathes, as 'one of the few White Muslims in New York. The Museum of Natural History shone her shooth.' A pause of wonderment. Again, English is made to seem happily arbitrary and odd. In some scene he wrote for Diane Keaton and himself, he calls her 'fetching'. 'Fetching?' he gets her to say; 'Fetching what?' Incessantly running up against some word or phrase that clasps him into radiant bondage, he first wanted to call *Annie Hall* (1977) by the word *Anhedonia*, meaning the inability to experience pleasure. It gave no pleasure at all to United Artists.

Bananas is a fine piece of nonsense about a banana republic called San Marcos, 'The country that, though small, has the highest rate of hernia in the world.' Woody's gift for word-displacement is very much an outcropping of his work in nightclubs. He has the gift of making 'minor lateral sclerosis' sound like a camera movement, death, or a small and beautiful daughter whose mutters are a joy around the house.

In *Love and Death* (1976) he casts himself as an undersized Russian of Napoleonic times. Huddled under a colossal fur coat at a very cold table, he asks his offhand beloved, Sonja, whose command of words like 'epistemological' the character admires, 'What's for dessert?' 'Sleet.' 'Oh, good,' he says as she swoops about graciously in more and more furs, thinking of love, death, Russia, this epistemology, who knows. Diane Keaton as Sonja tells him that sex without love is an empty experience. He feels that, as empty experiences go, it's not bad. 'Shall we to bed?' a man impersonating Napoleon says, in a Woody exchange, to Sonja. 'Shall we *what* to bed?' says Sonja: Woody's script, Woody's view. Lucidity is all. Comedians who deal in sexual uncertainty can be dire, like comedians who trade on pretending to be cowards, because both sorts profit by affecting to have qualities that they secretly despise; but Woody Allen makes haplessness about love seem one of the conditions laid down for living, just as he makes fear of death seem one of the conditions laid down for dying.

In *Manhattan*, he falls in love with a teenager. 'I'm forty-two,' says the Woody character. Amused by himself, horrified by himself. 'I'm taking out a girl whose father I could beat up. I'm dating a girl who does homework.' All Woody's films reflect aspects of his 'real' character. His apprehension: in *Sleeper* he is told they'll restructure his brain, 'his second favourite organ', though he has stopped kidding about sex by now. His helpfulness: on the set with actors, he is a marvel. He will sit endlessly through the most apparently unimportant wild-track rehearsal, perched on some prop, listening again and again, whistling between takes to keep the pace up ('It's all taking twice as long as it should,' he will say, upbraiding only himself), eventually giving a single director's note. I watched him spending hours with a gifted small-part actress playing a Jewish suburban housewife who tells a worried anecdote about a neighbour whose arteries froze as she was lifting a cup of tea to her lips. The take wouldn't come right. Eventually Woody leant down beside her and said softly, 'Remember you're telling your family a story.' It was the one acting note she needed.

Woody's films have always reflected his decorum and his hard-won resolve. More and more now, they reflect his simplicity. In *Hannah*, his hypochondria has matured into no joke. The straight political sense he brings to his life starts increasingly to mark his movies, which are both sobering and blithe, with a voice like no one else's. In *Zelig* (1983), the hero he wrote and plays is an epitome of the man some people still imagine him to be: a timid soul who can inhabit the vessel of any personality that comes his way. He shot it as a documentary, mixing Second World War footage with his own narrative. In an unforgettable, terrifying hilarious moment, Zelig is seen with Hitler and Goebbels and Goering at the Nuremberg rally of them all. The commentator says, as a circle appears around the near-hidden figure, that the untrackable hero now turns up here after all his other metamorphoses. Zelig waves shyly to the crowd, jumping to be seen. I'm here. It's me.

'Isn't the film about the charm of a man without a personality of his own?' said an earnest seeker after pigeonholes. 'No,' said Woody, 'it's about the kind of personality that leads to fascism.'

Woody – for real and in film's *alter ego* – takes punctuality as seriously as any other kind of straight dealing between people, however funny he makes it. In *Manhattan*, he is furious with the Diane Keaton character for being late for a movie. They stand in a queue where some know-all starts lambasting Bergman. The character played by Woody, much of his own stripe, mutters, 'One more kick at Ingmar Bergman and I'll knock his brains out.' Through his chum's lateness, they miss the beginning of the movie. At that point in *Manhattan*, which is one of the best of all America's romantic comedies and bang-on about a not-quite-real Manhattan – a Manhattan visibly idealized, as befits a tale of love – the Woody–Diane relationship is strained by his forcing her to see *The Sorrow and the Pity* yet again because at least she's still on time for that. She says 'Fuck'. The usually self-censoring scriptwriter (Mr Allen) has the hero (Mr Allen) say appreciatively, 'I like the way you express yourself. It's pithy and degenerate.'

'It is in the matter of religion that thought has caused me the most disappointment,' Bertrand Russell wrote in his notebooks when he was twelve years old. Well, says Woody Allen, going ahead from fifty, we might as well carry on with thought. No one who wasn't petrified by mortality could make comedies so palliatively serious about the straits we inhabit. God, if he exists, has been described by a Woody-written character as an underachiever, presumably because of the Deity's failure to put an end to the difficulties that comedy tries to see us through. Woody Allen is an agnostic with intent to know, though he has to be fobbed off with a maybe. 'I know maybe is a very small reed to hang your life on, but it's all we have.' To be going on with, there is humour, sense, and the prodigal grace of art. Like most of us, Mr Allen finds himself guilty, but with an explanation.

* * *

'Most movies are like pre-digested food because they are mere re-enactments of something that happened (if ever) back at the scripting stage,' James Agee once wrote. If anyone isolated the biggest single difference between the real films and the dead fish, he did it.

Nothing else in comedy has quite the same thrashing vitality as the kind of film that delusively seems to have been created at this moment, in front of the camera. Nothing in cinema is more depressing than the kind of comedy that obviously died two years ago, the day the last page was ground off someone's typewriter. In the presence of an animated corpse like this the difference is simply that nothing is happening in the present; you are aware only of the poor cadaver's anxious past, the yellowing script, the conferences, the boneheads' little improvements, the academic worries and the academic solutions that were found for them before ever a shot was taken, in the interests of creating a narrative that made sense on the page.

Narrative in the cinema, especially comic narrative, is not

heavy reading. If you write down the narrative line of a great film comedy it often looks fragmented and elliptical; it is only on the screen that it becomes powerful and organic. Anyone who can create this kind of formal life is a born director, and it needs prodigious talent, character and nerve to do it: to store up the energy of a film so that it can explode when the cameras are on it.

'Action is the language of the screen, and the instant present is its tense,' wrote James Agee, again. No one understood this precept better than his friend John Huston. *The List of Adrian Messenger* is a riveting comedy in thriller guise put together like a game of poker. In the pre-credit sequence an unseen man working late in an Aldwych office is tersely murdered by a dandy who sabotages the lift. Immediately, Clive Brook as a sporting octogenarian marquess is leaning against a mantelpiece having tea after hunting, with his grandson – played by John Huston's son Tony – and his daughter, Lady Bruttenholm, pronounced Broom.

All through the picture one seems to be coming into rooms where conversations have been going on for a long time. Huston's films declare him to be, among all the things he was, a master of light pressure in comic narrative. One of the guests produces a list of eleven men, including himself, most of whom have already died in uninvestigated accidents. Shortly afterwards he helps out a vicar with his excess baggage at an airport counter; the luggage darkly disappears on a conveyor belt, and while the plane is blowing up the vicar goes quietly into an airport lavatory, takes out a pair of contact lenses and peels off his genial mask to emerge as Kirk Douglas.

You guess then that the dandy, too, is Kirk Douglas. Half the people in the film are obviously in disguise; whenever you see a gipsy, or a tramp with a skin like a hen's leg, or a countrywoman who looks like Donald Wolfit playing Widow Twankey, you are *supposed* to guess that it's Kirk Douglas. The trick is that you're only sometimes right.

There is a very good lizard-eyed performance by George C. Scott as a high-class detective – his English accent gets better as the film goes on – and the scenes about grand country life are absolutely right. So is the mixture of etiquette and violence in the hunting scenes. This was a folly work in Huston's life, obviously made for his own entertainment out of his own Irish country life. The casual authority of it is unmissable.

* * *

Spike Milligan programme heard in the car. Spike Milligan, an instinctive man of wild sense, famous through the Goons. He was in a railway station waiting-room accompanied by a cough. Someone else, also waiting, had a cough. This other cough the man had caught himself. Spike had a free one he'd got in the local National Health doctor's waiting-room, where everyone was giving coughs away to each other any day of the week. Both men specialized in waiting. In various places. One said that of course he was an avant-garde waiter, as opposed to all of the traditionalists who waited *for* something. He just waited. Not for anything in particular. A purist.

A comment on the National Health Service that the Tory government is dismantling. Labour mantled it. Anyone of Spike Milligan's nature is a born satirist. Political satire is social satire. What else? *Polis* can only mean the state of mortals in society.

Robin Williams, the man of America's conscience in confused days, at his best standing up to be counted, is what is called a stand-up monologuist. He bounds on stage apologizing for having got to the wrong place. He had been stopped by a man asking how to get into the Metropolitan Opera House. 'Lots of money.'

Robin Williams as Jesus: 'I'm not a carpenter this time, I'm a sheet metal worker and don't fool with me.'

* * *

Record of a rascal hunter. He crouches over his newspapers and Congressional Records, the irreplaceable I. F. Stone, political maverick and unique muckraker, our Swift, our saving comic ironist. His spectacled eyes and pen-sharp nose are fixed as close to documents as Mr Toad's to the steering wheel in *The Wind in the Willows*, when Mr Toad is spiritedly studying the road and honking an ancient motor horn, much as Stone has sounded alarms in handprinted broadsheets and rapscallion articles unmatched in English-speaking political affairs for two centuries. The marvellous nuisance-man of Washington hunts down fallacies in newsprint which even editors miss from one week to the next, and finds rascals in bound volumes that bore other reporters into a doze. He consumes print with an intensity as maniacal as Mr Toad's in burning up the road, partly because of a deafness that led him to read instead of listen. Stone seems to grasp at this disability with a tacit and stirring thanks for the way it focuses his senses. Head down, he quickly tears out scraps of the dozens of newspapers and magazines he regularly reads, being too impatient to use scissors, and orders them by a system that looks more like piling than filing. Yet he can find a reference in ten seconds: or immediately if it is in his own mind, where it is usually stored.

An unobtrusively deft documentary called *I. F. Stone's Weekly* recorded the way he works. It was made by Jerry Bruck Jr with a lot of Stone's own fanaticism. The film commands a moved respect for its hero, who has been a loner all his life, yet who has sustained a contagious sort of conviviality in his reporting. When people started subscribing to the newsletter called *I. F. Stone's Weekly*, which was a single-man job if ever there was one, they felt among friends because of his company. His voice carried. He sounded always as if he had air, repose, and comrades around him, even in the McCarthy days, when no newspaper would employ him. He had long since been forced to resign from the National Press Club for trying to entertain a Negro judge at lunch there. He was one of the first to go into the high-level lies about the Tonkin Gulf. No man has ever been more adept at hunting down bland whoppers, at detecting the hidden hush-money for pressmen that is implied in their dining with canny political figures whom they might otherwise be free to bombard tomorrow, and at reporting world affairs with a mixture of scrupulous worry and the guttersnipe humour that is the sinew of America. The mixture is heartening, rare in life, unequalled in the history of modern lone reporting, and, above all, brave. Jerry Bruck shows us this modest man racing through bookshops for foreign newspapers and magazines, picking up books and dropping them again in the same movement as he looks for another to add to his pile, getting his newsletter off the presses (with a voice-over interpolation from the printers about his paying bills almost before they are sent). At an unaccustomedly swanky ceremony, to give Stone the Polk Award, he thanks people for 'my first Establishment award' and promptly goes on to talk exclusively about the forgotten achievements of George Polk in reporting the Greek struggle against 'our first Vietnam'.

The famous *Weekly* began with a tiny circulation. Until it was discontinued, in 1971, the circulation manager was Stone's wife. She is seen saying briefly, in the midst of feeding the Addressograph, that if her husband stopped to organize his files he wouldn't have time to do his reading. There is a shot of Stone sending requested back issues of the *Weekly* himself, walking to the mailbox laden with batches of them. Another week one sees him darting excitedly for records that a young assistant, later worn out by Stone's energy in research, admits to finding boring. Stone must have fatigued junior helpers by the dozen into taking to their beds. He is always virtually alone.

Stone tells the audience about the day when he started tracking down a lie about an underground atomic testing which 'really began in the mind of that scientific screwball and real nut Edward Teller, because as we got close to an agreement with the Russians, he began to say, "Suppose they test underground, or suppose they test on the dark side of the moon . . . How will you know?" ' Stone got his regular *New York Times* the next morning. As he puts it in the film, the *Times* wrote that underground tests the day before conformed 'to the expectations of the experts, meaning Teller and Latter . . . that the test would not be detectable more than two hundred miles away'. But somewhere Stone got a city edition of the *Times* with a shirt-tail saying that Toronto had detected them. In the late city edition, he found other shirt-tails, one from Rome, one from Tokyo, saying that they had detected them. 'I thought, gee, I wish I had enough money to cable to those places and find out what's going on.' But he hadn't so he stacked all the stuff in his basement, this elating man who can detect casuistry thousands of miles away yet hasn't the cash to send a cable about atomic testing. He waited. Events developed. The great powers came close to a test ban. The USSR offered listening posts about 580 miles apart. 'Two days later the Atomic Energy Commission, which is in my opinion the most mendacious government agency in Washington, released to the press a report saying that tests could not be detected more than two hundred miles away.' The obvious purpose – obvious to Stone, that is – was to make a liar out of Harold Stassen, who was negotiating with the Russians for President Eisenhower, and to undercut agreement. Stone says that he said to himself, 'I've never been on a seismology story before,' and he discovered by telephoning around town that the Commerce Department's Coast and Geodetic Survey has a seismology branch. So he jumped into his car. 'And they were so glad to see a reporter. I don't think they'd seen a reporter since Noah – since there was a tremble from Mount Ararat when Noah's Ark landed and there was a wide squiggle on the seismometer.' We are glad to see a reporter, Mr Stone: all the rest of us, who have read you all these years, and we thank Mr Bruck for this footnote to your nobility and funniness.

* * *

Federico Fellini is a master of the festive, of boon nights and false noses. He is not to be found by analysis. 'Signor Fellini,' says an interviewer in the middle of Fellini's *The Clowns*, 'what message are you trying to give us here?' A bucket instantly falls over Fellini's head, and then another over the interviewer's. Splat, wham. Trip over a basin of paste, explode another clown's explodable trousers, turn the fire hose on the elephant. We are in the circus world that Fellini has often taken to be the world itself, as in Gelsomina's march behind the musicians in *La Strada*, and the gay, idiotic strolls along the beach in *I Vitelloni*, and the moonstruck mask of Giulietta Masina exchanging stares with us in *Cabiria*, as if she were a clown who had clambered into the audience. It is the buffoon's world, the arena of mock gladiators, where combat is mortal one minute and gone the next, the Inquisition that doesn't count because the fatal questions proceed like a schoolboy riddle in some dream of rudeness from long ago. 'What message are you trying to give us here?' says the film. A bucket over the intellect, please. 'How do you lose ten pounds of fat?' goes the schoolboy catch. 'Cut off your head.'

The film starts with the sight of a small child in a nightgown – obviously the small Fellini – leaning out of a window in the dark. There is a joyful vamp-till-ready by Nino Rota. Ropes screech. The circus big top is going up. Prisoners listen from the local jail. The circus draws children and convicts because it sabotages authority. The ringmaster is a figure of pomp without power. The white clowns – the symbolic grown-ups in the scheme of clowning, with blanched indoor faces and black lips and majestic sneers – are overdressed, over-privileged, and no match for the clowns called the *augusti*, their impossible charges, who wear the same dirty costumes the whole time and refuse to recite a nice poem when the vicar comes to tea. Of all the water sloshed around in circuses, the augusts slosh the most. They are the kindergarten criminals, and crime pays in gallons. Their energy includes an empty, splendid braggadocio that Fellini must always have doted on and found touching. It is there in the swagger of his wife, Masina. *The Clowns* – commissioned by Italian television – is slightly a documentary-within-the-entertainment, with Fellini himself appearing as the head of a camera unit recording retired clowns, but mostly a spectacle, with young Italian clowns playing the tricks and wearing the make-up of famous forebears. The spectacle is full of showing-off undaunted by fatuity. Jungle men come on and ripple their muscles before doing no harm whatever. The ringmaster keeps helpfully interjecting things like 'Anyone with a weak heart had better leave.' The strong man challenges a large opponent called Miss Mathilde, who looks much like Brünnhilde, though with tights slightly baggy above her sandals, and breastplates like two pressure-cooker lids. 'And now,' announces the ringmaster, 'in a *terrible experiment*, the fakir will be buried in the glass coffin.' It all seems very Italian. I once saw a magnificently costumed policeman in Florence directing traffic as if he were Napoleon, although the traffic was already successfully following identical commands of tame mechanical traffic lights. He was a figure of military brilliance, with a massive chest, though not much leg.

Fellini is not saying that the circus represents anything else, not indulging the sawdust-among-the-sequins heartache, not making any point except that he adores clowns. The subject is extravagant; the match of style to subject is exact and tonic. We are pitched into the entertainment like tumblers. There are clowns all over the place. This is Fellini pure. In the ring or out of it, say his films, nothing is absolute. He believes profoundly in the redeemable, and clowning is the system where there is always another chance and where damage never matures. It is his native land, and we are in it. Clowns with tear ducts like water pistols, clowns with exploding cars, clowns with hammers, clown dramas with single lines of dialogue like 'The cow's loose!' to introduce some ideal muddle, clowns promising to make the smelliest cake that ever was, clowns pumping themselves up in the red-and-yellow-striped sweaters, clowns who cry softly to themselves and bay in the ring like dogs at the moon.

After a while, that turn is over. A Fellini bent on homage and learning goes with a camera unit to talk to great clowns in old-age homes. They can remember little. They seem more absorbed by their canaries. He looks at the film of one of the historic performances, but it breaks and burns in the projector. Another rare fragment of the film is run for him by a tidy-minded woman archivist who winds up the insufficient record of a career as if it were a remnant of ribbon in a draper's shop at closing time. We are told that the best clowns are Spaniards and Italians, and then there is a sombre cut to a young tiger being trained. With the switch from the real life of recollections to the real life of a circus in rehearsal, the ancient ritual of entertainment has a moment of seeming satanic. Fellini's colour photography – by Carlo di Palma – sometimes has the same effect. Now and then, the sumptuous tone is disquieting. 'The clowns didn't make me laugh. They frightened me,' says a child in the film, speaking for Fellini. The picture will suddenly darken for a moment, as if a bird's wing had covered the sun.

Fellini makes connections between clowns and village dunces which look as if they were first made when he was small. There is an image of a fool tramp being threatened by a countrywoman with a scythe. Another of a midget nun, always in a hurry on some task, who says that the saints don't trust anyone much. Another of a drunk's wife: 'You should drop dead, and I for marrying you.' The dirty threats of clowns, their dedicated scuttling on peculiar errands, their savagery about midgets, and the eternal abuse by the elegant white clown of the unemployable bungler he is coupled with sometimes remind Fellini all too much of things outside the circus. Clowns express a peasant dislike of those who don't work, and a peasant cruelty to the abnormal. There is a wonderful shot of a villager creeping along a wall and being jeered at by the local kids. He can be panicked into behaving like this only by seeing war films; then he goes slightly mad, and puts on a soldier's uniform and acts as if he were in occupied territory. In fact, of course, when the clown characters in any of Fellini's other films chance to look around them they always find themselves in the most heavily occupied territory imaginable. But the moments swiftly pass, and they are back in their own beguiled systems. Like much else that is lyric in Fellini, *The Clowns* celebrates quick recovery in its characters, and the film itself has that gift. The mood spins upward fast. Antonioni cherishes the enervating and hangs on to it with the grip of some high-strung insomniac insisting on eight hours' restlessness in bed every night; Fellini shakes off melancholy in a second and behaves as if he wanted the day never to end.

Like Claudia Cardinale in *8½*, Fellini's clowns express the idea of something unspoilable. Nothing alters in their world. Nothing hurts. Mistakes are blissful. A clown bashes another one with a hammer. 'You missed,' cries the hammered one in triumph, but holding up a finger with a swelling as big as a grapefruit, and then, after a second hit has wrecked a second finger, he yells, still more victoriously, 'You missed again!'

But these immune people we are watching, who seem to have no age – we also hear about terrible accidents to them, and some of them are very, very old. Fellini gives his film double vision. For half an hour at a time he makes clowns seem the theatre's version of dunces and lunatics, but when we suddenly see real dunces and real lunatics they are not like the clowns at all. There is a scene in an asylum. Up above, clowns fly on high wires, anxious to divert, playing Lear's Fool; below sit real fools with catatonia, closed in on themselves, clenched like sea anemones. The sequence has a piercing gentleness and no grotesquerie. There is a wonderful observation of nerve being mustered in a vacuum when a woman patient draws the edges of her coat together and raises her chin. Fellini once meant to make a film about a *vitellone* young doctor working in an asylum, to be called *The Free Women of Magliano*. He wrote an account of it in *Cahiers du Cinéma* in 1957. If he had made it, I daresay he might then have glamorized madness, and he could have been accused of joining the giddy quest for enlightenment in the psychotic and the stoned, which is a direct parallel to the taste of the Romantics nearly two hundred years ago; all the same, the essay suggests a thicker sense of character than that, like a novelist's.

Fellini's clowns are discards of modernity. So are all the characters he has cared for most in films, sometimes risking banality. The richness and speed of his gift rescue *The Clowns* and make it a glory. Clowns are his pagan seers, like the character played by Richard Basehart in *La Strada*: divining anarchists, convivial, without guilt. Fellini is the most pre-Freudian of directors. If his characters are unhappy, any cure has nothing to do with 'adjusting'. The augusts in their run-down clothes are cheeky losers without complexes, and they are also not political in the slightest. They embody revolt, not revolution. The white clowns, sumptuously dressed and stern, like popes, are the authoritarians who are their other half. The complicity of opposites is a cause of endless trouble, but so is marriage, so is family. The augusts suffer squalls of weeping. Their eyelids are sometimes as red as their noses. Nobody pays any heed. One of them cries into a bucket;

another says cheerfully, paddling, 'Oh, good, your sorrow will refresh my feet.' Fellini's film is full of blithe cross-purposes and bathos. The script-girl in the film-within-the-film is a rotten typist who tears a sheet of script as she pulls it out of the typewriter; a projectionist can't work a projector. Nobody minds. *The Clowns* happens in a world of not-minding. The aptitude for fun is virgin and carnival, as it is for a moment in the hand-linking scene near the end of *8½*. There is a chaotic circus funeral for one of the clowns: a loafer severely eulogised as having been unfaithful to his friends, and a torment to the gas-and-electricity company. The funeral march mysteriously turns into a triumph. Everything is correctable. Coloured paper shoots down from the roof – for once, enough paper streamers. The soundtrack rustles as the procession pushes through the ribbons. At his best, Fellini catches the look of loss on a million faces, and, beyond that, a kind of felicity.

Though it was only morning, Fellini made a celebration not long ago of a run-through in New York for an evening-at-Lincoln-Center gala in his honour that night. He sat happily in the stalls of the huge hall, practically alone, vigilant for companions, at a technical rehearsal at noon. Nine hours later, or thereabouts – considerably thereabouts because considerably Italian, multiplied by the internationalism of delays in anything to do with film – he was to be honoured.

Fellini looked round at the place, lit only by a half-power string of lights around the first tier, and said 'I didn't know it would be so expensive to reproduce Kafka. We are at the Day of Judgment. Our witnesses cannot be heard. Nothing is serene. Are the patrons well? Everything is like a Swiss clinic for nervous disorders.'

The Kafkaesque sound of unknown feet climbing up the stairs turned out to be the far-from-Kafkaesque sound of the well-known feet of Marcello Mastroianni. Pink shirt, straw hat, eyes a less pungent pink by courtesy of drinks on Pan Am the night before. The troupe had come from Rome. Immediate vivacity. Alberto Sordi appeared. Anouk Aimée was already there, a glory in this Valhalla, which looked as though it had been ordered on the telephone by Mussolini. 'The acoustics are terrible,' shouted Mastroianni cheerfully. (No music, though: only voices, his not to be sneezed at.) But the late Nino Rota's music for Fellini's films was started off in our heads by someone humming one of the vamp-till- ready themes from *8½*.

The celebration itself: the hall was packed, with clips from Fellini's films raising spirits to life again after the sombre effect of queues of deadly limousines. An adroit young interpreter gallantly made quick choices about when to translate. Anouk knew how to speak in short enough phrases for her to cope with. Mastroianni looked quickly at the blank screen to see if he was blocking a shot and then spoke well, wildly, funnily, and unstoppably: Italian in full flood, with the translator dropping any attempt to chip in. Giulietta Masina, ravishing, with platinum-blonded hair and a glittering white satin dress, made a deep bow with arms stiffly away from her, a gesture totally like her own in *Cabiria*. Then she spoke of the magnificent roles her husband had given her, eyes barely moving from his box, and went on to say that having spoken of herself as an actress she wished to speak of herself as a wife, having spoken of nothing else anyway. They have been married for forty years and she is always there, not speaking, tiny, hidden by a mink three times as big as she is, visible only as a pair of huge eyes that are a clown's, with a clown's make-up added by nature. Fellini's spirit took over the hall: the spirit of a troupe, the merriment of gangs of friends watching the life of a capital city both swanky and sordid as seen from the bottom of the heap. Genius, Fellini said once – about Picasso, I think – is irruptive, inarguable, joyous.

The hotels were having a strike in New York. This first fretted a preoccupied film-maker in a hurry to get back to editing his next film, and then amused him. 'Americans are supposed to be efficient and *Italy* is supposed to have strikes.' This particular hotel had taken a theatrical way out. Every day the staff changed uniforms, and thus their union identities. At any moment the chef might carry the luggage, the doorman might become the manager, incorporating new-boy nerves with a touch of Italian pomp. Who knows if the manager made the beds or who cooked.

'I love American breakfast,' said Fellini, sharing a pork sausage. 'As to uniforms, you understand the Italian need for uniforms. We get exhilarated by them. During the war I was at school and there were very infectious military parades. For a private citizen, in peacetime it was always the ultimate aspiration to wear a uniform and medals. For an Italian the great triptych is, *scusi*, Jesus on the Cross to the right, who of course is a uniform in himself, Mussolini in the middle with a saucepan on his head, and the Pope on the left, very well dressed. I am not being sacrilegious. I myself am guilty of a uniform' (he meant the famous black bear coat and black hat).

8½ is often taken to be autobiographical, with Mastroianni as Fellini in the role of a famous film director with a block that flourishes into a great film willy-nilly. The use of first-person narrative is a deliberate artistic device: there is a sense in which Fellini would be autobiographical even if he were telling the life story of a sole. *8½* is a rueful account of a peculiarly contemporary kind of man, imaginative, openly greedy, riddled with the bullet-holes of self-accusations, and almost dying of neurotic sloth. The only work I can think of that has the same grim comic capacity of inturned comprehension is Evelyn Waugh's *The Ordeal of Gilbert Pinfold*.

In *La Dolce Vita* the journalist hero is taken up with the allure of a sham chic world that he knows only from the outside. He is like Fellini's loathed *paparazzi*. He lined them up for the opening of events at Lincoln Center for a communal press call to allow photographers to click away at his actors and himself in their box. The device transformed the motley gossips into a crowd that had the mongrel bravado of one of Fellini's own set-ups. Suddenly the photographers looked like the dinghy full of small-town citizens in *Amarcord*, amazed by the sight of a giant liner on a cellophane sea: the worldly photographers seemed endowed with the excited innocence of the little boy who acts the child Fellini at the beginning of *The Clowns*.

La Dolce Vita's hero is the envier enticed; in *8½*, the film-director hero is the regional man describing a ravelled past that he tries to turn into a circus. Living in the bedlam of preparing for a big picture, he hasn't an idea in his head. Sets are already being built, rival actresses are acting their heads off to each other in the pretence that they have parts, but no one has seen a page of the script. His imagination is drowned in memory. He recalls the huge hips of a cheerful woman innocent of slimming knowledge whom he saw doing a rumba when he was a small boy, and the punishment he got afterward from the priests at school. Coming up gasping from his daydream, like a dolphin close to talking, and shaking the drops of water off himself, he thinks perhaps he may at least have rescued something from the ocean bed. A severe critic figure who seems to be working on the film thinks not; the literal-minded are not of Fellini's stripe.

In all cases, Fellini knows instinctively that the artist is an outsider, a witness. Perhaps to be 'provincial' is the essence of being an artist, especially in Italy, this Milan/Rome obsessed country. Naples doesn't count. Naples is a stranger to the fabricated country, loyal chiefly to Sicily and to strikes about Northern-made matches that don't light. Florence and Venice don't count as recorders of Italian unity: their histories are particular. Flooding of irreplaceable libraries, on the one hand, a gradual sinking into the Adriatic on the other. Fellini himself comes from Rimini, born there in 1910. He started off in films as a writer and a gag-writer (like Woody Allen, his fellow in films whose deepest works play death's fool), then assistant director, then director.

'I'm not taking us down in shorthand,' I said, because he thought the sausages should be eaten and there was a lot of mixed grill hovering.

'Thank God,' he said, eating fast. 'So we can talk.' He made a pile of vitamin tablets. 'These two are for *calma*,' he said. 'Sexual *calma*.'

'It's still quite early morning.'

'I mean excited. Then this next pill, a very large iron pill. And so on and so on.' He sorted the pile into a colour spectrum. 'I am too full of ideas about wanting to get on with a film, and as a guest of a new city it is quite wrong to have these ideas.' Pause. 'An idea for a film comes first out of the mind like a very fine piece of thread. One thinks, and perhaps it becomes a piece of string. One goes on thinking, and then perhaps it becomes a rope. A tax man once asked me where I got my ideas. Those are his words, you understand. Walking along a street, I said. A street located in which country? he said. That would determine the point of tax origin, he said. He had a very pleasant face, but a thin mouth, a money mouth. The only street I could place him in was a street in Rome, the origin I suppose of *Satyricon*, where I looked down at a paving stone and thought suddenly that beneath it was ancient Rome still alive.'

He spoke again of Rimini and of the value of being regional. 'Provincial. One is allowed to loiter.' That brought him, with a flick of his long fingers, to Los Angeles. In Los Angeles, of course, where producers have constantly turned down the idea of financing new films by this matchless man, he was also not allowed even to loiter. 'Last time I loitered in Los Angeles it was early in the morning, one of my favourite times when I am not officially working. I was in Los Angeles for an Oscar. A policeman picked me up, tapping me on the shoulder, gently enough, and took me in what seemed to be just another black limousine to the police station. I was quite honoured. The scribe of crime there asked me my name without looking up. "Fellini," I said. He shook his head. "I am here for an Oscar," I said. More disbelief. Still no looking up. "Whistle a theme from *La Dolce Vita.*" Very stern. So I did and I was driven back to my hotel with high festivity and now it was a real limousine, I think, though that may have been my imagination because of the wonder of it all and the vehicles may have been the same. A cop convinced by our far-away Nino Rota was my only witness for the defence and I can't even whistle well.'

We spoke of *Ginger and Fred*, the film that he thinks of as some sort of sequel to *La Dolce Vita*. *Ginger and Fred* is not about Ginger Rogers and Fred Astaire, but about two down-at-heel vaudeville characters who can imitate them. In the film the couple achieve their triumphant facsimile in a TV-studio set. From the usual television mess of cables and half-eaten sandwiches, their tap-dancing routine emerges.

Fellini is patiently amused by cineastes' gobbledygook. In one short film, *Toby Dammit*, he leaves around on the sound-track some finely chosen mutters. 'The first Catholic Western . . . A cross between Carl Dreyer and Pasolini, with a touch of John Ford . . . The two outlaws represent contemporary anarchy and irresponsibility.' And then something about the costumes: 'Both Piero della Francesca and Fred Zinnemann.' His tenderness is expansive and funny. An interviewer in *Toby Dammit* asks a pale, worried actor whether he considers himself a neurotic. 'It's my only quality,' he says, clinging to others' view of him, though he has much more mind than an intellectual girl interviewer crawling in and out of camera shot on all fours.

Fellini, master of festivity, loves and thus creates people who know that the present is made of the past, which gives them knowledge of an eternal now. He reveres clowns, circuses, the fragile and unfortunate, life's lighteners. This thoughtful man: one of his heroes is Jung, for his archaeological dig for unknown energies under the rubble of 'fears, lack of alertness, neglected damage'.

'Jung is one of the great travelling companions of the century,' he said, in a remark that sums up his films' assumption that we are together; villagers collected in a dinghy watching the passing of a brightly lit liner with oblivious passengers, or performers in circus's chaos and union. No one is ever going to forget *8½*'s final scene in the circus ring, with the people of the film-maker's past called down by megaphone to walk together round the ring, like circus elephants holding each other trunk by tail with a rebellious baby elephant at the back. If a small elephant declines to follow the mob, he has Fellini's fellow-feeling. His complicity with the oddities of life is his characters': fluently comic, sober, merciful, determined not to be desperate, with a droll and perfectly earnest belief in paradise and damnation that sends certain moments soaring off into the blue of art with no sound of engines running.

8½ is even more obviously autobiographical than most of Fellini's films; it is also without explicit timeliness, so that it got hard criticism for not being *engagé* enough. I remember walking on the Aldermaston March – the English Easter march in favour of unilateral disarmament – and trying to pass on my admiration of the film to a better athlete, who was striding away his holiday in heavy nailed boots, carrying a knapsack of austere provisions and notebooks of political jottings. He took a mountaineer's glucose tablet for energy, looking at me in a way that made it clear that an admirer of *8½* was a very minor peak to conquer, and said that the film left him unsure of how Fellini felt about the separation of Church and State.

Fellini's *Amarcord* is even more beautiful and detailed than *8½*, and free of the playful toying with the ugly and the outlandish which has made some of his latest films seem impure products. It is perhaps the most dreamlike film he has ever made, though it is actually no dream film. It is about a childhood obviously close to Fellini's, at the start of Fascism, recalled by a fifty-year-old man brought up in a small town. The recollections overlap, as real-life events do. Pranks, family rows, the remarks of town oddities, the coming of Fascism in the guise of something like an uplifting Boy Scout troop seem to flow into one another. The central family consists of Titta (Bruno Zanin), standing for the adolescent Fellini; a tired mother; a self-dramatizing father, wearing a straw hat that he keeps stamping on while telling his relatives not to dramatize; a small brother, who looks at life as if through a blaze and out to the other side; and a thin, unbalanced uncle, less insane than others think. This Dostoyevskian character, though he has been committed to an asylum, is said to have been always more clever than his brother at school. Attenuated now into an unshaven figure with a wise, taciturn, occasionally polemic face, he has extra inches of ankle and wrist sticking out of his Sunday-best suit like the ends of sentences that impatient families have never allowed to be heard. Though apparently mad, he is perhaps less deceived than anyone else.

The season is changing. The witch of winter is ritually burned in a bonfire. Spring is arriving. Fluff balls fill the air like the feathers of moulting ducks. The town unmarried beauty, who lies about her age and weeps now and then for a husband, wears her red beret at a more dauntless angle. Everyone fancies himself and indulges in grandiose fibs that take in no one. A man who is supposed to be playing in the local seaside-resort orchestra, belonging to a dated hotel that looks about to be shipwrecked, enacts the local Lothario to a surprised but grateful visitor and asks her, 'Are you Polish? Only Poles have such fiery eyes.' Sex is much talked about by the elderly, in tones of undiminished optimism, and tentatively approached by Titta, who makes a valiant attempt to woo the local tobacconist. A colossal Amazon of a woman who wants to be carried about as if she were flying, like a Dumbo mother with the aspirations of a Zeppelin, she howls in ecstasy when the gasping boy manages to lift her off the ground. Pressed against her fluffy V-necked sweater, he twists his head round for air. There is an unmistakable Fellini moment when the excited woman, heaving with pleasure after the boy's repeated and Herculean successes in lugging the screaming sandbag about, strides ahead of him and raises the roll-up metal shop door for him as if it weighed no more than a piece of paper, saying solicitously that it's too heavy for him.

Boys at school undermine the mannerisms of their teachers. A master who talks meditatively of the Romans but concentrates mostly on keeping his cigarette ash as long as possible turns furiously on a small boy who has had the wit to bang authority's desk just when the ash is at a crucial point. Another master, pedagogically mysterious in his habits, chooses to teach in a hat and overcoat and to prowl round the classroom without looking at the boys. While an angelic-looking child manages to blow a raspberry at his schoolmaster every time he is taught a Greek letter that, according to the demonstrating master, involves placing the tongue at a particular place on the palate, the rest of the town is getting caught up in the early days of Fascism. Rows of young boys and girls and ranks of hopeful, poverty-stricken old-age pensioners wait for the arrival of a Fascist general. Their salutes, like his arrival, are obscured by a cloud of smoke. The only dissident is Titta's father, head of a bricklaying firm, who tries to turn up for the occasion in a Socialist tie. It is taken off him by his infuriated wife, for reasons of civic safety rather than of pro-Fascism. All the same, an old-fashioned phonograph bravely rigged up on top of a tower emits shocking sounds of Socialist music. His employees, if they had the money, or the time to think about it, would be Socialist to the core. One of them, nicknamed Brickhead, has written a poem: 'My grandfather laid bricks.

My father laid bricks. I laid bricks. But I got no house.' He laughs. Someone asks the name of the poem. 'Bricks', he says.

Uncle Teo, the madman, is taken out for a rare spree in a carriage driven to the family's farm. Courtesies are exchanged. On the way, Uncle Teo eats biscuits and shows the family the stones in his pockets. The family arrives at the farm. Things slowly disintegrate. Uncle Teo climbs to the top of a tree and yells, 'I want a woman!' over and over again. Male members of the family get a ladder and climb it to try to get him down. Each one in turn is hit on the head by a well-aimed stone, about which a great deal of fuss is made. 'What an eye! He hasn't missed once!' exclaim the watching children in admiration, absently swatting themselves hard because of the mosquitoes that seem to send most of their scuttling elders, apart from Uncle Teo, into such a state. He has a grander spirit. He stands at the top of his tree undisturbed, uttering his oratorical cry for a woman from his crow's nest of a soul. Uncle Teo may be mad, but he would never be a Fascist. He is at last brought down by a bustling midget nun, who swiftly climbs the ladder and says, 'Get down! Enough of this madness!' She and the other attendants at the asylum have been called for in despair by the hysterical relatives, who have tried everything to entice him down, including a fake departure without him, though Uncle Teo is a canny visionary who wouldn't care about the trick anyway. There is a life elsewhere, he visibly thinks. Told in the carriage on the way to the farm that he can catch a glimpse of blue sea if he looks over there, he stares fraternally at the sky instead. The asylum attendants understand him. 'One day he's normal, the next he isn't. Happens to all of us,' says one of the male nurses. Uncle Teo's solemnity, good sense, and feeling of awe are typical of Fellini's comedy. They are shared by an almond-seller who dreams of a wonderful harem ('Oh, what abundance!' he exclaims, red-nosed and excited) and by the wide-eyed small children of the movie. One of them, going to school with a satchel on his back in a fog, falters and halts when he suddenly sees a wonderfully beautiful, soft-nosed white buffalo appearing out of the whorls of mist.

The fluff balls are soft, the snow is soft, and the eye of the film looks softly upon the little town's ceremonial occasions. There are many excitements. There is the bonfire, for instance. There is a communal voyage in small boats to see a grand liner called the *Rex*. It takes a long time to get to it, but everyone makes the effort. The girl of the town puts on a white sailor suit instead of her usual red dress, and a white beret replaces her red one. We have seen her going to bed in the first one: a gesture that seems to be a mark of the town's sense of the dashing, which is uncrushed by poverty or Fascism. There are always bad things to deal with, after all. The trip out to see the liner is an event. The dolphin species is talked of in words of wisdom. 'My dentist says it's a very sentimental fish,' someone says contemplatively. The town girl in her sailing kit finds her longing for someone to talk to over a cup of coffee momentarily assuaged by the community spirit. The liner is overwhelmingly beautiful; it is a brightly lit continent full of the debonair and the well-off. 'What does it look like?' asks an engagingly irritable blind accordionist, restlessly lifting his dark glasses and frantic for a report. All the same, he can catch the sense of Italianate fun: small-town, self-important, full of braggadocio in ways that Fellini understands and loves. What a worthwhile trip! What a triumph! Then the town is again covered with snow. 'We had a record snowfall this year, excluding the Ice Age,' says a character who sometimes acts as a narrator.

Amarcord is an economical film about small-town bravery. It often sends shivers down the spine. Fellini has surely proved himself good enough by now to be trusted by sceptical bystanders. To make such an atheistic, wonderstruck, affectionate work as *Amarcord* is very difficult. It is anecdotal yet all of a piece, comic and stirringly hospitable. Once in a while, one wants to shake someone by both hands and say 'Well done.'

Fellini's *And the Ship Sails On*, set in 1914, celebrates, with suitable love, the *folie de grandeur* of opera. We are actually on a liner, as we can only long to be in *Amarcord*. A band sees us off. It is like the Venetian scene in Verdi's *Otello*. The stately guests upstairs move with operatic organization, bound in dignity to bury a great singer ('Hildebrande, one of the great voices of our time'); below decks the chefs hustle in speeded-up action. Music in the end controls everything. The chefs stir in tempo. Upstairs, an astrologer, blinking like a baby, says to the privileged, 'A surgeon discovered that star.' Everything is newborn in the film, movingly about the apparently jaded.

Not for nothing that this is 1914. 'Get the news.' But what we are concerned with is music. The funeral coach of the great singer. *La Forza del Destino*. Sailors on deck turn round as the music brings them another and possible world. They gather on the rails above the stoking deck, while obedient motion in the kitchen accompanies allegro tea-room music for the first-class passengers. There is 'Ave Maria'. A famous dancer dances. A seagull flies in. The Master of Ceremonies, the familiar of Fellini's imaginings, wonders to camera what all these people are doing and asks our pardon. A blind, musical woman refuses compassion and orders her sandwiches as though she could see. Everyone in this film has sight, of a sort, and how much sharper if he will listen.

Below decks, the stokers are sweating. A tenor from first class at the rails. There is wonderment. 'La donna è mobile'. A rhinoceros is gently raised, a great hulk that has to be hauled up by chains fixed by the bare-chested stokers. Music carries its weight. Care is taken.

The Triple Alliance is on deck. It is, after all, 1914. Serbs, roped off, invite the hermetic first-class guests to dance. Some of the wish for communion has its way. In the kitchen, a Russian basso profundo sings a tone out of tune to soothe a live chicken about an experiment. He softly puts her to sleep. Or perhaps a cockerel does. The rhinoceros, in the meantime, has been properly hosed down, this great hulk of life so alien to the operatic entrepreneurs whose income comes from a more fastidious and staged vision of mortality. With the hosing, passengers put up umbrellas. The rhino's legs are dangling. Chefs wash it from buckets.

On the third night out from land, some trickery with time and alliance made possible by music takes over. The guests gather at the rails and watch the stokers, who take the big singing parts in snatches of Verdi operas that bring up thoughts of Géricault and Delacroix, except that their ship is no *Shipwreck of the Medusa* but a ship made safe by music's concord.

★ ★ ★

Shakespeare was the most Italian of English dramatists. Impossible to prove a negative: impossible to prove that he *didn't* go to Italy. Who wrote better of boon nights, midnight flits, the stuff of opera; no wonder that Verdi so leapt to Falstaff. Falstaff's friendship with Hal is one of the great comic peaks in dramatic literature: comic in the sense that the friendship is in mortal hands, not subject to the gods, and has a human bloom.

As Auden once said, if it is true that *The Merry Wives of Windsor* stemmed from Queen Elizabeth's wish to see Falstaff in a comedy, then she proved herself a good critic, for his presence in the history plays is strangely wrong. Falstaff is a non-finite figure; it is impossible to imagine him as a child, and one knows at once that his death at Shrewsbury is only shamming. He is a character who exists simply because he *is*, and therefore remains disturbingly outside the temporal world of the plays in which the other characters are incessantly aware of death and exist only through dynamic action. One notices his alien character acutely in the relationship between himself and Prince Hal. At the beginning of *Henry IV*, the prince is apparently much like him, an accomplice in arrested childhood who also seems to be beyond time; but before we are halfway through Part I, Hal has succumbed to his nature and left the knight behind. When Falstaff asks: 'Art thou not horribly afraid, thou being heir apparent?' we know that he has no conception of what it is like to have a sense of the future, and that his crony's metamorphosis leaves him wondering. His immunity to the passions of the play is sealed by the laughter he sets up. For laughter is an act that immediately suspends passion, removing one from the continuum of purposive activity as effectively as a sneeze. When Falstaff appears, the ambitions that drive the play are suddenly paralysed.

The Royal Shakespeare Company aptly opened 1966 with

the two parts of *Henry IV*, the double play that is one of the great marvels of the canon. No other work of Shakespeare's has the same extraordinary twin mesh of historical and personal ethics. The sense of a kingdom on the edge of change is engulfing. Politically the play is even more complex than *Coriolanus*, more expansive, less jaded; and the course of the friendship between Prince Hal and Falstaff is recorded with feeling far beyond *Romeo and Juliet*. In the capacity that *Henry IV* expresses for simultaneous pain, magnanimity, and the comic sense of what abides, one sometimes seems to be in the presence not of one man's creative process but of the imagination of humanity itself.

Ian Holm's brilliant Prince Hal, a cool, trim watcher, made the betrayal of his past with Falstaff seem a deeply rooted act of temperamental necessity instead of an expedient piece of ditching by a new monarch. Quite early in the play, Hal has begun to inspect himself and to cast off his old judgments. He is no longer altogether made rapt by Falstaff. The roisterers in Eastcheap are sometimes a whole world for him and sometimes nothing but a tiny faction of subjects.

The final scene when he refuses to recognize Falstaff was stunningly prepared for in the deathbed scene with his father, which Hal played drunk. It was a piece of production insight that made instant sense of Hal's mistake in thinking his father already dead, which becomes a vulgarity that makes him sober for the rest of his life.

Henry IV is about power, friendship, the blooming of fun, the smothering of conscience; but most of all it is about occasion and timing. The old king – a fine performance by Tony Church, red-eyed and querulous – has come to power by fostering a moment of public opinion. His enemies in Northumberland, Scotland and Wales are motivated not only by envy but also by a suspicion that he has dangerously misread the clock of the State. It is because Falstaff behaves as if he were immortal that he becomes a sacrifice: the people who survive are the ones who sense the machinery of time moving on.

Hal becomes a good king when he knows that something is over, and Hotspur has to be killed because he is a 'Mars in swaddling clothes', arrested at a stage of infant aggression and thinking that the engine of England can be driven by brute strength. The losers in the play think that power is something static, like the throne itself; the victor knows that it is a process.

In such a scheme, Falstaff is elegiac from the start. He is funny not because he is simple but because he is hideously shrewd, screwing up his eyes when he is in a fix because he has a horribly intelligent double vision about himself. He pretends to be irritable when he is abused or caught out in a lie, but he is really rather gratified by insults; they are a sort of compliment to his baby's ego, which is ravenous to be noted and intrigued by any mirror that is held up to it. Hal's insults are a game to him.

Jokes about his size give him no pain because they are never aimed at the cause of it; other people take it that he is fat because he is greedy, but he himself feels swollen by the heroic banishment of melancholy ('grief blows you up like a bladder'). He boozes to warm his blood, so he tells himself, and to sharpen his wits for Hal's sake; and in the prince's presence in Part I he seems indestructible, alive with the young man's affection and almost floating with fatness.

But in Part II his mass acquires leaden weight; and in the scenes without the prince, the joker begins to lose his way. His sensuality becomes wan, his body aches, and his gout draws on. A hole is cut in his boot for his swelling toe, and his movements hurt him. With Doll Tearsheet on his lap he revives for a moment with thoughts of bed, but in the next half-line he is gripped by self-disgust and fear of death. Apparently safely wrapped in an eternal present, in fact he feels the chill of mortality more keenly even than the king. He is like a toddler gifted with some appalling edge of adult apprehension.

'I shall be sent for soon,' he says furiously after banishment, telling himself that the king's betrayal was only a passing mood; 'at night.' Their ancient nights are what he yearns for all existence to be like, out of time, drowned in sack, a limbo of private life and immortal licence; but for Hal they become a dream to be shaken off, a deceiving infancy that he leaves behind to see his avid boon-companion as a profane and surfeited old man.

Like all Shakespeare's greatest plays, *Henry IV* is immensely complex and also very simple. To a child seeing it, and a production with understanding of its comic apparentness, it might shake down into a series of pictures: a crowned father in a narrow black bed envying a political enemy for his son; a prince mimicking his father's disappointment while he is sitting in a fat man's chair in a tavern; grown men pretending to be children around a tarred gibbet in a screaming wind, and an archbishop playing deadly politics in a wood with rooks cawing over his head.

The vision of the play opposes, with comedy's timelessnes, the friendship of a prince snatched into history and a patient commoner not on power's escalator.

Orson Welles's idea of making a composite film about Falstaff – called *Chimes at Midnight* – is typically popular, serious and to the point. Apart from his other gifts, he had the uncommon great flair for fixing on central figures whom a great many people are going to recognize and respond to.

Falstaff is one of the most instantly moving characters in Shakespeare, because he is gifted in a way that is bound to bring him pain: a creature born outside time whose genius is wholly for friendship, contracted to love an ambitious mortal prince who is going to outgrow him. Hal knows that their relationship will alter as soon as the old king dies, but Falstaff unconsciously believes that it will last forever, like all the other good things, jokes and capon and sack and nights of limitless congeniality.

He sees no end to them, no reprisals, no pang beyond the cure of carousing and sleep, for he lives without a twinge of the foreknowledge of change that nags in the bone of the people around him. The key word is *Midnight*: spells run out, licence over, an endless, brilliant evening suddenly irrecoverable. Falstaff's alacrity to go to the crowning of his crony when we all know that Hal is due to rebuff him is one of the nearly unbearable things in Shakespeare, like most of *Lear*.

The Shakespearean scenes are laced together in the film with narrative passages from Holinshed. Falstaff is Orson Welles himself, wearing a brambly halo of white hair and a false nose eroded like rock under a waterfall. The old king is played by Gielgud with great beauty. Margaret Rutherford is Nell Quickly: her 'cold as any stone' speech about Falstaff's death from *Henry V* is as stirring as anything that this poignant and self-forgetting actress has ever done. The dashing editing catches friendship thawing, especially in the passages of Falstaff's night sprees, and in the amazing battle scene, where thrashing bodies freeze in mud-clad death like the running men who were calcified in flight by the lava of Pompeii.

Comedy lies in the rooted, the idiom of language. Our zoo-talk. Everything then, if authentically heard by the writer, goes at the pace of quick-witted zoo-citizens. The great question of Shakespearean comedy is, where should it be placed? Many the scenes of the mechanicals in the *Dream* we have seen fouled up by Mummerset talk, Mummerset being the rustic lingo assumed by the actors without a fitting chance to sound as if born within sound of Magdalen bells.

Much Ado loses its comic wits when it tangles with women's rights, hardly in Shakespeare's mind, which steadily accorded them. His abiding sense of humour was wonderfully funded by Franco Zeffirelli, who had the dazzlingly simple idea of placing the play exactly where Shakespeare laid it himself: not in an elocutory limbo, which is where it usually happens, but in Messina. This is bound to raise hackles. Whenever a producer seizes on a specific social context for a Shakespearean play instead of letting it roam between the rural forelock-tugging of Mummerset and a sort of mock-Tudor department store for the well-heeled, he will always be accused of wrecking the poetry.

There exists now a passionate small faction that almost seems to wish that Shakespeare had nothing to do with the theatre. Denying that he was an actor, and numb to the plain vulgar theatricality of his genius, the party members sometimes seem to be striving for the day when productions of his plays can be limited to tutorial readings. Robert Graves's 300 changes for this *Much Ado* came into the category of scribbling on the Koran; this applied especially in the case of anyone refurbishing an obsolete joke. The guard-word of the Shakespeare-to-be-read-as-literature agitators is 'gimmick', and the main plank in the platform is a project known as 'letting the verse speak for itself', as though the plays were a prison for some literary characteristic on legs that sorely needed liberating from the human beings in whom Shakespeare incarcerated it.

Franco Zeffirelli passionately disagrees. What he responds to is exactly the opposite. It is their theatricality, their humanity, and their instinctive recourse to the concrete. In his *Much Ado* there was a rain of invention.

It has become a truism about *Much Ado* to say that it is made up of three fatally distinct stylistic units: the yokel machinations of Dogberry, the notion of romantic love in the Hero–Claudio plot, and the freebooting anti-romanticism of Beatrice and Benedick. When the play is produced, as it often is in England, with Dogberry speaking like a yokel actor advertising eggs on the telly, a repining Hero out of refined drama-schools, and two classical stars trying to make the small-town banter of Beatrice and Benedick sound like Oscar Wilde, no wonder *Much Ado* is held to be organically a failure. But Zeffirelli had the blessed simple-mindedness to see the characters not as sources for critics' puzzles, but as the citizens of a single small town; and the moment the play is localized, it meshes precisely.

Instead of being the proponent of a distant ethic of love that now lies pickled in troubadour poetry, Hero becomes a wretchedly believable girl trapped in a perfectly recognizable Sicily where the same ferocious code of chastity endures to this day. Beatrice for once seems credible as her cousin. In Maggie Smith's performance she was not the usual alien sophisticate, free of the rules that bind Hero, and unrelatedly caustic, but a product of the same culture who simply happens to have more spirit and a pelting tongue. Placing the play as exactly as this at once makes sense of the Hero–Claudio drama: in logic it is absurd that the accusation against Hero is unanswered (as Lewis Carroll once complained in a letter to Ellen Terry, why didn't anyone use the abundant material for an alibi?), but in Sicily this is a slur enough.

Zeffirelli tore into the play as though it were a fiesta. It was rather like the way Beecham used to belt into the Hallelujah Chorus: the pouncing speed was breathtaking. The play began and ended with a local brass band, wheeling past an enthralled populace on a stage rimmed with fairy lights like a small town welcoming a hero. The Latin sense of self-importance was rife, and so was the endearing Latin unconsciousness that to anyone else this sense might well be conspicuously unfounded. The military characters wore magnificently brave uniforms that had obviously never sniffed battle, and Leonato a mayoral suit apparently tailored for a duck.

The men were mostly dashing, especially Robert Stephens as Benedick, even if the pomp of their chests did tend to run out towards the ground, the costume designer having done miracles in turning Englishmen into no-leg Latins. The women were unimaginably plain, especially Hero, and Beatrice was blithely blowsy. Dogberry/Frank Finlay sweetly seemed to see himself as Napoleon in a greatcoat. The character's furious tears about his insulated position as a householder were so accurately Italian that they almost settled the question of whether Shakespeare ever went to Italy. Not for years had the human substance of Shakespeare been reflected like this in a production.

There was one extraordinary moment, inexplicable except in the unique terms of what can happen in a theatre, when the light held and then slowly faded on Don Pedro sitting alone, smoking a cigar and simply looking after Beatrice and Benedick. The moment swivelled the mood of the play, a pause full of death set into a gala ending, and it demonstrated the balance of feeling that was the commanding gift of the production. Half the time the characters' obsession with wooing was made to seem absurd; but if romanticism is to be mocked, love is made to seem mortally serious. The 'Kill Claudio' can never have worked with more sardonic energy.

More of the carrying truth of the rooted. In Luigi Barzini's book on *The Italians* there is an interesting page about the national use of the words *sistemano* and *sistemazione*. Italians *sistemano* unruly nature, mountain torrents and spoiled children; mothers want to *sistemare* their daughters with steady husbands. Streetwalkers and high-born mistresses yearn for a *sistemazione* that will allow them to pose as widows and bring up their illegitimate children respectably; industrialists long to *sistemare* competition through cartels. The land of misrule and scrambling improvisation dreams of itself as imposing order and stately master-plans. It is genuinely comic, like a man yelling at the top of his voice in praise of restraint.

'*Ti sistemo io*' ('I will curb your rebellious instincts') is a common Italian threat that sums up Petruchio's piece of swagger in Zeffirelli's film of *Taming of the Shrew*. Petruchio's bullying is funny as soon as the play is firmly planted in Italy, because he is then a hot-air disciplinarian whose ability to curb his shrew occurs in the midst of bouts of yelling and chaos in himself. His stabs at a masterful coolness are more like fatigue and about as impressive as hangovers in the life of a drunk.

Franco Zeffirelli's film with the Burtons has the same brilliantly obvious comic source as his production of *Much Ado*; he simply took Shakespeare to have meant precisely Padua when he wrote the word, and he makes the cast behave literally like Italians. They are buffoons dreaming of dignity, careful tacticians with a picture of themselves as heroic risk-takers, romantics believing in their talent for logic and *sistemazione* as devoutly as fat Neapolitans believe lasagna verde is slimming because it is coloured with spinach.

The film is very captivating. The editing of the brawl scenes is a bit like vaudeville. The picture is enticing to look at, with a sunny-natured opening scene in a gauzy drizzle, high shots of rapt onlookers and crankily angled passages, brownish tints through the reds, and Burton in a bucolic make-up that looks like a Venetian portrait, when it isn't obscured by his great foot kicking over a goblet on the table. (The photography is by Oswald Morris and Luciana Trasatti; art directors, Giuseppe Mariani and Elven Webb.)

Michael Hordern as Baptista, father of Elizabeth Taylor's exquisite Shrew and Natasha Pyne's pastoral Bianca, looks sick at the havoc but keeps cheerful. 'How speed you to your wooing?' he bawls nonchalantly to Petruchio, who is staggering about on the roof of a house with one boot off-balance, vilifying some happy cats and a far-from-wooed Kate. The bond between the lovers is one of benign disgust. Their discontent has nothing dismal in it, but merely the blessed adrenalin for another good day of battles. Every now and again the fury is reined back and there is a pause of sweetness between them, like the finely felt moment when the Shrew tempers Petruchio's violence and kisses him on the nose.

The jibes in Zeffirelli's film leave no wound, because they are about nothing private; they are simply variants on a community convention, devised by two virtuosos of insult flailing about for a way of making the awful admission that living together might work. It is a feat of this production to make it seem purblind for anyone to grind on with the old saw about *The Shrew* being a male suprematist tract. The play's last part can seem boorish; but Zeffirelli fastidiously twists it around, mostly by Elizabeth Taylor's performance, which quietly sends up Petruchio for putting her through hoops. In the end the triumph is really hers, and it is one of emotional taste, because she chooses to tell the steady truth about love in the banquet scene where everyone else is effect-making. It is a debonair way to end a gentle-spirited film.

Zeffirelli and his writers have cut the Christopher Sly induction and done a lot else to aggravate library purists; what the film proffers instead is buoyancy, control of mood, Shakespearean performances where the actors unusually seem not to be listening to what they are saying but tumbling out with what they are thinking, and some joyous comic sequences about the Italian character, especially the wedding. The congregation's mood quickly switches from piety to seething boredom, and a priest hoping to *sistemare* the noisy couple loses his nerve in the face of a Petruchio who has dropped off into a sloshed doze on the altar-rail.

Italians – and the Romans and the great Latin and Greek dramatists before them – knew that married couples can live through exactly the same situations and interpret them completely differently under each other's noses. It is one of the most tried and true jokes in drama. Shakespeare, an Italian by wished parenthood if ever there was one, enjoyed the knowledge full well. Zeffirelli's comprehension of

Shakespeare's light irony about such deep differences between the genders is anciently laid. A lot of the comedy in the *Lysistrata* depends on the fact that the women in it regard their own bodies politically, while their husbands insist on browsing about them physically.

Divorce Italian Style, in which Marcello Mastroianni first emerged as a very funny character actor, concerns the situation of the *Lysistrata* gone considerably haywire. The husband, a Sicilian aristocrat, is a lugubrious lecher who loathes his wife and waits alertly until she is asleep before he comes to bed. The wife, on the other hand, a sprightly and monumentally imperceptive woman, inhabits such a different world that she thinks it necessary to keep him at bay by pretending that she has headaches every night. She is frightened he will suspect that she has a lover; he turns gratefully away to dream of finding her one.

Part of the wit of Mastroianni's performance is that he makes the man seem such an *intimidated* sort of cad. As he lopes around the corridors of his crumbling family palace, smoking through an ivory cigarette-holder and somehow making even his suit for Mass look like a pair of satin pyjamas, he seems the most low-pressure bounder imaginable. Everything is an effort, and most things make him despondent. He saves his energy for dodging into the lavatory to look through opera glasses at the legs of his schoolgirl cousin, with whom he is glumly besotted. Only Italians, I think, with their carried voice of passion breaking music's bounds, can make glumness in love funny. One doesn't believe it. At any moment they are going to soar into an aria beyond any gainsaying.

Mastroianni's hair, which breaks into an oily surf of curls over his collar, is combed carefully flat. In spite of his brave attempts to look like Ronald Colman, he has a ruinous stoop that makes him look like a St Bernard dog badly in need of the brandy round his neck. His wife, whom he married for the sake of her hips, has a face that has since driven the iron into his soul. Her hair grows in low eaves, like a Victorian curate's; her eyebrows meet in the middle, and her moustache is as luxuriant as his own. On such a hirsute head her girlish expression seems horrifyingly unsuitable.

In one scene on the beach, when she has buried herself up to the neck in sand for the sake of her arthritis, the head is left bobbing and smiling, still making demands and chatting brightly. Her husband looks as though he is going to be sick.

He must murder her. As a devout man he can do nothing else; divorce would be an unthinkable sin, even if it were possible in law. He decides that the way to do it is to abuse his own honour. If he can only arrange to be cuckolded, thus allowing him to kill her in a passion of apparent jealousy that every Sicilian will understand, he shouldn't go to jail for more than four years. With the election coming, which means a general amnesty, it will be even less.

The script is written partly by the director, Pietro Germi. It is slyly sceptical about the bombastic ideals of honour, manliness, and religious propriety that are upheld in South Italy, coexisting cheerfully with a working practice that allows people to be expedient, cowardly, and respectfully enthralled by scandal. The film is gravely photographed, and designed in an overblown baroque style that is self- importance without self-knowledge. Mastroianni's performance gives the whole picture a kind of doomed but hopeful eroticism that is rather like the comic tone of *Lolita* or Wertmüller. And of Goncharov. Italians and Russians have things in common apart from music: they are earnest in gloom, but a communal sense of high days sustains them to the skies willy-nilly.

Comedy of social circumstance, reported with a grave no-comment that rises into the satiric and farcical: Lina Wertmüller's *The Lizards* begins very much like a nineteenth-century novel, the kind that satisfyingly tells you straight away that Mr B, an apothecary of middle height with blue eyes and a pronounced chin, lives in the small town of X with his wife and three daughters. The information at the start of the film is physical and precise. The lizards of the title live in a little town in the South of Italy; their lives are rather like the lives of Fellini's *vitelloni*, though their class is more like the provincial middle class of Chekhov.

Antonio, the son of a notary, is a languid law-student idling away his youth in endless talk of deferred evacuations to Rome and unlaid but lusted-after girls. The film begins at siesta time, the point of melting will that is the standing condition of the town: the shutters are up, the fields and parlours are full of snores, the landowner's widow is doing her accounts and a bad girl's five illegitimate children are sleeping the sleep of the good, packed into a bed like brisling. You watch Antonio with his friends, sauntering in the warm air, playing cards; you see them eyeing the marriageable girls, who are mostly ugly and obliged to seem shy, and yearning after the ample and beautiful local jade, whose bra size they guess to be at least forty-two.

The film is really an account of a town, a place where nothing happens but the arranging of marriages and the hysterical satisfying of empty forms of honour. Time crawls like a snake on a stone, broken up by absurd brawls that are never about the real crisis beneath: people are full of anguish, and the anguish runs into the sand. There is one beautifully composed shot of three generations of women that is as eloquent as anything in Jane Austen about the marriage market. The old grandmother is looking on; the grand- daughter is desperately unhappy; and the mother, obsessively tidying the shapes of two buns of laundry as though she were making bread, has nothing to say to help her. Satiric sense is finely in pitch.

* * *

The presiding spirit – genius – of the Beatles remains for good their comic common sense and music. They break the glass by letting us in on the dolts they have to deal with in their films. When a reporter in *A Hard Day's Night* asks one of the Beatles what he would call that hairstyle he's wearing, he replies blandly: 'Arthur.' Comedy never explains. Like the slipped vowel in their own name, the way the Beatles go on is just there, and that's that. In an age that is clogged with self-explanation, this makes them very welcome. It also makes them naturally comics. They accept one another with the stoicism of clowns. None of them tries to tell you that their peculiarities are a sign of the traumas of modern man or because mum did the wrong thing at six weeks. In Alun Owen's script, which has such a lynx ear for their own speech that their ad libs are indistinguishable in it, they behave toward one another with the unbothered rudeness that is usually possible only between brothers and sisters. It is this feeling that you are looking at an enviable garrison of a family that is at the root of the Beatles' charm. I don't believe it is just the Lennon–McCartney numbers, good and sweetly odd as they are. When Richard Lester was shooting the numbers in the film, the kids in the Scala Theatre were yelling so loud that they did not realize they were listening to six new hits months before anyone else. The only thing that could have finished the Beatles with the fans, it seemed to me then, would be if they had seemed to split up as a family.

A Hard Day's Night has no plot. What it has instead, which is plenty, is invention, good looks and a lot of larky character. The narrative is simply a day in the Beatles' lives. Their situation is pure comedy: four highly characterized people caught in a series of intensely public dilemmas but always remaining untouched by them, like Keaton, because they cart their private world around everywhere. Whether they are in a train carriage or at a press conference or in a television studio, the Beatles are always really living in a capsule of Liverpool.

As a piece of grit in the narrative Alun Owen has given Paul a scratchy old grandad (Wilfred Brambell), about whom the nicest thing that anyone can say, and even this seems doubtful, is that he is clean. Grandad resents their unity and manages to create a fair amount of chaos. His jibes slide off Paul, John and George, but they find a victim in Ringo, who is already worried enough about his shortness, and the size of his nose. They are also the last straw for the boys' distraught manager (Norman Rossington), who is conducting a war of nerves with John that is lost from the start because John hasn't got any nerves.

Like John's book *In His Own Write*, and like Richard Lester's own *Running, Jumping, Standing Still Film*, *A Hard Day's Night* is full of slightly out-of-focus puns, both verbal and visual. For instance, a Beatle will make a dive for someone's square tie and ask in a dim, Harrow School way, 'I say, did you go to Harrods? I was there in 1958.' Or John Lennon in a bubblebath will suddenly see a handshower as a submarine periscope and start playing war films. One of the best sequences, as in *The Running, Jumping, Standing Still Film*, is a fantasy in a field. Lester obviously adores fields. This one inspires a jump-cut speeded-up sequence mostly shot from a helicopter in which the boys horse around, do a square-dance and lie down with their heads together in close-up as though they were swimmers in an old Esther Williams picture. There is a marvellous feeling of liberation about this sequence, as with some of the dances in *West Side Story*. Technically *A Hard Day's Night* lifts a lot from *cinéma vérité*: in the use of hidden mikes, throat mikes and handheld cameras, for instance. But if you compare it with a real piece of camera truth-telling like Granada's Beatle film, *Yeah, Yeah, Yeah*, made by the Maysles brothers in America, it's clear that Dick Lester's hasn't very much to do with *cinéma vérité* in its character.

A Hard Day's Night is better described, perhaps, as a piece of feature journalism; this was the first comedy in England that had anything like the urgency and dash of an English popular daily at its best. Like a news feature, it was made under pressure and the head of steam behind it has produced something expressive and alive. If this is personality-mongering, it is also very responsive to personality and eloquent about it. Ringo emerges as a born actor. He is like a silent comedian, speechless and chronically underprivileged, a boy who is already ageless with a mournful, loose mouth, like a Labrador's carrying a bird. He seems a very precisely Liverpudlian Labrador. Precision of roots: Fellini's amplitude, Falstaff's piercing Englishness, Zeffirelli's sense of the Italian abiding in Shakespeare, Germi's grasp of solemn *omertà* on the steps of the Church; the Beatles' English cheek and blood-brotherhood fun; comedy demands precision of locality. Maybe it is most festive when we feel people clustering around the parish pump. The feeling is contagious in Slav comedy. The word *zemlya* in Russian means ground, soil, country, all three, and its translation to the other Slav languages has the same tone as in Russian: quizzical, doting, 'Which direction is ahead? Have a pickled herring.'

For an essence of festivity, Ivan Passer's *Intimate Lighting* (bad translation of the Czech) is a wonder. The film has a character that will one day belong as definably to post-1960 Czech films as certain domestic qualities mark the Dutch school in painting.

The immediate material is the Czechs' passion for music. The provincial people in the film take music as seriously as the English might take a project about saving an old train: the difference between *Intimate Lighting* and an Ealing comedy has something to do with the director's attentiveness to the characters. At the opening of the film the members of an amateur orchestra are rehearsing hammer and tongs to get themselves up to scratch for a visiting soloist from Prague. In the first passage a wind player commits a harrowing note for the nth time. The conductor, grim with control, says, 'We'll drown you afterwards.'

When the soloist arrives, he stays with an old friend from the Conservatoire days whose dulled family life now appals him. In his eyes, it visibly reduces mostly to squabbles about who is to have which joint of the goose and tactics about keeping the peace with Grandpa. People's tetchiness becomes genuinely comic in the film because it is made dogged and not self-aware. A string quartet fumes with civil war without even stopping playing. 'Either we play or we fight,' says one of them, carrying on with the score.

Intimate Lighting has an adorably funny scene when a string quartet member gets fed up with the interruptions of a disembodied arm that keeps holding up kittens for attention outside the window during rehearsal. About music the Czechs like to be serious. The characters in this film address themselves to music rather as Chekhov's people address their furniture, hailing it every now and then in a sort of elegiac vocative. 'People say you can travel the world with one sad song,' says a character in a funeral cortège behind a brass band, suddenly revived by melancholy. 'If this car ran on tears – my goodness . . .' He falls excitably silent, like a Chekhov character struck by the tragic sense implicit in the family bookcase.

The characters are possessed by music, bossing a girlfriend about companionably to the sound of a motor-horn, enthralled when drunk by the musicality of a pause between

Grandpa's snores. Under their sealed-off idiosyncrasies they express a feeling of seriousness about life, regret about lost chances, the blight of bodies that time and hard work have spoilt for old pleasures. There is one little scene, when a stout grandmother making a bed suddenly tries to demonstrate a ballet position she could once do, that I suppose only a Slav film could achieve with such a true mixture of ridiculousness, grief and lightness.

The Beatles, in *Magical Mystery Tour*, and the best of their musical successors – who include the Bee Gees – tell us, 'Nothing is real. And nothing to get hung up about.' The shining comedy *Sgt Pepper's Lonely Hearts Club Band* is the underlining of those words. It is a benediction laid upon everyone who has ever loved the musicianship of the Beatles, who seemed to incarnate – perhaps through our own wish, and growingly with a sense of self-parody – all that was free and witty in the gifted rock groups that have been clasped to the heart of an era dissident about the worth of orthodox get- ahead values.

Sgt Pepper's Lonely Hearts Club Band relies on vagrant sympathies to link the Beatles to the Bee Gees. It works because of the writing, Henry Edwards; the director, Michael Schultz; the director of photography, Owen Roizman; the producer, Robert Stigwood; the arranger and director of the music, George Martin. Among them, they saw the way to create an evanescent world that, because it depends on music, can never disappear. How could they contrive to have the Beatles' own music (the music here was written by Paul McCartney and John Lennon, with one song by George Harrison) pouring out of the Bee Gees and other guest stars – including Peter Frampton – the ethic of whose music has also been to run against the grain of a moneygrubbing society, collecting more than a generation of passionate loyalists as it goes? The endeavour is won technically by following an early edict of the Beatles: that there is nothing you can say that can't be sung. We are in a fairyland where almost the only speaking is done by the beneficent, gravelly voice of George Burns as the mayor of a town of innocence called Heartland, USA, overseeing a bandstand that is the centre of the place. Practically all the other words are sung. Even George Burns's voice is mostly off-camera, the voice of an unseen aging maverick from an older society who shares the feeling of audible and younger people that music endures. When the seen characters are speaking – which is very seldom – they mouth silently, to carefully obvious post-synching. Another of the answers is that the figure of Sgt Pepper is made to seem an immortal one. He presides over the film, and has lasted through most of the troubled twentieth century, including the twenties, the Depression, the Second World War, the fifties. By now, he has become a weathervane. But a weathervane of some importance, who leads from the era of the Beatles to the era of the Bee Gees.

The Bee Gees, with their air of freedom from constraint, lay a hand of entrancement on the citizens of Heartland, who cling around the fabled characters of the film. They cling, just as we do – like magnetized iron filings – to the love of music and feeling of the perdurable which this commemoration of the Beatles produces. All shall be well. But then a telegram from Hollywood arrives. A villainous film magnate called B.D. – Big Deal – Brockhurst (played by Donald Pleasence), the greedy chairman of Big Deal Records, who is shot always in leery close-up, offers them the world. Come to Hollywood. They accept, with no feeling of peril. Peril does not exist in this sphere. Music will keep the players and singers safe from rapacity. The band – Peter Frampton and the Bee Gees – goes off to Los Angeles, where it is met by B.D. in a six-wheeled silver roadster in which the players sit facing one another with a magically steady table between them set with decanters of booze, which they proceed to drink in a charmed way that never makes them drunk. The only thing approaching tragedy in the film is that the original Sgt Pepper's Band instruments are stolen from a museum by Frankie Howerd, as Mean Mr Mustard, an intentionally caricatured representative of worldly interests, played with a flustered fussiness like that of a bargain-hunting housewife at a sale. But everything is reversible. Even a suicide leap from the top of a building is reversible, by a magic bolt of lightning from a gold-suited, gold-booted accomplice who is within this world: the falling man is stopped in mid-air by the marvel of film – and of music

– to fly back up to the top of the building. There exists no disappointment in this circle of music lovers which is not to be healed, no grief which lacks the balm of music that Dryden spoke of long ago in the words set by Handel's *Ode for Saint Cecilia's Day*. When 'Strawberry Fields' – the Peter Frampton character's girlfriend – dies, she is encased in a glass casket, the other musicians mourning in black, singing and playing with a beauty that erases sadness.

The film is an uncumbersome statement of comedy against the ordinary, against trudging impulses. It takes the liberties of music. Like music, it observes no limit to the distances that can be crossed. An immediate cut to another dazzling place, another scheme of things, is like the interrupted cadence in music, when the return to the tonic is delayed but promised. The musicians wear magical suits, boots that will take them anywhere; a couple of kisses on a hugely magnified spinning record; boring worldly activity is speeded up with wizardry. Jokes are made at the expense of 'adult movies' belonging to the Mustard Motel, which also offers 'rooms by the hour'. How grubby, this world of the moneyed, how slow, when the people of the world of the film know how to change the colour of things as rapidly as music does when it shifts three half tones downward into the relative minor.

And all the time there is the background amity of George Burns, this ally from the world of the musicians' elders, this alien who understands the ethic that the stick-in-the-mud and the thrifty mistrust. The instruments come back, with the help of computer intelligence and computer messages: the very inventions that people who don't respond to the Beatles and the Bee Gees and all the rest find so foreign. It is almost an image of the wonder of the computer memory bank that this most musical film, filled with the imagery of wonder, should restore to us some of the melodies that we so responded to when the Beatles were in their heyday. We might have thought them lost without this picture, which calls them to life as computer memory can call up messages of long ago. Here is 'Lucy in the Sky with Diamonds' again, as reviving as it ever was; here is 'With a Little Help from My Friends', a key to the message of years ago which we might have feared flown to the winds. The film speaks to anyone who has a feeling for the amazement of music and to anyone who has a feeling for the convivial, the blithe, the debonair which was conveyed by the marvellously confident sense of companionship among the Beatles decades ago. Not for nothing did they bring to us the air of a family of brothers beyond transience: not for nothing does this film re-embody them. Musicality lasts. Wit lasts.

Index